Vital Holiness: A Theology of Christian Experience

INTERPRETING THE HISTORIC WESLEYAN MESSAGE

by Delbert R. Rose, Ph.D.

The contents of this study are divided into three major divisions. Part One covers the origin and development of the Christian movement in America which is known today as the Christian Holiness Association.

Part Two is a biographical study of Rev. Joseph H. Smith, a Methodist minister who was a product of the Christian Holiness Association and who became its chief expositor-evangelist.

Part Three is the theology which Rev. Smith taught for more than sixty years. The theology of Christian experience herein presented is therefore representative of the Wesleyan interpretation of the New Testament standard of holiness.

The entire book is written in such a way that it will not only be of vital interest to scholars, but will also prove fascinating to the average reader.

ABOUT THE AUTHOR...

Delbert R. Rose was born in Corunna, Michigan. He graduated from Cleveland Bible Institute (now Malone College) and received his B.A. from John Fletcher College. He earned his M.A. and Ph.D. degrees from the State University of Iowa. Kletzing College conferred upon him the D.D. He also did graduate study at Garrett Evangelical Theological Seminary, Asbury Theological Seminary, Union Theological Seminary (N.Y.), New York Theological Seminary, and the University of Kentucky.

After serving as pastor and full-time evangelist, he taught at Kletzing College, served as Dean-Registrar and Professor of Theology at Western Evangelical Seminary, and was a member of the faculty at Asbury Theological Seminary for twenty-three years. He has written two volumes in the Aldersgate Biblical Series (vols. 37 and 39) and has been a frequent contributor to **The Herald** and **The Asbury Seminarian**.

He is a member of the Evangelical Theological Society, the Wesleyan Theological Society, and the International Society of Theta Phi. He was ordained deacon and elder in The Michigan Conference of The Evangelical Church which denomination later merged with the United Brethren in Christ. Through the merger in 1968 he became a ministerial member of the Detroit Conference of The United Methodist Church.

In January, 1975, he became Dean-Registrar and Professor of Biblical Theology at Wesley Biblical Center, Jackson, Mississippi.

Vital Holiness: A Theology of Christian Experience

INTERPRETING THE HISTORIC WESLEYAN MESSAGE

Delbert R. Rose

BETHANY FELLOWSHIP, INC.
Minneapolis, Minnesota

To
Dorothy
whose name means "gift of God."
As a devout Christian, a faithful companion,
and a helpful critic,
she has fulfilled her name
in my life.

Vital Holiness: A Theology of Christian Experience
by Delbert R. Rose

ISBN 0-87123-539-0

Copyright © 1965 by Delbert R. Rose
Third edition copyright © 1975 by Delbert R. Rose
All Rights Reserved

Published by Bethany Fellowship, Inc.
6820 Auto Club Road, Minneapolis, Minnesota 55438

Printed in the United States of America

Preface to the Third Edition

For several years this book has been out of print, but since several influential persons have shown interest in its continued availability, I have asked Bethany Fellowship to republish it. While a rewriting of parts of the volume would doubtless improve its readability, I have decided to make only minimal changes in its content.

Inasmuch as the National Holiness Association, recently renamed the Christian Holiness Association (CHA), has passed through several organizational changes, this document does not attempt to trace the developments within the movement over the past twenty-five years. The official history of the CHA is now being written by the nationally recognized church historian, Dr. Timothy L. Smith.

The following basic changes have been made for this third printing of my doctoral dissertation. While on file at the State University of Iowa under the title, "The Theology of Joseph H. Smith," I published its first and second editions under the title **A Theology of Christian Experience**. For this edition I am adding two significant words to the title which pinpoint the central thrust of the theology of Joseph H. Smith and the movement he championed throughout his fruitful life, namely, **Vital Holiness**.

The "Appendix B" in the previous editions has been re-

PREFACE

placed by an up-to-date listing of those schools, colleges and seminaries which are currently auxiliary to the Christian Holiness Association. This changed list is important because several holiness schools have either changed their names, merged, or ceased to operate, while several new ones have been founded, within the past quarter of a century.

"Appendix D" is new in this edition and contains two important matters: first, "The Constitution of the Christian Holiness Association" which sets forth the purpose, doctrinal emphases, membership possibilities, and organizational structure of the Association; and second, the list of member-denominations as well as those not officially members but which are active participants in CHA.

The most requested improvement for the book has been the compiling of an index which appears in this edition. Also, a few typographical and factual errors have been corrected.

A large body of holiness literature has appeared within the past twenty-five years, most of which has been listed for us in a comprehensive bibliographic study authored by Charles Edwin Jones, Ph.D. His volume, **A Guide to the Study of the Holiness Movement** (918pp), appeared in 1974, with The Scarecrow Press, Inc., of Metuchen, New Jersey, and The American Theological Library Association co-sponsoring its publication.

There is a revived interest today in Wesleyana studies. Several graduate students are preparing theses and dissertations in this area. The whole of Wesley's **Works** are in process of being re-edited for publication, and the Wesleyan Theological Society—the theological arm of CHA—yearly publishes **The Wesleyan Theological Journal.**

In his presidential report to the 107th Annual Convention of CHA, held at the Sheraton-Biltmore Hotel, Atlanta, Georgia, April 2-4, 1975, Dr. B. Edgar Johnson declared that CHA currently represents over three million persons in North America and approximately five million around the world. With over 10,000 congregations, at least 16,000 ministers, around 2,000 annual camp meetings, and more than 2,000 missionaries ac-

PREFACE

tively working in the world, CHA's constituents are making an impact little recognized by many church leaders today.

In that same report President Johnson made a timely appeal to the CHA conventioners. "Without 'fondling a dead past or carressing antiquity' one wonders if the answer to our present situation is not **to remember.** Original purpose was clear. Its reason for being and method of achieving its purpose were incorporated in its first name—'The National Camp Meeting Association for the Promotion of Holiness.'

"We had a method—the campmeeting, and a message—holiness. And, our priority was right. The **message** was the **thing** and the **method** only a **means**," he continued. "A return to the message... could turn the vast army represented by CHA into a nation-transforming and world-affecting agency." It is my prayer that this book will be the means of calling many of the CHA constituency "**to remember**," and to impart vision and incentive to those of this generation in the holiness movement to serve this present age as faithfully as our spiritual forebearers served their respective generations.

Delbert R. Rose

Wesley Biblical Center
Jackson, Mississippi
May, 1975

Preface to the Second Edition

In August, 1952, this volume was first presented to the School of Religion and Graduate College of the State University of Iowa as a doctoral dissertation, in partial fulfillment of the requirements for the Ph.D. degree. It is on file at the University library under the title *The Theology of Joseph H. Smith*.

The contents of this study are divided into three major divisions. Part One covers the origin and development of the Christian movement in America which is known today as "The National Holiness Association." The developments and changes which have transpired in this Association since 1952 will be treated in another volume now under preparation by this author.

Part Two is a biographical study of the Reverend Joseph H. Smith (1855–1946), a Methodist minister who was a product of the National Holiness Association and who became its chief expositor-evangelist. Smith was a longtime associate of Dr. Henry Clay Morrison, founder of *The Herald* (formerly *The Pentecostal Herald*) and of Asbury Theological Seminary. Dr. Morrison chose to write of Smith in the following terms:

> It has been my happy privilege for many years to labor in camp meetings, conventions and revival meetings with Rev. Joseph H. Smith, a member of the Philadelphia Conference of the M.E. Church. He is a great New Testament teacher. I have known of no man who

could state the fundamental doctrines of the gospel of Christ more clearly and make them more inviting, give them finer emphasis, and gather from them larger fruitfulness, than this beloved and honored brother, Joseph H. Smith. He, like myself, has grown old in this blessed service of spreading scriptural holiness over these lands. He has been a man of great courage, of remarkable calm under trying circumstances, a wise counselor, and I have associated with no man that was more free from adverse criticism, or unkindly remarks about his fellowmen, friend or foe, than this same beloved Joseph H. Smith.

Part Three is the theology which Smith taught in his earnest promotion of the Holiness Movement for more than sixty years. The theology of Christian experience herein presented is therefore representative of that which has been proclaimed in the literature, through the schools, at the camp meetings, and in the churches at home and abroad which have emphasized the Wesleyan interpretation of "the New Testament standard of piety."

The only changes of consequence between this volume as it is now offered to the reading public and the form in which it was first presented at the State University of Iowa are to be found in the concluding chapter, in the footnotes and bibliography, plus a few minor corrections in the original text. The concluding chapter in the volume omits the section in the dissertation on "Conclusion" and "Suggestions for Further Study." Instead of having the footnotes entered at the bottom of each page as at first, they are now listed at the end of the volume. Instead of entering by title in the bibliography each devotional article, Bible study, and sermon as it appeared in the successive issues of the various periodicals for which Smith wrote, the name and the volume of each publication has been listed. The footnotes may be referred to for specific titles under which his writings appeared.

The author is deeply indebted to all those publishing

PREFACE

houses, libraries, and offices which so willingly shared their files and books for research purposes when the data for this volume was being gathered. My thanks is due those holders of copyrights on publications herein quoted which have aided in the preparation of this study.

The author wishes to express his sincere appreciation to Professor M. Willard Lampe, the esteemed former director of the School of Religion at the State University of Iowa who counseled him throughout his graduate studies and provided recommendations during the preparation of this investigation and who upon its completion suggested its publication. The late Dr. C. W. Butler, former president of the National Holiness Association and for many years an intimate friend of Joseph H. Smith, gave the author valuable information concerning and insights into the character and ministry of the man Smith and the Movement he represented, both of which figure largely in this study. Without the sustaining encouragement of his wife, Dorothy W. Rose, the writer would not have been able to complete his graduate studies and have written this volume. She was the capable typist of the major portion of the dissertation. To Reverend and Mrs. Robert Buswell, the writer is indebted for urging the printing of this volume in multilithed form and for assuming the major responsibility of preparing the "masters" for a multilithed edition, published by The Seminary Press of Wilmore, Kentucky, in 1958.

Aware of its many imperfections and limitations, this volume is released with the prayer that it will be an incentive to many to live wholeheartedly for Him who died for them.

DELBERT R. ROSE

Asbury Theological Seminary
Wilmore, Kentucky
January, 1965

Contents

Chapter	Page
ONE—INTRODUCTION	15
THE PURPOSE	15
Statement of the Purpose	15
Importance of the Study	16
LIMITATIONS OF THE SUBJECT	18
METHOD OF PROCEDURE	18
DEFINITIONS OF TERMS	20
ORGANIZATION OF THIS VOLUME	21
TWO—THE NATIONAL HOLINESS ASSOCIATION	23
THE EVANGELICAL AWAKENING	23
The Holy Club	23
The Holiness Movement	24
The Earliest Achievements	25
THE DECLINE OF WESLEYANISM	27
Wesley's Struggle	27
American Methodism Drifts	28
THE AMERICAN REVIVAL OF WESLEYANISM	30
The Sustained Witness	30
The Revivalistic Witnesses	31
The Palmers	31
Prominent Associates	47
The Channels of Revival	47
The National Camp Meeting Association	48
John A. Wood	48
John S. Inskip	53
Inskip's Successors	67
THREE—JOSEPH H. SMITH, 1855–1946	79
EARLY LIFE	79
CONVERSION AND CALL	81
ENTIRE SANCTIFICATION	85
HIS FIRST SERMON	86

CONTENTS

The Preacher's License 88
Home Missionary Labors 90
Conference Membership 92
Full-time Evangelist 93
The Evangelistic Institute 99
Evangelizing Methodism 107
National Holiness Association Work 112
Author 114
Bible-expositor Evangelist 117
    Dean of Holiness Expositors 117
    Expository Principles 118
    Expository Aims 120
    Emotional Appeals 120
    Evangelism's Field of Operation 121
    Evangelism Threatened 122

Missions and Schools 125
    His Missionary Outreach 125
    His Educational Concern 127

Memorabilia 130

FOUR—THE GOSPEL OF GRACE AND GLORY 137

The Starting Point 137
    His Theology Methodistic 137
    His Authority Biblical 138
    His Pattern Pauline 139
    His Ministry Evangelistic 139
    His Doctrine Experiential 139

The Glory and Grace Mediated: Revelation to Man 140
    The World as Revelational 140
    The Written Word as Revelation 141
        Scholarship and the Scriptures 142
        The Scriptural Doctrine of Scripture 143
        Revelation and Inspiration 144
        Inspiration and Illumination 147
        Illumination and Interpretation 148
        The Central Figure in Scripture 150

FIVE—THE GOSPEL OF GRACE AND GLORY (*Continued*) 151

The God of Glory 151

CONTENTS

His Nature 151
His Attributes 152
His Tri-personal Being 152

THE GLORY OF GOD MANIFESTED: CREATION AND PROVIDENCE 153
   In Heaven and Earth 153
   In Angels 155
   In Man 156

THE GLORY MARRED: THE RUIN OF MAN 158
   Origin of Evil 158
   Original Sin 159
   Twofold Nature of Sin 161
   Penalty and Effects of Sin 163
   The Extended Probation 164
   The Cursed Earth 164

SIX—THE GOSPEL OF GRACE AND GLORY *(Continued)* 167

THE GOD OF GRACE MANIFESTED: REDEMPTION FOR MAN 167
   The Person and Work of Christ: The Lord of Glory 167
      The Law of God 167
      The Gospel of Grace 169
      The Gracious Redeemer 169
   The Person and Work of the Holy Spirit:
      The Spirit of Grace and Glory 179
      The Strivings of the Spirit 180
      The Illumination of the Spirit 181
      The Birth of the Spirit 182
      The Witness of the Spirit 184
      The Sanctification of the Spirit 187
      The Guidance of the Spirit 190
      The Gifts of the Spirit 193
      The Unity of the Spirit 195
      The Intercession of the Spirit 198
      The Grieving of the Spirit 200
      The Supply of the Spirit 202

SEVEN—THE GOSPEL OF GRACE AND GLORY *(Continued)* 203

THE GRACE OF GOD REALIZED: THE RECOVERY OF MAN 203
   Grace for Individuals 204
      Justification 206
      Sanctification 219
      Glorification 235

CONTENTS

The Glorious Church 239
    The Fact of the Church 239
    The Foundation of the Church 241
    The Features of the Church 244
    The Function of the Church 249
    The Faith of the Church 254
    The Failure of the Church 257
    The Future of the Church 257
THE GLORY OF GOD MANIFESTED ANEW:
    THE RESTORED GLORY OF MAN 258
The Two Hemispheres of Glory 258
The Glorious Appearing of Christ 259
    Glorified in His Saints 260
    Judgment Against Sinners 261
The Glorious Kingdom of Christ 263

EIGHT—SUMMARY 265

THE DISTINCTIVENESS OF THIS STUDY 265
SUMMARY 266

APPENDIX A 269

APPENDIX B 271

APPENDIX C 273

APPENDIX D 275

FOOTNOTES 279

BIBLIOGRAPHY 311

INDEX 319

CHAPTER ONE

Introduction

World War II occasioned in England the re-study of John Wesley, the great revivalist of the eighteenth century, and his doctrine of superlative piety or Christian perfection.[1] That this English evangelist has had unusual significance since his day is evidenced by the fact that

> With the probable exception of a few statesmen and scientists, perhaps a general or two, John Wesley has received more attention from the pens of biographers and has had more written about him than any other Englishman of the eighteenth century. Time seems scarcely to have affected men's interest in him.[2]

While Wesley has been studied again and again, it has seemed strange to this investigator that some of his American followers have received so little attention. Yet their contribution has been a part of the sustained influence of Wesleyan thought and institutions. One such figure in American Methodism has been the Reverend Joseph H. Smith, 1855–1946.

The Purpose

Statement of the Purpose

Smith was a product and a promoter of a revivalistic movement generally known as the American Holiness Movement. While this trend in American church life has had many facets, Smith was most fully identified with that group which organized in 1867 as the "National Camp-meeting

Association for the Promotion of Holiness," but which is known today as the "National Holiness Association."

An official history of this eighty-five-year-old organization has not yet been written, and the biographies and the autobiographies of its recognized leaders have been but few. Consequently, considerable ignorance prevails concerning the nature and doctrines of the organization. It has had little if any treatment in the majority of books and monographs on American church history, and even books covering the "sects," with which it is usually classed, give it but sketchy treatment.[3]

It has been the central purpose of this study to gain an understanding of the theology of the man who has been the most widely recognized and respected teacher of the movement known as the National Holiness Movement, and thereby also to discover the genius of the Association he represented.[4]

Importance of the Study

Smith's life touched the founding fathers of the National Holiness Association, under whom he was schooled in thought and methods, and also the majority of the younger, contemporary leaders of the organization, whom he also deeply influenced. No other man in the movement has shared with Smith that distinction. He gave more years of consecutive service than any other leader to the specific purpose of promoting "scriptural holiness" through the various channels of this organization. No other American holiness leader with membership in one of the major Protestant denominations has enjoyed such widespread prestige within his own communion and at the same time shared so much of his ministry with interdenominational and denominational holiness bodies.[5]

While the reading public is somewhat acquainted with Joseph Smith, the founder of the Mormon Church, it cannot be said that it is equally informed on Joseph H. Smith, the chief expositor-evangelist of the National Holiness Association. The latter's name has never appeared in *Who's Who in America, Who's Who in Religion, Who's Who in Methodism,* or in any of the dictionaries or encyclopedias of American biography. While, if all his writings for periodicals and books were collected and published, he would have left no less than a volume a year for sixty years, yet most of them have been unnoticed by or lost to the present generation.

This study is further justified by the fact that most of the current writers on the philosophies of religion in America are acquainted with Calvinistic "Fundamentalism," but seem unaware of an Arminian "Orthodoxy" which does not share all the views of Fundamentalism against which liberal philosophers and theologians so strongly protest.[6] Smith claimed to be orthodox and therefore represented a segment within American Protestantism to which some outstanding scholars give little or no recognition.

The perennial interest in the theme of Christian perfection has been manifested again by the recent studies among both the Lutheran[7] and Methodist scholars,[8] by the current public demand for reprints of the older classics in "perfectionistic" literature,[9] by the rapid growth of the contemporary "Pentecostal Movement" with its perfectionistic emphasis, and the recent rise of "dialectical" theologians who challenge Wesleyan perfectionism, denying the possibility of perfection in this life.[10]

When R. Newton Flew was engaged in research for his book *The Idea of Perfection in Christian Theology,* the noted Catholic layman, Friedrich von Hugel, greatly encouraged him "to study more closely the type of piety revealed in the autobiographies of early Methodists...."[11] Although Smith lived later than the period to which von Hugel referred, he no doubt would have ranked well as one of the early Methodists in piety and zeal for the cause of spreading "scriptural holiness over these lands."

The revivalistic periods of American church history have usually produced a measure of unity for considerable sections of Protestantism. With the growing interest and activity in ecumenicity in the western world, it would be a grave oversight to ignore those revivalistic movements which have been potent forerunners of the modern ecumenical movement. Walter M. Horton has intimated that a crisis faces the Protestant churches today as to what treatment shall be given the lesser but significant groups in Protestantism.[12] Smith's revivalistic activities and affiliations make him a representative of one of these "lesser" groups.

LIMITATIONS OF THE SUBJECT

While the central purpose of this study has been theological, nevertheless, it has been necessary to discover the specific historical framework of the movement within which Smith took his place as a leader. Therefore a skeletel view has been presented of the rise of "Wesleyan perfectionism," its progress, decline and revival in American Methodism, and the formation and work of that movement which has striven to perpetuate the doctrines and evangelistic spirit of John Wesley.

The biographical study of Smith has been necessary to discover the type of Christianity he labored to produce. Like Wesley his thought was shaped by his religion and his religion by his thought, which he sought to derive directly from the New Testament.[13]

The theological section of this study has developed that doctrine which was central in Smith's teaching and related it to the major phases of the theological "system" he embraced and expounded in his evangelistic endeavors.

METHOD OF PROCEDURE

The materials for this dissertation have been gathered from widely scattered sources. In addition to engaging in the regular library research, the investigator for this study has visited the publication offices of various "holiness" periodicals, the libraries of a number of "holiness" colleges and Bible institutes, the headquarters of the National Holiness Association to examine the official minutes of the organization, and the homes of relatives and acquaintances of Joseph H. Smith.

Since no official history of the National Holiness Association has been written, this study has drawn heavily upon articles which have appeared in holiness periodicals, written by the foremost leaders in the Holiness Movement. To present the movement as nearly as one of its accredited leaders, such as Smith, would have done it, has been this writer's intent.

Smith left no autobiography, nor has anyone attempted his biography. Such data as have been available have been gleaned from various articles, written sermons, books, letters, official minutes, and personal interviews. In presenting the biographical data on Smith, the method of Wesley's noted biographer, Luke Tyerman, has been largely followed. Tyerman wrote, "I have tried to make Wesley his own biographer." [14]

In formulating Smith's theological position, the procedure has been to study at first-hand his published sermons, Biblical expositions, devotional meditations, addresses, and other written articles to discover inductively and set forth what Smith derived from the New Testament as that "primitive Christianity" he sought to revive or reinstate within those areas of Protestantism in which he and his colleagues ministered.

> What is the central ideal for the present life? And is it the will of God that by His grace we should attain it? These are questions which ought to be raised incessantly and for which Christian theology may reasonably be expected to provide an answer.[15]

The answers to the foregoing questions were the hub of Smith's theology, and the conclusions he reached he sought so to phrase as to make them understandable to all classes and conditions of men.

The central purpose of this study has not been the

proving or disproving of the scriptural soundness of Smith's views, but rather the determining of what has been, and what has not been, the theology championed by Smith and by over two generations of "holiness" preachers in America who have more or less identified themselves with the National Holiness Association and looked to Smith as an official spokesman for them theologically.

In setting forth Smith's interpretation of the Bible, it has not been deemed necessary always to quote the texts or portions of Scripture from which he derived his point of view. At certain junctures, however, the scriptural quotation or references have been given.[16]

Definition of Terms

On the whole Smith accepted the traditionally Wesleyan usage of theological terminology. For him the Christian life was initiated and developed by processes and crises. The first crisis he called, in its total change, the "new birth" or "conversion," but within that change were the pardoning, justifying, regenerating and assuring aspects. He also referred to this epoch as the "first work of grace." The second crisis he termed "holiness," "entire sanctification," "a pure heart," "Christian perfection," "perfect love," "full salvation," "the baptism with the Holy Spirit," "the second blessing, properly so-called," "a personal pentecost," or the "second work of grace." This he held to be "scriptural holiness." [17]

Until the rise of the present "Pentecostal Movement," Smith, with others in Methodism and American holiness circles, was accustomed to speak of this "second crisis" as one's Pentecostal baptism and to hold special meetings for its promulgation which were called "Pentecostal Meetings." Such meetings were held by various National Holiness Association leaders, including Smith, at Annual and General Conferences of Methodism as late as 1909 or 1910.[18] Following the rise (early in the twentieth century) of the "Tongues Movement," often referred to as the "Pentecostal Movement," with its teaching that speaking in tongues is the necessary evidence of the Spirit's baptism, the word "Pentecostal" was for the most part laid aside and the words "holiness" or "full salvation" were more frequently used to describe the theological position and to label certain meetings and ministers advocating the strictly Wesleyan interpretation of the Scriptures on holiness.[19] The National Holiness Association leaders considered "twentieth-century Pentecostalism" an unscriptural perversion of the doctrine of the baptism with the Holy Spirit.[20] Because of their doctrinal differences the leaders of the two movements have not publicly fraternized until the recent formation of the National Association of Evangelicals in 1942.[21]

Smith's theology was captioned by him as "the gospel of grace and glory." By "glory" he meant the real person and the nature behind that person, expressed in the form of works. God's glory centers in His nature, but it is His "nature overflowing the bounds of His own selfhood," in His creative and redemptive activities, that man beholds the divine glory.[22] Man's glory lies in his highest honors and deepest delights coming through honoring God and delighting in Him forever.[23] The "gospel" is the fullest revelation yet given of God's glory and of man's recovery from sin and shame and sorrow to attain his chief end—to glorify God and enjoy Him forever—all of which has been made possible through the person and work of Jesus Christ.[24] "Grace" is the unmerited favor of God extended toward sinful man through Jesus Christ, by which man may be brought into holiness and happiness forever.[25]

Organization of This Volume

This study has been divided into three major divisions. Following the introductory chapter, chapter two covering the first division has been devoted to the historical antecedents and organizational activities of the National Holiness Association with attention having been given to the leading personalities involved. Chapter three, covering the second principal division, has been a biographical study of the foremost expositor-evangelist of the Association, Joseph H. Smith, in which his background, religious experience, ministerial labors and goals, and character have been assessed. In chapters four through seven, the primary purpose of this study has been developed in the setting forth of the theological system which Smith regarded as the central teaching of the Holy Scriptures and the teaching which the National Holiness Association was especially obligated to propagate throughout the world, beginning with Methodism. The concluding chapter has reiterated the distinctive features of this study and summarized its findings.

CHAPTER TWO

The National Holiness Association

THE EVANGELICAL AWAKENING

Early eighteenth-century England was not a period for religious optimism among "the faithful." A careless clergy, an empty ritualism and emptied churches were extremely depressing to such zealous persons as Samuel and Susannah Wesley, occupants of one of the rectories in the Church of England. Among the nineteen children born to that manse were two sons whose influence has been felt around the world.

The Holy Club

While these two sons, John and Charles Wesley, were at Oxford University, John an instructor and Charles a student, they banded themselves together with a few other serious-minded collegians and methodically began the pursuit of holiness through Bible study, prayer, and good works. So regularly did they observe their regimen for devotion, study, and service that they were dubbed "Methodists" by their university associates—a nickname which has stuck.[26]

Methodism was born in a heart struggle for holiness under the roof of one of the great intellectual centers of the English-speaking world. From that "Holy Club" at Oxford, later removed to London, came not only John and Charles Wesley, founder and hymnologist respectively of Methodism, but also the flaming evangelist George Whitefield, known as the greatest preacher of the eighteenth century.[27]

While John Wesley's first assuring religious experience is dated as beginning May 24, 1738,[28] he had really begun his search for "inward holiness" in the year 1725.[29] The anomaly to the modern evangelical mind is that Wesley should have been so intent in his pursuit of sanctification or holiness before he had definitely experienced what evangelicals have taught as the initial stage in salvation or justification by faith.[30]

The successive stages in Wesley's spiritual pilgrimage have not fallen within the special concern of this investigation. However, the consequences of Wesley's "heart-warming experience," manifested in his evangelistic passion, his spiritual discipline, his doctrinal teaching and his religious, moral, and social impact upon the western world, have had direct bearing upon the movement with which this present study has had to deal.

The Holiness Movement

The "Holy Club" at Oxford was the initiation of a "holiness movement" within the established church. At the beginning neither Wesley nor his colleagues had any intention that their simply organized pursuit for personal, inward holiness would ever result in a new denomination outside the pale of the Church of England.[31] Wesley's sole objective was to save his own soul and those of others who might receive help from him.

On January 1, 1733, Wesley preached a sermon before the University, in St. Mary's Church, on the theme, "The Circumcision of the Heart." He described that change thus:

> It is that habitual disposition of the soul which, in the sacred writings, is termed holiness; and to which directly implies, the being cleansed from sin, "from all filthiness both of flesh and spirit;" and, by consequence, the being endued with those virtues which were in Christ Jesus; the being so "renewed in the image of our mind," as to be "perfect as our Father in heaven is perfect."—Vol. i, p. 148.
> In the same sermon I observed, " 'Love is the ful-

filling of the law, and the end of the commandment.'"
It is not only "the first and great" command, but all
the commandments, in one.... In this is perfection, and
glory, and happiness: the royal law of heaven and
earth is this, "Thou shalt love the Lord thy God with
all thy heart, and with all thy soul, and with all thy
mind, and with all thy strength." The one perfect good
shall be your one ultimate end....

I concluded in these words: "Here is the sum of
the perfect law, the circumcision of the heart. Let the
spirit return to God that gave it, with the whole train
of its affections. Other sacrifices from us He would not,
but the living sacrifice of the heart hath He chosen.
Let it be continually offered up to God through Christ, in
flames of holy love...." Have a pure intention of heart,
a steadfast regard to His glory in all our actions...." [32]

That sermon was the first of Wesley's published writings, and he "scrupled not" to term this standard of Christian experience as "perfection." Writing forty years later, after having tested his doctrine in the laboratory of Christian experience, Wesley affirmed that he had not had to materially change his view of the Biblical teaching on the theme and experience of "inward holiness" or "Christian perfection." [33]

Through the hymnology of the Wesley brothers, the writings and sermons of John Wesley, the discussions at the earliest "Methodistic" conferences, and the preaching, writings, and testimonies of those converted to the Wesleyan interpretation and type of religious experience,[34] the modern holiness movement, of which the National Holiness Association is a direct product, took its rise.[35]

The Earliest Achievements

Wesley's ministerial record after 1738 has been one of undiminished amazement to the students of church history. Yet it was forged on the anvil of hardship, self-denial and much bitter opposition to his doctrine and methods. He endured it all because he believed God had raised up the people called Methodists to "spread scriptural holiness over these lands." [36]

Wesley's formal organization of the Methodist societies included, among other groups, the feasts, band meetings, and the class meetings—a sort of social confessional in which the spiritual ills of Christians and the further culture of new converts might be cared for. These class meetings became "schools of holiness" in which the believers were to be hastened on to their full privilege and duty—becoming entirely sanctified.[37] Wesley's own recommendation to his co-laborers was this: "Therefore, all our preachers should make a point of preaching perfection to believers, constantly, strongly and explicitly; and all believers should mind this one thing, and continually agonize for it." [38]

By 1789, at the last Conference of Methodism attended by Wesley, it was shown that in fifty years of "holiness preaching," 240 Methodist societies had been formed with 541 itinerant preachers and 134,549 holding tickets as evidence they were members in good standing.[39] But the moral and social influences upon the Isles were not so easily tabulated. This same Methodistic root was transplanted to the American colonies in the 1760's and had flourished to the point in 1790 where 57,811 members, ninety-seven circuits, and more than 165 traveling preachers were reported in Methodism on this side of the Atlantic.[40] These earliest American-Methodist itinerants kindled revival fires wherever they went and were apparently to a man devoted to the task of reforming the continent and spreading scriptural holiness over these lands. In writing of them Gaddis affirmed that "personal salvation seems everywhere to have been regarded by the Methodist revivalists in terms of a first and second work of grace." [41] They were promoters of that movement which had begun at Oxford, spread to all England, Ireland, Scotland, and Wales, and which was to test its strength in the cities and frontiers of the New World.

The earliest religious influences in American Protestantism, except the Quaker influence, were anti-perfectionistic.

Calvinistic, Lutheran, and Anglican thought had largely molded religious thinking before Methodism arrived, and it was a serious question as to whether or not Methodism with its "perfectionistic revivalism" would continue to sweep America as it had the land of its birth.[42]

While the Methodists were assembled at General Conference in Baltimore in 1800, a holiness revival broke out under the leadership of the preachers attending the Conference and spread it up and down the coast, with so many being sanctified that Abel Stevens has called it a "Pentecost."[43]

That holiness continued to be emphasized within early American Methodism is further evidenced by the fact that her preachers were *advised* to read often Wesley's *Plain Account,* and after 1816 for many years were *required* to read it as a part of the Methodist Course of Study. By 1808, when Methodist standards of doctrine were fixed, there had been grafted into the tree of American religious life a dynamic, denominational body whose most distinctive doctrine was that of Christian perfection or scriptural holiness.[44]

The Decline of Wesleyanism

It has become a truism that for any movement to maintain its original ideals and zeal beyond a forty-year period is a rare exception. The whole religious history of ancient Israel was marked by advances, declines, and great revivals. Methodism has been no exception to this pattern.

Wesley's Struggle

All who first rallied around Wesley did not maintain the high level of piety with which they had begun. Two or three of the original Holy Club conspicuously failed to live up to their earlier vows, and one, who married a sister of Wesley, was "pronounced by the historian of the club an 'unmitigated scamp.' "[45] All movement was not forward and upward.

After forming the Methodist societies, the class meetings became the occasion for close examination of the faith and conduct of their members. Not all could report progress; some had failed, and backsliding was not uncommon. "Some of these were reclaimed, and others were expelled... 'that, as far as in us lay, the scandal was rolled away from the Society.' "[46]

> Formerly we thought [wrote Wesley], one saved from sin could not fall; now we know the contrary. We are surrounded with instances of those who lately experienced all that I mean by perfection. They had both the fruit of the Spirit, and the witness; but they have now lost both.... There is no such height or strength of holiness as it is impossible to fall from....[47]

In spite of these failures, Wesley ever stirred up his preachers to press the message he declared God had raised up the Methodists to proclaim. Whether preaching in the 1740's or writing letters at the close of his itinerant life (1791), Wesley exhorted, "Whenever you have an opportunity of speaking to believers, urge them to go on to perfection."[48] When Wesley died he had no fears that there would ever cease to be a people called "Methodists," but he did fear their departure from the "grand depositum" of doctrine and experience divinely committed to them.[49] His fears were not unfounded.

American Methodism Drifts

One of the by-products of a frontier evangelism in America was the camp meeting.[50] While originating among the Presbyterians, the camp meeting grew in such favor with the Methodists that within the first two decades of the nineteenth century it became a peculiarly effective institution in the spread of Methodism.[51] However, Presbyterianism soon repudiated the camp meeting because of the emotional excitement which it engendered, but Methodism increasingly exploited its possibilities. Paul H. Douglass has affirmed that

It was not long before every presiding elder's district held such a meeting. It has been estimated that by 1812 at least four hundred Methodist camp meetings were being held. The Methodists even brought the institution from the Western frontiers to the conservative East. Even in staid old New England the camp meeting took root and flourished.[52]

With Methodism's literature definitely keyed to the pitch of "holiness unto the Lord," her class meetings veritable "schools of holiness," and her camp meetings powerful instruments[53] for the "precipitation" of the experience of perfect love, it has become an enigma to some that she should soon drift from her original course.

But with the growth of the anti-slavery agitation, doctrinal controversies between the denominations, religious fanaticisms in the name of perfection, and reactions to the autocratic character of the Methodist episcopacy, there came a decline in the spiritual fervor and holiness emphasis of the Methodist Church.[54] Her bishops warned of the dangerous trends of her people in 1840, but seemingly little was done to change that trend.[55] And even though the Finney revivals were calling Christians to perfection and some successful Methodist evangelists and leaders were strongly pressing the message, yet Methodism as a whole continued to "fall away."[56]

So far had Methodism moved in 1860 from her original standards and earlier practices that

> Camp-meetings, which had been a great power in the Methodist Church, and in which tens of thousands had been converted and sanctified, had so far fallen into disrepute, that the church papers were earnestly discussing the propriety of wholly abandoning them.
>
> For several years prior to 1867 . . . there was a growing opposition to the subject of entire sanctification as a distinct experience. This opposition came from both pulpit and pew, and was often met with at the local camp-meetings. The opposition became at times so violent that in many places the professors of this experience found little or no sympathy or encouragement at these annual meetings.[57]

THE AMERICAN REVIVAL OF WESLEYANISM

During the second quarter of the nineteenth century, when the ministers of Methodism were becoming less and less insistent upon the original emphasis of Wesley, some eminent witnesses to Wesleyanism continued to appear within the ranks of the church.

The Sustained Witness

The names of Wilbur Fisk, Stephen Olin, Timothy Merritt, James Caughey, Nathan Bangs, and Bishops L. L. Hamline and E. S. Janes have been connected with the best in nineteenth-century Methodism. Nathan Bangs became "the father of the missionary work of the Methodist Episcopal Church" and one of its trusted historians.[58] James Caughey, a member of the Troy Conference, became a successful evangelist in many places throughout the United States, Canada, and Great Britain. So effective were his meetings in the chief cities of Ireland and England that 20,000 were converted and 10,000 sanctified.[59] Under Caughey's ministry abroad William Booth, then but a lad, "made transactions with God which led to his world-wide ministry."[60] Wesleyan University at Middletown, Connecticut, the oldest of Methodist colleges in the United States and the mother of Methodist colleges, has been proud to own as her presidents Wilbur Fisk and Stephen Olin. "Great names such as Fisk and Olin have adorned its history," wrote Luccock and Hutchinson.[61] Olin's name has gone down as one of the most influential delegates to the meeting which founded the Evangelical Alliance in London in 1846.[62] Timothy Merritt, assistant editor of the *Christian Advocate,* was held in highest esteem in his day.

> No man has been taken from New England Methodism, who had a higher claim to an honorable memorial among us than had "Father Merritt.". . . He was a learned man, a man deeply read in divinity and philosophy, critical in his observations, powerful in his analyses, of untiring application, deeply experienced in the things

of God, always exhibiting the fruits of the Spirit by the patience of faith and the labor of love.[63]

Bishops L. L. Hamline and E. S. Janes were elected to the episcopacy at the General Conference of 1844. Janes was conspicuous in the centenary celebration of Methodism's coming to America and her founding of Drew Theological Seminary as a memorial of that event.[64]

Thus, college presidents, editors, general officers, bishops, and evangelists, as represented by the foregoing persons, were among those who continued to testify and speak out for holiness or Wesleyan perfection during the period of Methodism's drastic reaction to her own doctrine.[65]

The Revivalistic Witnesses

Henry Worrall, the son of members of the Established Church, in his fourteenth year, heard that Wesley was to preach at Bradford, England, at five o'clock one morning. Stealing away from his home near Bradford, he hurried to hear one of the most talked of preachers in England in his day. Wesley's sermon "enlightened" him, and, upon attending subsequent meetings, he was "converted" in Methodist fashion. "He joined the Society, and received a ticket certifying his membership, from the hand of Mr. Wesley." [66]

A dozen years later found Worrall in New York, where he married a Miss Dorothy Wade, and to that union were born sixteen children. Two of these children, daughters, were to fill as real a role in reviving Methodism's "most distinctive doctrine," as the two sons of Samuel and Susannah Wesley had in formulating and promoting it nearly a century earlier in England.[67]

The Palmers. Sarah,[68] the oldest of these two Worrall daughters figuring in this study, sought God at the age of ten but did not profess conversion until her thirteenth year. Shortly after her conversion at a camp meeting, her class leader gave her a copy of Wesley's *Plain Account of Christian Perfection* which quickly led her to seek "a clean heart."

At a subsequent camp-meeting session she sought and professed to obtain entire sanctification.

In 1831, Sarah married Thomas A. Lankford of Richmond, Virginia, a successful businessman who never evaded official responsibility within the church and whose religious faith was one with his wife's. Among the several religious duties which Mrs. Lankford had come to perform each week was that of conducting a "social meeting," or prayer service, in each of two Methodist Episcopal churches in New York City. To conserve her energies, Mrs. Lankford proposed to her husband and to her brother-in-law, Dr. Walter C. Palmer, that these two prayer meetings be united in one and be held at the Palmer-Lankford home which the two families shared together. The suggestion was approved, and in August, 1835, Mrs. Lankford opened a prayer meeting which later became widely known as "the Tuesday Meeting." [69]

The first "Tuesday Meeting," held at the Palmer residence, 54 Rivingston Street, was a significant one. Forty women, representing the Mulberry Street and the Allen Street Methodist Episcopal Churches, assembled and followed a simple order of singing, Scripture reading, prayer, and testimony. The afternoon reached its peak when the wife of the Reverend Timothy Merritt[70] of the Methodist Book Concern in the city arose and said, "For thirty years I have been a seeker. This afternoon Christ is *my* Saviour. Never before could I say it without fear...." [71] That testimony, along with the testimonies of many others, sealed the matter for Mrs. Lankford that her proposed change of the meetings from the churches to her home was a spiritual success. Although she did not foresee it, she had founded a weekly assembly which was to touch the outmost posts of Methodism and deeply affect other evangelical denominations.

Mrs. Phoebe Worrall Palmer, a younger sister of Mrs. Sarah Worrall Lankford, had not yet entered into the experience of "perfect love" when the first Tuesday meeting was held in her home. Like Sarah, Phoebe had sought the Saviour in childhood. But as Phoebe moved on in her Christian pilgrimage defects and dissatisfactions within her experience began to appear. Class meetings, private prayer, and public services did not satisfy her spiritual hunger.

At nineteen years of age, Phoebe married Dr. Walter C. Palmer,[72] a young physician, the son of devout Methodist parents in whose home had been held for years a weekly class meeting of their church.[73] Walter C. Palmer had been converted at the age of thirteen and remained thereafter a loyal "believer" and faithful worker in the church.[74]

Although Dr. and Mrs. Walter Palmer were active and participated in the "great revivals in Allen Street Church," by 1835 neither of them had attained that "perfect love," which Mrs. Lankford was promoting through the "Tuesday Meeting" within their home. When Mrs. Palmer had reached the place of utter abandonment to the life of faith, irrespective of religious feeling, she too entered into the fullness of the Spirit. "... Oh! into what a reign of light, glory and purity was my soul at this moment ushered! I felt that I was but as a drop in the ocean of infinite love, and Christ was all in all...." [75]

While both Mrs. Lankford and Mrs. Palmer enjoyed moments of great ecstacy of religious feeling, these came only after they had fully determined to live without them, should that be the divine will. After having struggled over the matter of "pious feelings" themselves, both of them ever after made their public appeals to faith in the "immutable Word" of divine promise as that which is requisite to finding "purity of heart." Emotion was never emphasized as an object of pursuit or as the highest evidence of grace.[76]

Dr. Palmer, a graduate of the College of Physicians and Surgeons in New York City, was deeply influenced by the testimony of his wife and sister-in-law. Without protracted struggle, Dr. Palmer soon "consecrated his all" to Christ and believed he was accepted. The "witness of the Spirit" was given, and from that moment on he was a constant witness to Christian holiness.[77] With Dr. Palmer's enlistment in the cause of "scriptural holiness," this oustanding "lay trio" moved forward until their deaths, in promoting "the central idea of Christianity" through the Tuesday Meeting, camp meetings, church revivals, holiness conventions, and the printed page. Thus, a "layman's movement" to produce revivals of holiness was under way fully twenty years before the Layman's Revival of 1857–58 and the rise of D. L. Moody, the noted lay evangelist of the last quarter of the nineteenth century.

Possessing greater gifts for leadership than her sister Mrs. Lankford, Mrs. Phoebe Palmer soon became the recognized leader of the Tuesday Meeting, which continued until December, 1839, as a gathering only for women. After Mrs. Lankford moved to Caldwell-on-the-Hudson in 1840, Mrs. Palmer took full responsibility for the Tuesday meeting until her death in 1874.[78]

In December, 1839, Dr. Thomas C. Upham, professor of Mental and Moral Philosophy and tutor in Hebrew at Bowdoin College, Brunswick, Maine, was in New York City, superintending the publication of one of his books. Mrs. Upham had accompanied him and was brought to the Tuesday Meeting by a Mrs. Cox. A few months prior to this, Mrs. Upham, a Congregationalist, had attended a Methodist Episcopal church in Maine and there had heard of holiness as a second crisis in Christian experience, obtainable now by faith. Seeking in private, she entered into the experience and became a witness to her husband and in public services to the "sanctifying grace of God." [79]

At the next Tuesday Meeting, Dr. Upham, with other gentlemen, was in attendance. Mrs. Palmer was present, and by her clear answers to his queries the obstacles for him were removed from the pathway of faith. On a subsequent evening he returned and reported to Mrs. Lankford his experience.

> I lay awake all night thinking, "is it safe to give myself to Christ and believe He receives just because the Bible says so?" Toward morning I decided to venture.

I renewed my consecration, which I had often done before, for I had determined to be a faithful servant; but the consecration was to be renewed with this addition: *to believe* it was accepted; and Christ gave Himself to me in all his offices.[80]

Upham was ever grateful to Mrs. Palmer for her assistance in his spiritual odyssey. Of his religious experience in her parlor he wrote her that it was "in religion, the 'beginning of days'" to him. Mrs. Upham declared to Mrs. Palmer, "You have begotten him in the gospel." [81] Upham considered himself and Mrs. Palmer looked upon him as her pupil. So much so was this true that the learned professor was rebuked by his teacher in the faith when he turned to a Quietistic and an excessively mystical view of Christian experience.[82]

Having returned to Maine a united household in the faith of holiness, the Uphams opened their "Congregational" home to a weekly holiness meeting.[83] From the time of Upham's attendance at the Tuesday Meeting it became a mixed gathering of both the sexes and the several branches of the Protestant churches. Because of its success and inspiration, the Tuesday Meeting became a pattern for other "parlor meetings" throughout the eastern cities and into the midwest centers of population.[84]

Early in the history of the Tuesday Meeting a Congregational paper carried an extended report of it.

> Friends, we assure you that these meetings are not for sectarian or party purposes. A free, hearty, general invitation is extended to all. . . .
>
> Our very soul has leaped joyfully in witnessing how completely the Spirit of God annihilates the spirit of *sectarianism,* and leaps over the boundaries of Shibboleths. Here we see Methodists, Baptists, Presbyterians, Episcopalians, Quakers, United Brethren, and Jews in Christ, forgetting creeds, confessions, hair-splittings, and party distinctions, sitting side by side, drinking deeply of the one living fountain. . . .
>
> Not Wesley, not Fletcher, not Finney, not Mahan, not Upham, but the Bible, the holy BIBLE, is the first

and last, and in the midst always. The BIBLE is the standard, the groundwork, the platform, the creed. Here we stand on common ground, and nothing but the spirit of this blessed book will finally eradicate and extirpate a sectarian spirit.[85]

Dr. John A. Roche, at one time the pastor of the Palmers, wrote the following account for the *Ladies' Repository,* a Methodist publication for Methodist women:

It is one of the greatest spiritual centers in any land. It is attended by professors of religion, without regard to sex or denomination.... Probably in no church will there be found, from week to week, so many earnest believers drawn together, from different evangelical bodies. We doubt whether under any pulpit of our country, there sit as many ministers, for the single purpose of spiritual help. For successive weeks, we have seen there from twenty to thirty preachers of the Gospel. Among these are found Baptists, Congregationalists, Dutch Reformed, German Reformed, Presbyterians, Protestant Episcopalians, Methodists, and they mingle in the assembly, engage in the exercises, and assert their profit by the means. The privilege to speak, extends to all, and is as promptly embraced by some that are not of our church, as by any that are in it....

In this meeting are persons from all parts of the United States and British possessions; from England, Ireland, and Scotland.... Mrs. Palmer, when there, uniformly speaks, though she consumes no more time than would be allowed to another. It is not an unfrequent [*sic*] thing for a half dozen, and sometimes double that number, to profess to find the blessing for which they sought, in that place.[86]

Mrs. Palmer conducted the meeting above the level of debate, controversy, or mere lecturing. Anyone was at liberty to speak, sing, or propose united prayer just so long as it furthered the main object of the meeting—that of promoting holiness of heart and life among those in attendance.[87]

To this meeting came many of the great leaders of Methodism—Nathan Bangs, Stephen Olin, John Dempster,

L. L. Hamline, E. S. Janes, William Taylor, W. L. Harris, R. S. Foster, and others of the bishopric—as well as leading pastors and laymen from various congregations of the denomination. Methodism was being rejuvenated from within by the influences released during these parlor meetings in that great metropolis.[88]

Congregationalism, through Doctors Asa Mahan and T. C. Upham; Presbyterianism, through Doctors Ball, W. E. Boardman, and the Reverend Henry Belden; the Reformed Church, through the Reverend I. M. See; and the Baptists, through Deacon George Morse and the Reverend E. M. Levy; the Friends, through Sarah Smiley, David Updegraff, and Dougan Clark; and German Methodism, through Dr. William Nast, along with others from other communions—all felt the impact of the Tuesday Meeting upon their denominations.[89]

After Mrs. Phoebe Palmer's death in 1874, the Tuesday Meeting was continued by Dr. Palmer, with the assistance of Mrs. Sarah Lankford, until his death in 1883. Mrs. Sarah Lankford Palmer (second wife of Dr. Palmer) continued the meeting until her death in 1896. Thus, without interruption for sixty years, the Worrall sisters had maintained a "school of holiness" in their home, with as many as three hundred frequently in attendance, to which men and women came from many parts of the world.[90]

When Mrs. Lankford Palmer's funeral was held in 1896, the Board of Bishops of the Methodist Episcopal Church, in business session at Clifton Springs, New York, telegraphed the following message to her pastor, the Reverend Alexander McLean:

> Official duties detain us here. Her memory is precious to the whole Christian Church. Praise God for her holy life. Signed: John P. Newman, W. F. Mallalieu, J. N. Fitzgerald, E. G. Andrews, R. S. Foster, Thomas Bowman, C. D. Foss, S. M. Merrill, W. X. Ninde, H. W. Warren, Isaac W. Joyce, John M. Walden, C. H. Fowler, Daniel A. Goodsell, John F. Hurst, John H. Vincent.[91]

While serving as associate editor of the *New York Christian Advocate*, the Reverend Timothy Merritt[92] attended a "love-feast" at the Mulberry Street Methodist Church at which Mrs. Lankford was in attendance. After the service Merritt remarked to Mrs. Lankford that it would be well if the testimonies uttered at such services were published and thereby given wider influence. To this she agreed. From that conversation Merritt conceived an idea. Upon severing connections with the *Christian Adovcate,* Merritt returned to Boston and after prayerful deliberation determined to publish a magazine wholly devoted to promoting "Christian holiness." Mrs. Lankford agreed to furnish him an account of her experience for his publication. Finally, there appeared in July, 1839, a twenty-four-page periodical known as *The Guide to Christian Perfection.* The sole objective of the paper was to further Wesleyan perfectionism. The pioneer issue carried this statement from the pen of Merritt:

> We have, as Methodists, in general, adopted the views of the Rev. John Wesley on this subject; not because they are his views, but because he has given us the doctrine of the New Testament on this point, and that more clearly than any other writer within the compass of our knowledge.[93]

Thus was born the first independent-holiness periodical within the ranks of Methodism for the revived advocacy and widespread promotion of Wesleyan perfection.[94]

In 1840, the Reverend D. S. King, a Conference associate of Merritt's, appeared as joint editor and publisher of the magazine which soon changed its name to *The Guide to Holiness*. In 1851 the Reverend H. V. Degen became editor and publisher of *The Guide,* having had considerable experience in publication work while employed by the Methodist Book Concern in New York, where he had become acquainted with Merritt. When Degen's editorship began, the subscription list stood between twenty-five hundred and three thousand. Within the next decade the circulation steadily advanced until sixteen thousand copies of each issue rolled from the press. Checked by the war, it resumed its rise in 1865, when the Palmers purchased the periodical and published it in New York. By 1867 about thirty thousand issues per month appeared, and before the Palmers laid it down over thirty-seven thousand subscribers were reading monthly reports on the Tuesday Meeting at the Palmer household and other news concerning the reviving of churches and the spread of scriptural holiness around the world.[95]

The Guide exerted considerable influence in the awakening of the Methodist Church and other denominations to the message of "heart purity." Contributions for the periodical were early sought from those in the various denominations who were "following in the footsteps of Wesley," among whom were Dr. and Mrs. T. C. Upham and Dr. Asa Mahan.[96] The Reverend William Taylor, later Bishop of Africa, read *The Guide,* was deeply influenced by it as a young minister, and scattered it as tracts over his circuit. It had helped lead him into the experience and profession of "full salvation."[97] Along with many others, the Reverend S. A. Keen, an Ohio minister and later presiding elder and general-holiness evangelist for Methodism, was deeply influenced by *The Guide* in his search for purity of heart.[98]

In 1865, the Palmers purchased *The Guide* and another periodical published by members of the Pittsburgh Conference of the Methodist Episcopal Church, called *The Beauty of Holiness,* and combined them in an effort to unify the ranks and advocates of the holiness doctrine. For a time Mrs. Palmer was editor but later shared the editorship of the paper with Dr. Palmer, who continued as its editor after Mrs. Palmer's death in 1874. *The Guide* publishers become dispensers of holiness literature, written by Reverend James Caughey, Mrs. Phoebe Palmer, William McDonald, J. A. Wood, Dr. Asa Mahan, Professor T. C. Upham, and others whose writing conformed to the Wesleyan interpretation.

Mrs. Palmer's pen reached many she never met. Her writing career began in the early forties and continued until

1874. She wrote mainly for four periodicals—*The Christian Advocate and Journal, Methodist Magazine, Ladies' Repository,* and *Guide to Holiness* (earlier called *Guide to Christian Perfection*). Her books numbered not less than twelve different titles, several of which ran through many editions in England, Canada, and the United States. Her book *The Way of Holiness* alone passed through fifty-two editions within forty years.[99]

Mrs. Palmer also carried on an unusually large chain of correspondence with men and women within the Methodist Church and with many beyond its borders. She conducted *gratis* a "soul clinic by mail," and later published many of these letters, without disclosing the identity of the correspondents, in order to meet like spiritual needs in the lives of her readers. Although her pen was very active, she was forced to write in her diary on March 1, 1873, "The demands of my correspondents are far beyond my ability to meet, either in time or in physical endurance. I write enough to make volumes, yearly, a large portion of my letters being to persons I have never seen."[100]

> Inasmuch as the Bible is not a sectarian book, she wrote, or holiness the mere doctrine of a sect, it has been my aim to present it as the absolute requirement of the Bible, and the binding upon all, of every name, rather than as a mere doctrine of a sect. In doing this, I have kept closely to Bible terms—Holiness, Sanctification, and Perfect Love.[101]

Not only did people *come* to her for counsel and instruction at the "Tuesday Meeting" and through letters of inquiry, but Mrs. Palmer *went* to them through the printed page and a public ministry.

Three years after her profession of purity of heart, Mrs. Palmer began a series of "evangelistic expeditions" which did not terminate until the last year of her life, thirty-four years later.[102] At first within her home city, then out into the surrounding states and Canada, for four years in the British Isles, and from coast to coast in the United States after 1865, she answered calls to present the message of perfect love and revival. Wherever she went revivals were kindled and often hundreds were converted and sanctified in or as a result of her services.[103]

At first Dr. Palmer took a month's vacation each year from his medical practice in New York in order to accompany his wife and assist in her evangelistic labors. After 1859 he turned from his lucrative medical practice to devote most of his time to promoting revivals and "spreading scriptural holiness over these lands." [104]

Mrs. Palmer visited camp meetings in the summer and various churches, schools, and Christian homes in the other months of the year to conduct holiness meetings. In 1845 she with Mrs. Sarah Lankford visited Wesleyan University, Middletown, Connecticut, ministering to both faculty and students on the theme of "present holiness." In not a few of these contacts many ministers, including Methodist preachers and presiding elders, Baptist and other denominational ministers, were won to Christ in "full salvation." [105] In Boston she led a member of the House of Representatives into "the rest of perfect love," and preached to Presbyterians, Episcopalians, and Unitarians, as well as to Methodists, where "the deepest interest prevailed." [106]

During the fourth decade of the century, Mrs. Palmer sensed a rising tide of interest in this "most distinctive doctrine of Methodism." On October 27, 1844, she wrote in her diary, "I am rejoiced, indeed, that it is becoming more a matter of experience with our ministers. Dr. Olin now enjoys the blessing." [107] That very year she had taken great courage in the possible triumph of her work by the elevation of L. L. Hamline and E. S. Janes to the bishopric of Methodism, men whose faith and testimony were one with hers in an hour when she estimated that not more than one in fifty in her denomination professed the attainment of the grace of entire sanctification.[108] She wrote these bishops personal letters in which she expressed her inner conviction: "... *I have a divine conviction on my mind, that you have been specifically raised up for the promotion of holiness in the church....*"[109] She further expressed the view that the lack of a definite experience of holiness among the Methodist ministry hindered the progress of the church as nothing else.[110]

In 1851, after having traveled in evangelistic labors through the New England and mid-Atlantic states, Mrs. Palmer wrote of her faith and convictions to Mrs. Mary D. James as follows:

> Never has my mind been so arrested to the importance of the fact that it is for the want of personal holiness, that so little is done by the laity, in the work of soul-saving. Ministers cannot do the work of the people in this department.... O, for a holy ministry, and a holy church.[111]

She strove not only for a sanctified ministry but also for the establishment of the laity in personal holiness and soul-winning service within the churches. She was out to raise up a "Laity for the times." Under that caption she wrote a series of articles for the columns of *The Christian Advocate and Journal* in 1857,[112] the very year the Layman's Revival broke out in New York.[113]

The part which the Palmers played in "the second evangelical awakening" seems to be little recognized if not unknown to many students of American revivals. Dr. J. Edwin Orr in his book *The Second Evangelical Awakening in Great Britain* gave some credit to the Palmers for the nineteenth-century awakening,[114] but seemingly had not sufficiently examined the evidence for the large part they had in preparing the minds of laymen and ministers both in the States and in Canada for the outburst of revival which came to both sides of the Atlantic.

For five consecutive summers previous to the Layman's Revival, the Palmers had been holding camp meetings in the province of Ontario, then known as Canada West. Their very first visit there in 1853 was unusually fruitful.

> The mayor of Kingston was powerfully blest, over *five hundred* professed conversion, and nearly as many obtained the full assurance of faith. That meeting gave new life, and a fresh impetus to camp meetings in Canada. The Wesleyan Methodist Conference reported an addition of *six thousand* that year,—mostly from the region where the camp-meeting had been held. . . .
>
> From that time forward, Dr. and Mrs. Palmer attended four camp-meetings in Canada, every summer, for a number of years in succession. . . .[115]

Nowhere on this side of the Atlantic did the Palmers reap larger harvests in conversions and in believers entering entire sanctification, than in Methodist circles in Ontario, Canada.[116]

The summer of 1857 found the Palmers in camp meetings in both Upper and Lower Canada. At the Brighton camp two hundred were saved and scores were sanctified. Mrs. Palmer expressed her conviction about Christian holiness for believers in these words:

> O, I do wonder that the attention of the Christian world is not more concentrated on this all-important experience, the attainment of which, should it become general, would soon bring about the conversion of the world to God.[117]

At Millbrook Camp the altars were filled with seekers for either pardon or purity. The services sometimes kept the Palmers busy from eight in the morning to near midnight.[118] At St. Andrews, near Montreal, hundreds were moved upon visibly while the Palmers addressed the people. At Prescott, with five or six thousand present, Mrs. Palmer pressed for decisions, and over two hundred names were taken of those who had found either pardon or purity.[119]

On October 7, the Palmers arrived in Hamilton, C. W., with plans laid to leave the next morning for New York. Two of the three ministers in the city brought their midweek prayer meeting groups together with a view to having the Palmers address them. Of that service Mrs. Palmer wrote to her sister Mrs. S. A. Lankford, "And while talking in the meeting, I felt a divine power pressing me mightily to urge upon the people to set themselves apart at once, to work for God in promoting a revival." [120] About thirty accepted the challenge, and the Palmers agreed to postpone their departure for New York. The ten days which followed brought nearly four hundred new recruits into the Christian fold, and many were sanctified.[121] A like series of services were immediately held in London, C. W., in which another two hundred were "added to the Lord," and hundreds professed having received the baptism with the Holy Ghost.[122]

Summarizing the results of the campaigns that summer and fall in Canada, in a letter to Bishop and Mrs. Hamline, Mrs. Palmer wrote:

> Never have we witnessed such triumphs of the cross as during the past summer and fall. I think ... not less than two thousand have been gathered into the fold, at various meetings we have attended. Hundreds of believers have been sanctified wholly, and hundreds have received baptisms of the Holy Ghost, beyond any former experience.[123]

Before the close of 1857 calls came from many quarters in the eastern United States, Upper Canada, Bermuda, and the British Isles for the Palmers to conduct special services there. They had become an integral part of that extraordinary revival which in the year 1858 was to sweep every state in the United States, "adding a million converts to the churches, accomplishing untold good, yet being utterly free from the fanaticism which had marred earlier American awakenings." [124]

In June, 1859, the Palmers began evangelistic labors in England which, with the help of other evangelists, precipitated a movement in the United Kingdom similar to the one in America. That awakening "affected every county in Ulster, Scotland, Wales, and England, adding a million accessions to the evangelical churches, accomplishing a tremendous ... social uplift, and ... home and foreign missionary activity." [125]

The Methodist Quarterly Review, reviewing the Palmer's work abroad, stated:

> In some *three score* places where Dr. and Mrs. Palmer labored, the power of God was wonderfully displayed.... In many towns, all denominations shared in the precious work... ministers and laymen, bowed at the same altar, and became witnesses of perfect love. When theatres are emptied, rumshops closed, policemen left idle, blasphemers taught to pray, defrauders compelled to make restitution, and thousands of awakened souls made joyful in the Redeemer's love, the work must be confessed to be of God.[126]

Dr. Orr has called this the "Second Evangelical Awakening," a new thesis still unrecognized in its fullest dimensions by most historians.[127] The fifty years which followed constituted "a distinct and definite period of the expansion of the Christian Church," and was marked by evangelism throughout.[128] D. L. Moody, Evans Roberts, R. A. Torrey, Wilbur Chapman, "Gypsy" Smith, and others of the non-perfectionist churches, along with the evangelists of the National Camp-meeting Association for the Promotion of Holiness, pressed the claims of Christ upon the English-speaking world.[129]

Mrs. Phoebe Palmer closed her labors in New York, the city where she had begun them, in 1874. As she ended her nearly forty years of useful life, Dr. T. Dewitt Talmadge declared that she had lived to see the whole Christian world awakening to the importance and place of the doctrine of Christian sanctification. Said he,

> Twenty-five thousand souls saved under the instrumentality of Phoebe Palmer! ... Oh, that the name of Phoebe Palmer might be one of the watch-words to rouse up the church universal! The Methodist Church cannot monopolize her name. She belonged to that church, she lived in it, she died in it, she loved it; but you cannot build any denominational wall high enough to shut out that light from our souls... let the story of her life and death thrill all nations.[130]

Dr. Palmer continued to promote the interests of *The Guide to Holiness* and, with Mrs. Sarah A. Lankford Palmer's assistance, the Tuesday Meeting. In 1877, Mrs. Sarah Palmer was invited to conduct holiness meetings at Methodism's leading summer assembly, the famed Ocean Grove Camp-meeting, Ocean Grove, New Jersey, which she continued to do for eighteen consecutive summers, with never a fruitless meeting.[131]

Upon the death of Dr. Palmer, *The Guide to Holiness* was continued under the editorship of the Reverend George Hughes, a Methodist minister who had become the first secretary of the National Camp-meeting Association for the Promotion of Holiness in 1867. Dr. Palmer saw the danger of carrying organizational activities for the promotion of holiness to the point of producing schism. This he carefully avoided by working, as had Mrs. Phoebe Palmer and her sister, in connection with the regular channels of Methodism. "Let us not forget that the M.E. Church was established to spread scriptural holiness over these lands," he declared, and entreated thus:

> It will not be thought presumption in one who has been identified with the cause for nearly half a century to affectionately exhort all lovers of Holiness not to have anything to do with any movement that tends to distract the Churches, and bring the witnesses of full salvation into collision with the pastors.[132]

Holding these views, the Palmers did not become members of any of the holiness associations, although they did attend and at times participation in the National Camp-meetings for the Promotion of Holiness.[133]

The Reverends William McDonald,[134] George Hughes,[135] and A. Atwood, early promoters of the National Camp Meeting Committee, agreed that the Palmers did the pioneer work for the revival of the holiness doctrine within Methodism through the Tuesday Meeting, the *Guide*, and their evangelistic and literary efforts, which finally resulted in the forming of the organization which is known today as the National Holiness Association.

Prominent Associates. Against great opposition in some quarters the Palmers had pressed for a return to "the faith of the fathers" of Methodism. With no organization to back them or funds beyond their own to sustain them, they championed throughout the land the cause of a holiness revival. "Those cooperating with them were stigmatized as 'Palmerites,' " and not a few felt they must strongly resist the emphasis of their teaching and meetings.[137] In spite of criticism they still enjoyed the approval, personal friendship, and attendance at their meetings of the "elect" of Methodism, such as Bishops Hamline, Janes, and William Taylor; Doctors Bangs, Olin, Kidder, Peck, and Lowrey; the Reverends Alfred Cookman, James Caughey, John S. Inskip, and many others. Bishop Matthew Simpson's commendation of Mrs. Phoebe Palmer added to the lustre of her name within Christendom.[138]

Beyond the borders of Methodism, Professor Thomas C. Upham and Dr. Asa Mahan, Congregationalists, were among their most noted associates. David Updegraff of the Friends Church, Dr. Charles Cullis of the Episcopalian Church, Dr. Boardman of the Presbyterian Church, all influential within their own denominations, could be numbered among their colleagues in the promotion of the holiness ideal.[139]

The Channels of Revival. Beyond the Tuesday Meeting and other like gatherings in the vicinity of New York, the Palmers had chosen the established services and organizations of the Methodist Church and the local ministerial associations in various areas through which to conduct their teaching ministry. Methodist district and state camp meetings, annual conferences, church and school revivals furnished them abundant opportunity to speak of Methodism's "grand depositum."

Books, tracts, and the monthly issues of the *Guide to Holiness* afforded large access to the minds of the religiously inclined. Some leaders of Methodism had written significant books which helped sustain the position of the Palmers. Bishop Hamline wrote *The Beauty of Holiness,* Dr. J. T. Peck (later bishop) wrote *The Central Idea of Christianity;* R. S. Foster (later a professor at Drew Theological Seminary and then bishop) wrote *Christian Purity;* J. A. Wood, a successful pastor, wrote *Perfect Love;* William Taylor wrote *The Infancy and Manhood of the Christian Life;* and James Caughey wrote *Earnest Christianity.* From beyond Methodism came Asa Mahan's *Christian Perfection* and *Baptism of the Holy Ghost;* T. C. Upham's *Interior Life, Divine Union,* and *Life of Faith;* Dr. Boardman's *The Higher Life;* I. M. See's *The Rest of Faith;* and A. B. Earle's *Bringing in Sheaves.* All of these publications heightened the acceptability of the perfectionist teaching.

By the close of the seventies, Dr. Palmer wrote in the *Guide* that up until about 1836 Christian perfection was looked upon mainly as a doctrine peculiar to the Methodist Church, but that Charles G. Finney's and Asa Mahan's discovery of it as a scriptural teaching had encouraged its acceptance in non-Wesleyan denominations.[140] The later holiness leaders recognized the Palmers as having been the pioneers in this wider interdenominational acceptance of the holiness doctrine,[141] whereas Gaddis attributes the revival of perfectionism to Finney's preaching.[142] However, according to Gaddis, Finney's perfection doctrine was more Wesleyan than anything else in its source.[143]

In 1896, Bishop William Taylor, world evangelist and Methodist bishop of Africa, wrote that the influence of the Tuesday Meeting had extended holiness work "through the United States, Upper and Lower Canada, England, Ireland, and Scotland. Phoebe, aided by her noble husband, became the evangel of that Holiness revival." [144]

The National Camp Meeting Association

John A. Wood. Just seven years prior to the first Tuesday Meeting there was born in Fishkill, Dutchess County, New

York, one who, in manhood, conceived an idea which was destined to outlive the Tuesday Meeting and yet reach larger numbers for the same *end* for which the parlor gatherings in the Palmer home were held. That one was John A. Wood, who at the age of ten experienced conversion and joined the Methodist Church in 1841. Shortly thereafter he was invited by a Congregational minister, the Reverend William Hill, to study under him in the preparation for the ministry. Wood accepted the offer and lived in the Hill home, assisting the pastor and studying under his guidance.[145] Hill, a former Presbyterian minister, while attending the Tuesday Meeting at the Palmer residence, "obtained entire sanctification" and became a promoter of the doctrine.[146]

While J. A. Wood could not escape the influence of Hill's personal life and teaching, yet he alternately chose, for the first nine years of his own ministry, either to ignore the Wesleyan doctrine of entire sanctification or to antagonize those who professed it.[147] Achieving the distinction in the Wyoming Conference of Methodism (New York State) of being a successful revivalist and evangelist, he was appointed to the Court Street Methodist Episcopal Church, Binghamton, New York. Wrote Wood,

> There were more entirely sanctified people in that church than in any half dozen churches in the conference. It was one of the best appointments in the conference and B. W. Goreham, Epanetus Owen, and other sanctified ministers had been their pastors, and Dr. and Mrs. Palmer had held meetings with them repeatedly.[148]

After a severe struggle with his own pride, the prayers of the "sanctified members" at Court Street Church prevailed, and J. A. Wood was "instantaneously sanctified" on the platform of the Kittleville camp meeting in the presence of his presiding elder, forty other preachers, and some three thousand people.[149] Thereafter Wood was always known as a holiness preacher.

During his last year at Binghamton (1859–60), Wood wrote and published a book entitled *Perfect Love*, which to the present has had a wide circulation in America and Great Britain—General Booth having bought the plates to print copies for his soldiers in the Salvation Army.[150]

On his way to a camp meeting at Red Bank, New Jersey, in August, 1866, Wood expressed to Mrs. Harriet E. Drake, of Wilkes-Barre, Pennsylvania, his concern about the opposition to "the doctrine and distinctive experience of entire sanctification" which he and others often encountered at some Methodist camp meetings. During the conversation Wood said he believed "that some camp meetings for the special work of holiness ought to be held."[151]

Having entered the experience of holiness under Wood's pastoral ministry and subsequently having opened her home for meetings for the promotion of holiness, Mrs. Drake readily approved of Wood's idea and volunteered to meet half the expenses of such a camp meeting if he would start one. Wood then suggested the idea to the Reverend William B. Osborn of the New Jersey Conference and informed him of Mrs. Drake's financial offer.[152]

Wood's idea of a special camp meeting for the promotion of holiness tenaciously laid hold of Osborn's mind, and the next April he traveled to New York City especially to lay the matter before the Reverend John S. Inskip, pastor of the Green Street Methodist Episcopal Church. Entering Inskip's study, Osborn said with great emphasis, "I feel that God would have us hold a holiness camp meeting!"

Inskip's response to the idea was enthusiastic. After prayer for divine guidance and help, a meeting of Wesleyan-minded men was held to consider the plan. Immediately a larger meeting was called, to be held in Philadelphia, June 13, 1867. Thirteen Methodist ministers signed their names to the call for the Philadelphia meeting and published the call in the church papers.[155] Only those who were in favor of "holding a camp meeting, the special object of which should be the promotion of the work of entire sanctification," were invited.

Meeting in Philadelphia on the day set, the ministers and

STANDING: J. W. Horn; J. E. Cookman; L. R. Dunn; A. Cookman; B. M. Adams; W. H. Boole; W. L. Gray; G. A. Hubbell; A. McLean

SEATED: W. B. Osborn; J. Thompson; W. McDonald (vice president); J. S. Inskip (president); George Hughes (secretary); S. Coleman; G. C. Wells

ABSENT MEMBERS: J. A. Wood; G. C. M. Roberts; W. T. Clemm

An Early
National Camp Meeting Committee
For the Promotion of Holiness

laymen present voted to hold a distinctively holiness camp meeting at Vineland, New Jersey, July 17 through 26, 1867, and appointed committees to prepare for and publicize the new venture. The movement sponsoring the camp was named "The National Camp-meeting Association for the Promotion of Christian Holiness."[156] The nature and aim of the proposed camp was prepared by a noted Methodist pastor, the Reverend Alfred Cookman:

> A general camp-meeting of the friends of holiness, to be held at Vineland, Cumberland County, New Jersey, will commence Wednesday, July 17, and close Friday, 26th instant.
>
> We affectionately invite all, irrespective of denominational ties, interested in the subject of the higher Christian life, to come together and spend a week in God's great temple of nature. While we shall not cease to labor for the conviction and conversion of sinners, the special object of this meeting will be to offer united and continued prayer for the revival of the work of holiness in the churches; to secure increased wisdom, that we may be able to give a reason of the hope that is in us with meekness and fear; to strengthen the hands of those who feel themselves comparatively isolated in their profession of holiness; to help any who would enter into this rest of faith and love; to realize together a Pentecostal baptism of the Holy Ghost,—and all with a view to increased usefulness in the churches of which we are members.
>
> Come, brothers and sisters of the various denominations, and let us, in this forest-meeting, as in other meetings for the promotion of holiness, furnish an illustration of evangelical union, and make common supplication for the descent of the Spirit upon ourselves, the church, the nation, and the world.[157]

At the very first service of the camp various ministers spoke of their strong convictions that this camp meeting was ordered by God and destined to exert an influence over all Christendom as well as initiate a new era in Methodism.[158] While many Methodists called the new camp meeting movement schismatic in spirit and divisive in effect, the founders of the Vineland Camp were encouraged by the fact that the then-famous bishop of Methodism, Bishop Matthew Simpson, brought his family to the camp meeting and with them his unconverted son, Charles. The influences of the camp resulted in Charles' conversion at the public altar. Many others were converted or entirely sanctified, results which led the sponsors to believe that their venture was a "success."[159]

In keeping with the wishes of those attending the Vineland Camp a committee of twenty-one persons was elected to arrange for a similar camp the following year. Pledging themselves to sustain each other and to employ all possible means of propagating the doctrine of entire sanctification, and never to answer the criticisms from others even if misrepresented, this committee organized for future action. They elected John S. Inskip as the first president of the organization to be known as the "National Camp-meeting Association for the Promotion of Holiness," and the Reverend George Hughes, its first secretary. Without incorporating (until 1899) or drawing up constitution and bylaws, these Methodist ministers and their successors were bound together in the specific work of promoting holiness camp meetings.[160]

John S. Inskip. On August 10, 1816, in the small but historic town of Huntingdon, England, the birthplace of Oliver Cromwell, John S. Inskip, one of fourteen children, was born to Edward and Martha Swanel Inskip. All of John Inskip's immediate ancestors were "nonconformists," but his father's religious life was short-lived. After professing Christian faith at eighteen, Edward Inskip developed a distaste for religion and embraced skeptical views.

Upon moving his family to America about 1820, Edward formed associations with "free-thinkers" and openly sought confirmations for his skepticism. Forbidden by the father to attend Sunday school, John's mother taught the children to read the Scriptures and recite prayers, inasmuch as she had retained a reverential attitude toward the Bible. However, through constant association with his father, John was won over to infidelity and, as early as fourteen, vigorously aired his skeptical views.

In his sixteenth year John went "with a sad heart" to the little Methodist Episcopal Church in Marshallton, Chester County, Pennsylvania, and heard sermons preached by the Reverends J. S. Taylor and Levi Scott (later bishop). Breaking away from his young companions, he sought religion at the Methodist altar, professed conversion and joined the church as a probationer that evening, April 10, 1832, without his parents' knowledge of it.[161]

Soon feeling the "call to preach," John entered Dickinson College at Carlisle, Pennsylvania, with the approval and support of his parents, whom he had won to the Methodistic faith. On January 31, 1835, John wrote to his "spiritual father" and former class leader, J. S. Burton.

> While I am adding to my literary knowledge, my prayer still is, Lord, increase my knowledge of Thy way and of my own heart. Last night... I commenced struggling after the blessing of sanctification.... I am now enabled to say, "The blood of Jesus cleanseth me from all unrighteousness!... The reason of my letter is, that by humble profession in the fear of God, I may not be so easily overcome by the enemy.[162]

Perhaps because of financial limitations, young Inskip did not remain long at Dickinson. Licensed to preach May 23, 1835 (the same year the Tuesday Meeting in New York was begun), he began his ministry on the Springfield Circuit in the Philadelphia Conference. In early Methodist fashion the young circuit rider promoted revivalism, and in the first two years of his ministry he, with the preacher-in-charge, reported more than five hundred conversions.[163] Soon Inskip's success won him appointments in Philadelphia churches. By 1846, he was pastor of Ninth Street Methodist Episcopal Church, Cincinnati, Ohio, under the episcopal direction of Bishop L. L. Hamline.

Inskip's experience of sanctification, which he dated January 30, 1835, seems to have been retained but a short time. By 1845 he was lamenting his lack of love and "great unfaithfulness." Bishop Hamline's personal example and public preaching of Christian perfection stirred up Inskip on the matter. The latter's high esteem for the bishop inclined him to consider anew the doctrine, but not without misgivings. He declared,

> There has been, however, so much disputing about this matter, that I fear but few either understand or believe it. And yet there is no truth more clearly revealed, or more plainly enforced, in the Scriptures. May my own heart feel its blessed influence! It is my sincere desire to know the true and right way. I know it is both my privilege and duty to be much better than I am.[164]

Even though publicly successful in a degree in winning converts and championing social and religious causes, Inskip continued to confess secretly his spiritual failures. Although elected president of the Cincinnati Preachers' Meeting, he accused himself of "too much of self and vain glorying," of "not possessing the humility and zeal becoming a minister of the gospel of Christ." He wrote, "Indeed, I come short in everything. As I advance in life, my imperfections seem to multiply rather than diminish.... Oh, for a pure heart! Oh, for holiness unto the Lord!"[165]

After successfully serving pastorates in Dayton, Urbana, Springfield, and Troy, Ohio, Inskip was forced to appeal to the General Conference for a vindication of his practice and advocacy of "family sittings" in church. Not a few ministers in the Ohio Conference viewed Inskip's practice as "a wicked prostitution of the church of God."[166] The opposition against Inskip, leading to his General Conference appearance for appeal, forced him into the limelight of American Methodism. Consequently, he received many calls to fill leading pulpits of his denomination. He accepted the urgent invitation of the congregation at Madison Street Methodist Episcopal Church, New York, and was transferred to New York East Conference in September, 1852.

The following summer found Inskip attending camp meetings where sanctification was preached and where many were experiencing this "deeper work of grace," and he wrote,

> ...I have reason to count myself one of the happy number. This gracious work was wrought in my heart, after the meeting closed, while engaged with a company of others in singing. I never can forget that moment. My peace since then has been uninterrupted.[167]

Just a few years previously he had had little place for the doctrine of Christian holiness and had so interpreted Methodism's relation to this doctrine as to nullify the Wesleyan emphasis. Ten days after returning from the Sing-Sing Camp Meeting, at which he professed finding sanctification, he recorded the following in his diary: "I begin to feel very different in regard to this peculiar feature of Methodism. It seems to me now, nothing is so interesting as the narration of Christian experience. I never had such a continuation of peace and joy."[168]

Between 1854 and 1858 Inskip served as pastor in three different Brooklyn churches, but was returned to New York City as pastor in May, 1858, serving at the Cherry Street Methodist Episcopal Church. During this time he was successfully winning converts in revival and pastoral efforts as well as promoting Protestant principles and anti-slavery sentiment.[169]

Inskip's successful camp-meeting ministry seems to have begun in the summer of 1860, when he preached at the Sing-Sing, Falls Village and Paulings, New York, camps, where he witnessed "the power of God visiting the people, and many conversions taking place as the result."[170]

Returning to the pastorate after a period as chaplain during the Civil War, Inskip continued his aggressive work of building up the congregations he served, yearly adding several new members who had been converted at his altars. But he did not preach entire sanctification nor witness to it to his people. Although having experienced this grace on two different occasions—at Dickinson College, in 1832, and also at Sing-Sing Camp Meeting in 1853—he had failed to maintain the heart enjoyment of the experience. His attitude toward this doctrine and those who believed and promoted it was one of complaint and criticism. His book, written in 1851, entitled *Methodism Explained and Defended* bodied forth his inner feeling and that of many other Methodists toward the holiness doctrine. While declaring Methodism's peculiarity among the other Protestant denominations consisted in its teaching "the possibility of man attaining a state of grace in the present life, in which he will be made free from sin ... *may be attained now*—at the present moment," [171] nevertheless he devoted most of his attention to the exposure of the real or imaginary faults of those promoting the doctrine. He called attention to their "practical inconsistencies"; he called them "wild and deluded enthusiasts"; he accused some of them of possessing "pride, irritability, and petulancy"; he impeached them for criticizing non-holiness preachers, for moodiness, for controversial influences, for contradictory theories of holiness.[172] Hastening to dismiss the subject, he wrote:

> Whether such a state, may or may not be obtained, at the time of justification—whether instantaneous or progressive—and many other similar inquiries, that have been conducted with unusual vehemency, are questions of but little consequence.[173]

While improving in his devotional life and promoting the spiritual interests of his hearers, he carried a strong prejudice concerning the subject of entire sanctification. However, Mrs. Inskip attended the Tuesday Meeting at th Palmers[174] and was deeply aroused to seek the grace of perfect love. In mid-August, 1864, the Inskips went again to the far-famed Sing-Sing Camp Meeting, where Mrs. Inskip sought, professed, and rejoiced in the experience of heart purity.

Mr. Inskip, although not surprised, was deeply opposed to what she had done. "Greatly afflicted and mortified," he returned to his Brooklyn pulpit only to find that Mrs. Inskip's testimony found approbation among leaders of his congregation. One "expressed the conviction that it was what the whole church not only needed, but should seek at once." [175] This spurred Inskip to call upon God for greater measures of the Spirit in order that "he might the more successfully lead souls to God." "He felt his need of 'more religion,' a 'deeper work of grace,' and a 'baptism of the Spirit.' But the idea of entire sanctification had become repulsive to him." [176]

Subjectively biased against the experience of heart holiness he sought to bypass that phrasing of it and achieve the *end* of a holy, fruitful life without the means which holiness preachers held before him for its realization.

The crisis came on Sunday morning, August 28, 1864. Much against his own feelings he was "led to preach" from Hebrews, chapter twelve, verse one. With much liberty and pointed appeals, from the pulpit

> He urged upon his people the duty and importance of immediate and decisive action. The culminating point was reached, and in the most vehement manner he exclaimed: "Brethren, lay aside every weight! Do it now. You can do it now, and therefore should do it. It is your duty at this moment to make a consecration of your all to God, and declare your will henceforth to be wholly and forever the Lord's!" He ... emphasized it with increasing earnestness. "Let us *now* lay aside every weight," he said, "and the sin which doth so easily beset us." ... and as he continued to urge the admonition, a voice within said, "Do it yourself." He paused a moment, and the admonition was repeated, "Do it yourself, and do it now." Must he turn away from his own teaching, and urge others to do what he would not do himself? He could, consistently, do nothing else but obey.... He was not long in deciding what course to pursue. In the same earnest manner he said: "Come, brethren, follow your pastor. I call Heaven and earth to witness that I now declare I will be henceforth wholly and forever the Lord's." Having gone so far as to give himself to God in an "everlasting covenant," his faith gathered strength, and "looking unto Jesus," he exclaimed with unutterable

rapture, "*I am wholly and forever Thine!*" ... The bliss, the peace, the triumph of that hour, he never lost sight of. It was to him a new life.[177]

That evening brought an answer to his prayer for greater effectiveness in soul-winning. Twenty came to his altar seeking salvation the first day he began preaching Christ as "present sanctifier," a day which marked the beginning of a revival at South Third Street Methodist Episcopal Church, Brooklyn.

> The revival continued until more than three hundred were converted, and a large number fully sanctified, and a special meeting for the promotion of holiness established and held weekly in the parsonage.[178]

Two weeks after becoming "wholly and forever the Lord's" Inskip attended for the *first* time (according to this investigator's findings) the Tuesday Meeting at the Palmers, and immediately engaged them to hold holiness meetings in his church.[179]

Convinced that the sanctification of the church meant the salvation of the world, he soon came to believe that God was calling him to a special task in the spreading of scriptural holiness. Anticipating opposition to his purpose to tell "at all times and everywhere" of "salvation complete and full," he determined to be firm and fearless, without being controversial or caustic, in his preaching.[180] Feeling that Methodism had declined in spirituality and power, Inskip was convinced that a revival of the doctrinal preaching of Christian holiness was the key to the success of the gospel. He was encouraged by the fact that the doctrine was attracting attention in the mid-sixties among many Methodist preachers.[181]

By the middle of the year 1866 (one year before the Vineland camp), it had become clear to him that he must further as never before *one thing*. Without knowing his future work, he recorded in his diary his firm resolve: "It is my purpose to devote the remainder of my short life to the all-important work of spreading scriptural holiness among men."[182] He then devoted himself to a careful study of the doctrine of full salvation. In the light of the thought and practice of his times he was convinced that three things were of utmost importance in promoting this doctrine.

> First, it is needful to show that the work is in addition to regeneration; secondly, that it must be obtained by faith; and thirdly, when obtained, it should be acknowledged. These points should therefore be frequently and earnestly pressed.[183]

While serving as pastor and seeing scores of professed conversions and sanctifications, Inskip's influence continued to widen. Dr. L. R. Dunn, a leading Methodist pastor of Newark, New Jersey, and Mrs. Amanda Smith, later a "world-renowned evangelist," were among two of the influential persons won to a holiness ministry through Inskip's labors.[184]

The bishops of the Methodist Episcopal Church in 1864 had declared that "a gracious revival of religion, deep, pervading, and permanent, is the great demand of the times."[185] They had addressed the General Conference, with fervent entreaty to the ministry, to turn their most thoughtful and prayerful attention to meet that demand.[186] Inskip's inner spiritual urges were now decidedly turned in that direction. He with others felt that initiating of the National Camp-meeting Association for the Promotion of Holiness at Vineland was with that end in view.

In the summer of 1868, the second National Holiness Camp Meeting was held at Manheim, Pennsylvania, in the very heart of the religious activities of the Evangelical Association, a Methodistic body, organized by Jacob Albright about 1800, to reach the German-speaking peoples of America with the gospel. One observer wrote:

> Representative men and women were there from nearly every state in the Union.... The Sabbath was a great day. Not less than twenty-five thousand persons were on the ground, including three hundred ministers. Bishop Simpson was present, and preached.... Mr.

> Inskip preached in the afternoon on Christian perfection... and greatly moved the vast crowds....[187]

Scores were reported as having been converted or sanctified. One called the Manheim Camp "a little Pentecost," and when asked for the reason he said

> ...he had come from a testimony meeting, where Methodists, Baptists, Presbyterians, Dutch Reformed, Congregationalists and Quakers, had spoken of the work of God in their hearts, and from the testimony given, he was utterly unable to distinguish the one denomination from the other. This was Pentecost.[188]

After the Vineland and Manheim camps, which had been initiated and arranged for by the National Camp-meeting Association, all other camps for many years were held at the invitations and under the auspices of the Methodist Episcopal Church, on grounds dedicated for such religious services. In sixteen years, fifty-two national camps had been held with as many more invitations declined.

After having served thirty-five years as a pastor, most of that time in metropolitan centers—Philadelphia, Cincinnati, New York City, Brooklyn, and Baltimore—Inskip felt constrained to take a supernumerary relation in the Conference and devote full time to evangelistic services. With the approval of Bishop Ames, Inskip left the pastoral ministry in March, 1871, to enter holiness evangelism, and accompanied the bishop on the latter's "official visits to several conferences in the Southwestern states." [189] At the St. Louis Conference Inskip held holiness meetings, and nearly the entire conference sought the baptism with the Holy Spirit at the altar. Like services were held, and similar responses were witnessed at the seats of the Kansas, the Missouri, and the Nebraska Annual Conferences that spring. So universal was the awakening and advance in the spiritual life of the ministers in the west that Inskip wrote: "Mrs. Inskip and I have greater confidence in the church than ever, and are more fully assured of success. Praise the Lord forver." [190]

At Omaha, Nebraska, in early April, Inskip and his wife joined a party of twelve other National Camp-meeting workers and friends to travel to California to conduct holiness meetings in Sacramento, Santa Clara, and San Francisco. With the National Camp-meeting Association's largest canvas "tabernacle" along with them, the party pitched the "big tent" in California's capital in late April, 1871. Its four-thousand-seat capacity was soon filled, with many people standing to participate in the services, but not without much disturbance from mockers, "ranters," and moral desperadoes. The results of the meetings were most varied and far-reaching. Gamblers and opium addicts, the ultra-rich and the poor, the ministry and the laity, Baptists and Presbyterians along with Methodists, were seekers at the altar in these meetings. In all, more than one hundred were newly converted, many reclaimed from a backslidden state, and at least two hundred sanctified wholly.[191]

The Santa Clara meeting seemed even more victorious to the evangelistic party from the east. There were as many altar seekers as at Sacramento, but the greatest victory seemed to be the well-nigh unanimous support the National Holiness leaders won from Methodist leaders in northern California. Presiding elders, leading pastors, the president and some professors of the University of the Pacific, and the editor of the *California Christian Advocate*, published their hearty support of the work and ministry of Inskip and his co-adjutors.[192]

In the San Francisco campaign all the Methodist churches in the city participated, and several from other denominations become interested in the holiness meetings. Leading ministers in the city, Dr. Benson, editor of the *California Christian Advocate*, Dr. Thomas, agent of the Methodist Book Concern in San Francisco, and other prominent men publicly sought and witnessed to full salvation. In Inskip's estimate this meeting far exceeded the successes of either the Sacramento or Santa Clara services.[193]

During Inskip's *first year* in full-time evangelism, he

and his co-laborer, the Reverend William McDonald, recorded that they had traveled more than twenty thousand miles, held about six hundred public services, and "heard more than seven hundred ministers and three thousand members profess that they had experienced the blessing of full salvation, to which was added the conversion of some twelve hundred souls." [194]

Not counting the many church revivals and tent meetings, the annual Methodist camp meetings and annual conferences in which he labored, Inskip himself presided at forty-eight of the fifty-two National Camp Meetings held between 1867 and 1883.[195] While distrusted and opposed by several, Inskip's leadership commanded the respect and confidence of not a few of the foremost leaders of his denomination. At the close of the Round Lake, New York, National Campmeeting in 1869, Bishop Matthew Simpson expressed his deep pleasure with the camp, its management, its spiritual results in "deep earnestness and piety... united with so much intelligent Christian action" and earnest calmness. He coveted the same spirit for the whole of Methodism.[196] The leading pulpits in Boston, New York, Philadelphia, Baltimore, Cincinnati, Columbus, and other cities called for and shared in the services of Inskip and McDonald as they moved forward in holiness evangelism.[197]

So outstanding were the successes of the Inskip-McDonald team that churches in Canada, Great Britain, and India called for their services. In 1875, under their ministry, Canadian Methodism experienced anew what she had known under the leadership of the Palmers about twenty years earlier. Several hundred found Christ, either in pardon or purity, with about one thousand seekers in the closing service at Montreal.[198]

Returning to the States in the spring of 1875, these two holiness evangelists, usually accompanied by Mrs. Inskip, continued their labor in churches, annual camp meetings of various Methodist conferences, "tabernacle" or tent meetings in the cities, and the National Camp-meetings for the Promotion of Holiness, until their departure for holiness evangelism abroad.

With calls from Ireland, England, Italy, and India, to hold holiness meetings in those countries, Inskip and wife, McDonald and wife, and J. A. Wood and wife, disembarked from New York City for an "around-the-world tour" on June 26, 1880. With them went the "big tent" for tabernacle meetings in India. Carrying with them letters of commendation from the New York East Conference, the New England Conference of Methodism, and Bishop Matthew Simpson, along with letters of invitation from the North India and South India Conferences of Methodism, the party of six confidently entered upon their mission of spreading scriptural holiness around the world.[199]

Stopping first in the British Isles, the evangelistic party labored one hundred days among the Methodists, holding more than two hundred public services which issued in not less than three thousand professions of salvation.[200] On November 16, 1880, these American evangelists arrived in India and were assured by the Reverends W. B. Osborn, formerly of New Jersey, and D. O. Fox, presiding elders of the South India Conference, "that most, if not all, of the preachers of the South India Conference, were earnest in their advocacy of holiness," and were anxious that the Inskip-McDonald-Wood team should make holiness their theme of preaching while in India.[201]

Inskip and his party conducted a large tent meeting prior to and simultaneous with the annual South India Conference in Bombay. As a result, the Methodists were greatly revived and passed unanimously a resolution approving the ministry and aims of these National Camp-meeting Association leaders. McDonald described one of those services in these words: "At one of the meetings, so far as we were able to judge, the whole conference, bishop included (Bishop Stephen M. Merrill), were on their knees at the altar, seeking the fullness of God." [202]

All classes—sailors, soldiers, and natives of Hindu and

Parsee backgrounds—were among the number converted and sanctified in the South India meetings. From Bombay the team proceeded to Allahabad, where not only many conversions took place, but every member of the Methodist Church there entered into "the enjoyment of the fulness of love." At the Annual North India Conference, Bishop Merrill presiding, the Inskip team held holiness services with the altar lined with seekers after purity.[203]

The party of evangelists were in India only eighty-eight days, traveling 2,622 miles through the heart of the country during that time and holding 130 gospel services, including those at the two annual conferences. As in Great Britain, Canada, and the United States, several hundred in total responded to the call for pardon and purity under their ministry.

While McDonald and Wood and their wives returned to the United States *via* Italy and England, the Inskips returned to this country by way of the Pacific Ocean. With the Reverend W. B. Osborn, Mr. Inskip carried on an intensive preaching mission in Australia concerning which he wrote these lines:

> During the eight weeks we remained in Australia, we travelled by rail about eight hundred miles, preached *eighty* sermons, and saw 2,500 people saved, about two-thirds of whom were converted, and the balance wholly sanctified. Among the last-mentioned class were a large number of ministers—travelling and local. On the whole we deem it the most faithful two months' toil we have ever been able to perform. To God be all the praise.[204]

By the time Inskip had returned to his Ocean Grove, New Jersey, home in June, 1881, his pulpit ministry had passed its zenith. For three more summers he conducted National Camp Meetings, but with declining health. Stricken with apoplexy in the fall of 1883, Inskip lingered in a semi-helpless condition until March 7, 1884, when he departed from this life at his Ocean Grove Camp-Ground home, Ocean Grove, New Jersey. Excessive labors had hastened his death.

He wrote of his loss of health, "Our mistake in over-doing is one we ought not to have made."[205]

Not only had Inskip expended his abounding energies in incessant preaching as an itinerant evangelist and promoter of camp meetings, but he had also served as editor of the *Christian Standard and Home Journal,* a weekly organ of the National Publishing Association.

In the early seventies several ministers and laymen had formed the National Publishing Association for the Promotion of Holiness for the purpose of printing and "flooding the land with inexpensive holiness literature." Placing Inskip as manager of that publishing company at a time when it was threatened with utter bankruptcy caused no little strain on his physical strength. But he successfully carried the responsibility, greatly reducing the indebtedness on the publishing house property at 921 Arch Street, Philadelphia, Pennsylvania, and paying up debts incurred in its current operation. Inskip's editorial work for the *Christian Standard* began in 1876 and continued until near the time of his death. He was succeeded as editor of this paper by Dr. E. I. D. Pepper who continued in that position until his death in 1908. Reverend E. S. Dunham of Ohio succeeded Pepper and edited the paper until its consolidation with *The Christian Witness,* in which publication he conducted for many years "The Christian Standard" page.

Inskip was convinced that not only the camp meeting, the church revival, tent meetings, and the holiness convention were necessary to the propagation of Christian holiness, but also that the printed page must be largely utilized in evangelizing the church for converts to the experience of holiness. At one time he proposed the raising of $10,000 for the printing and scattering of Wesley's sermons in tract form.[206]

In the annual meetings of the National Camp-meeting Association for the Promotion of Holiness in the fall of 1869, the matter of a monthly magazine for the purpose of correcting the many public misrepresentations of the views of the National Camp-meeting Association and of more fully presenting the Wesleyan view of holiness—which they all firmly advocated—was considered. A publishing committee was appointed, consisting of William McDonald, W. H. Boole, and C. Munger, who were to investigate the proposed project and publish, if they deemed it advisable, a monthly magazine called *The Herald of Perfect Love.*

Securing John Bent, a printer in Boston, to assume the whole financial responsibility of the publication for the first year on condition that McDonald would edit it *gratis,* the paper was launched in July, 1870, under the title *Advocate of Christian Holiness.* It continued until 1874 as the organ of the National Camp-meeting Association for the Promotion of Holiness, but without financial obligation to the Association. Within the first year eight thousand subscribers were signed up for the paper. By 1874, when it was purchased by the National Publishing Association and transferred to Philadelphia, it was circulating among ministers of all Protestant denominations, numbering in the thousands. Every member of not less than eight annual conferences of Methodism was receiving the paper. Through foreign correspondents in Canada, England, India, and China, it reported on the progress of the holiness truth in other lands.[207] The *Advocate of Christian Holiness* (later called *The Christian Witness*) and the *Christian Standard* did for the work of Inskip and his co-laborers what the *Guide to Holiness* had done for the "holiness cause" under the leadership of the Palmers.

Inskip's Successors. Not all of those who believed in and were sympathetic with the cause of spreading scriptural holiness associated themselves with the National Camp-meeting Association for the Promotion of Holiness. It early became a matter of great debate in some areas as to whether or not local, state, and national holiness associations should be organized. As early as the beginning of the Palmer influence, Dr. Jesse T. Peck, later bishop, had written that while special meetings for the promotion of holiness were not objectionable, since they were open to all, yet *"any organization of the friends of holiness, as a distinct work, is undesirable and highly dangerous."* [208] While the Palmers represented a group in Methodism which favored Peck's view, Inskip's successors were more favorable to simply organized associations with a view to promoting the holiness cause within and between denominations.

Among those who became more or less nationally known as definite promoters of the holiness revival between 1867 and 1952, through the camp meeting and literature channels established by the National Camp-meeting Association, were John Inskip, William McDonald, J. A. Wood, Alfred Cookman, W. B. Osborn, B. M. Adams, L. R. Dunn, W. H. Boole, William T. Harlow, Alexander McLean, John Thompson, A. E. Ballard, B. W. Goreham, Bishop Matthew Simpson, Bishop William Taylor, E. I. D. Pepper, Asbury Lowrey, Asa Mahan, William Nast, Deacon George Morse, Sheridan Baker, G. D. Watson, Joshua Gill, Daniel Steele, George A. McLaughlin, C. J. Fowler, E. F. Walker, David E. Updegraff, Bishop W. F. Mallalieu, W. B. Godbey, Joseph H. Smith, Dougan Clarke, M. L. Haney, L. B. Kent, Isaiah Reid, S. A. Keen, D. F. Brooks, John Wesley Hughes, A. M. Hills, Bishop W. T. Hogue, J. Walter Malone, M. W. Knapp, J. O. McClurkan, G. W. Ridout, C. W. Ruth, Seth C. Rees, A. L. Whitcomb, Bishop I. W. Joyce, Bishop J. M. Thoburn, Bishop J. H. Oldham, P. F. Bresee, B. Carradine, H. C. Morrison, L. L. Pickett, William Jones, "Bud" Robinson, B. S. Taylor, S. B. Shaw, Sarah A. Cooke, Millie Lawhead, Iva Durham Vennard, Beatrice Beasley, E. S. Dunham, W. H. Huff, S. L. Brengle, George Kunz, J. L. Brasher, C. H. Babcock, C. N. Dunaway, C. W. Butler, Andrew Johnson, Lela G. McConnell, John Paul, E. W. Petticord, T. M. Anderson, John Owen, Joseph Owen, J. C. McPheeters, Z. T. Johnson, Paul S. Rees, C. I. Armstrong, and H. M. Couchenour.[209]

William McDonald (1820-1901),[210] an influential member of the New England Conference of Methodism, succeeded Inskip as president of the National Camp-meeting Association in 1884. Carrying forward the program begun under Inskip, McDonald served as president until resigning in the early nineties, when he was succeeded by the Reverend C. J. Fowler. Fowler (*circa* 1848-1919), a member of the New Hampshire Methodist Conference, was early prejudiced against the holiness doctrine, but through the influence of Reverend George A. McLaughlin, Fowler was led to profess the experience of Christian holiness and became interested in the Holiness Movement.[211] Under Fowler's leadership the National Camp-meeting Association changed its name to the National Association for the Promotion of Holiness, expanded its membership privileges in 1894 to include ministers and laymen of all evangelical denominations,[212] incorporated in 1899, received women into its membership in 1907,[213] encouraged the organization of local, county, and state holiness associations as auxiliaries of the National Association, and extended its home and foreign missions' activities.[214]

McDonald's and Fowler's terms as president covered the most critical period of the National Association's history. Gaddis has divided the history of the Holiness Movement into three stages: the stage of undenominational movements (1867 to 1893); the stage of sect-formation (1893 to 1907); and the stage of consolidation (1907 to the present).[215] While Gaddis and W. W. Sweet have treated of the departure of many of the "holiness people" from the ranks of Methodism, yet they have not adequately traced the lines of the continuous Holiness Movement within Methodism.[216]

Leaders of the Holiness Movement attributed the rise of the sects to two causes: the tendency toward "wildfire" or fanaticism on the part of some of the holiness teachers; and the oppression of trusted leaders and laymen by their respective churches.[217] Whereas the Palmers and the movement under Inskip had stressed but two major themes—the justification of sinners and the entire sanctification of

Christians—some arose within the movement who stressed a fourfold gospel, namely, justification, entire sanctification, divine healing, and the second coming of Christ.[218] While numbers of teachers within the movement believed in all four emphases, nevertheless some maintained that the National Association was raised up to promote the holiness doctrine and that any innovation beyond that would divert from the central objective of the movement. At three successive general assemblies of holiness teachers—in Jacksonville, Illinois, in 1880 and in Chicago in 1886 and in 1901—the matter of the formulation of the holiness doctrine and its related teachings, and the status of teachers, were carefully considered. Of the 1880 convocation, Isaiah Reid wrote as follows:

> At Jacksonville the dew of youth was on us. We had not then met many of the issues that have since confronted us. The ecclesiasticisms of the day had not then so used their combined power to oppose the movement. The general public was eager to attend our camps and various meetings. We always had the benefit of large congregations. We also had the conscious uplifting that the knowledge of general unity and harmony brings the heart.[219]

By 1893 the internal differences over what should be preached in the holiness meetings, fanaticisms, oppression by the churches, and the conflict between theology and science within some churches, had occasioned a new era in the Holiness Movement.[220] Nevertheless, the foremost leaders of the National Association continually opposed anything that would tend toward the rise of a new denomination out of the holiness meetings which were held for salvation and fellowship purposes.[221]

While the early leaders of the National Camp-meeting Association were at work principally in the eastern and north-central part of the United States, the Holiness Movement had spread into the southern states as well. The movement received its first major impetus in the south from Dr. Lovick Pierce, father of Bishop George F. Pierce, who was sanctified in 1842, and thereafter sought to promote the doctrine among his associates. But the slavery question which had occasioned the split in Methodism, and the Civil War which left the south a defeated and depleted people, hindered the progress of the holiness doctrine. Writing in 1896 of the southern attitude toward the Holiness Movement, W. A. Dodge, founder of the famous Indian Springs Camp Meeting in Georgia, declared that "thousands have never touched it for the reason that they said it came from beyond Mason's and Dixon's line." [222]

Because of the Reverend A. J. Jarrell's visit to the Ocean Grove Camp Meeting, where he heard Inskip and was sanctified, the Holiness Movement was revived in the south early in the year 1880, when Jarrell invited Inskip and McDonald to hold meetings in his church in Georgia. Through holiness conventions, periodicals, camp meetings, and local pastors, the holiness cause spread for a time in Georgia, Florida, and the Carolinas. Then because of "mistakes" on the part of the holiness promoters, as well as oppression from several of the church leaders, the cause suffered great reverses.[223]

In the central south, the Holiness Movement was advanced by the labors of such men as John F. Winn, Beverly Carradine, B. A. Cundiff, A. A. Niles, John S. Keen, J. W. Hughes, H. C. Morrison, J. W. Beeson and L. P. Brown. At Meridian, Mississippi, a male and a female school were founded which in the first decade of the twentieth century became the largest holiness institution in the world, enrolling approximately one thousand students.[224] *The Pentecostal Herald*—founded and edited by H. C. Morrison—along with Asbury College, also greatly augmented the holiness cause in the southern states.[225]

In this area, the holiness forces sought to organize in a fashion similar to the National Association for the Promotion of Holiness in the north, calling themselves the Holiness Union of the South. This union was effected at Memphis, Tennessee, in October, 1904, and met for an annual convention in successive years in other southern cities.[226] It was the Holiness Union which sponsored H. C. Morrison in a world missionary tour, and underwrote the expenses of E. Stanley Jones during his first years as a missionary in India, and which financially aided the Cowman-Kilbourne missionary team in Japan.[227]

The Holiness Movement took root in Texas in 1877, and by the following year the Texas Holiness Association was organized and holding camp meetings from place to place. Favorite camp-meeting preachers among the Texan campers were three Kentuckians, W. B. Godbey, H. C. Morrison, and L. L. Pickett.[228] By 1908 the Reverend E. C. DeJernett appraised his state's movement thus:

> The evangelist has had an important part to play in the holiness work in Texas. While many of them were ordained pastors or preachers in the various churches when they got the experience and were then thrust out into the evangelistic field, yet most of the scores of evangelists in Texas were not preachers before they got sanctified, but were engaged in farming, wood-hauling, brick-making, selling goods, practicing medicine, etc.; but when they became Spirit-filled they, like Elisha, left the plow, etc., for the prophet's office.[229]

At the end of their first thirty years of work, the Texas leaders could report the following achievements:

> The Texas holiness movement is supporting a number of missionaries in different countries, the movement has two colleges—the Texas Holiness University and Plainview, one Bible School at Pilot Point, and several primary schools. It has four orphanages, two rescue homes, and four papers, viz.: *The Pentecostal Advocate, Holiness Evangel, Purity Journal,* and *Message of God* (in Spanish).
>
> The Movement has two enthusiastic organizations that meet annually, viz.: the Holiness Association of Texas, an undenominational and interdenominational organization, and the Council of The Holiness Church of Christ.[230]

About two years later, Dr. Godbey wrote that "the greatest campmeeting in the world, in Waco, Texas," founded partially through his efforts, attracted four thousand tenters to the campgrounds and an additional sixteen thousand for the various camp services.[231]

Doubtless because of the unschooled leadership in much of the movement in Texas, the following fanaticisms appeared, but did not continue as representative of the original or sustained teaching of the Holiness Movement: (1) the belief that salvation from sin is salvation from death; (2) the view that there is a work of grace subsequent to entire sanctification, called "the fire"; (3) the teaching that demons are God's servants sent into sanctified people to chastise them, one of which is the demon of sickness; (4) the feeling that "marital purity" must obtain in sanctified family life; (5) the insistence that holy people should not partake of pork and coffee; and (6) the preachment that all "doctors, drugs, and devils" are done with when one is sanctified.[232]

On the west coast, the Holiness Movement experienced advances such as the one under Inskip and his party, but also suffered serious losses. "Come-out-ism," queer views on the millennium, and some rash actions, turned the attitude of many against the movement. The rise of new holiness denominations, such as the Church of the Nazarene, organized in 1895, gave the impression to some that the movement was schismatic. However, the winning of Mrs. J. H. Glide, a Methodist lady in Sacramento, California, to the experience of holiness meant much to the movement both influentially and financially. Mrs. Glide was the wife of a millionaire and many thousands of dollars were channeled by her into the holiness cause. Doctors Carradine and Morrison deeply impressed Mrs. Glide through their holiness ministry on the coast, and consequently she gave thousands of dollars to the Asbury institutions in Wilmore, Kentucky, because of Morrison's influence.[233]

West of the Mississippi, the movement seemed to prosper

most in Texas and Iowa. The Palmers and Inskip had visited the area under Methodist auspices to hold holiness services. The first specifically holiness camp meeting west of the Mississippi was held at Kosta, Iowa, and the second, a National Camp Meeting, was held at Cedar Rapids in 1873. The Iowa leaders did the whole Holiness Movement a service in furthering the interdenominational aspect of the movement by making their association, organized in 1879, open to "sanctified" men and women of all the evangelical denominations. This association not only held camp meetings during the summers, but also holiness conventions throughout the rest of the year. They organized gospel "bands" of holiness evangelists which went from place to place, promoting their doctrinal beliefs.[234]

Just as the Texas Holiness Association and others east of the Mississippi had done, the Iowa Holiness Association (early known as the central northwest movement), published its own periodical, *Highway and Banner,* and established its own school, *Central Holiness University,* becoming the most fully organized area for the Holiness Movement in the whole nation.[235] They established a course of study for their evangelists and required each one to report at the annual camp meeting just as the pastors of an annual conference would be required to do. By 1906 the membership of the Iowa Holiness Association had reached nearly twenty-four hundred, its auxiliaries had climbed to forty county associations, and its eight gospel "bands" had reached out to hold services "in twenty-nine states and territories and one in a foreign field."[236] At their annual camp in Iowa that year people gathered from twenty-four states, representing twenty-six different denominations.[237]

In the spring of 1900, the Iowa Holiness Association extended an invitation to the National Association to hold an annual National Association camp meeting conjointly with the Iowa Holiness Association camp. At the 1908 joint-camp session of the two Associations, meeting at University Park, a suburb of Oskaloosa, Fowler reported the following concerning the National Association:

> The membership of our Association... is as follows: Ministerial list, 191 ... the list of laymen numbers 207 ... associate members number 359. ... The total number ... is 737. ...
>
> So far as I know, we are the only inter-sectional, international, interdenominational holiness Association on earth. ...
>
> The holiness movement is now many-sided. ... There is a danger and a great danger that attention will be given to one's local, sectional, divisional, and denominational interests, and be betrayed to lose sight of what is really the work of holiness itself. ...
>
> There are genuinely holy people in all Christian denominations, in local independent communions, in new ecclesiastical enterprises, and a great danger is ... that real holiness will be wasted or weakened in losing sight of a genuine catholicity, in one's zeal for some local or denominational interest. ...[238]

Fowler's report indicated that the Iowa Association had far exceeded the National in its membership, had entered the field of giving credentials to its evangelists, and even arranged a course of study for them with the stipulation that an annual report must be submitted to the Association. With this sectional thrust, along with the one expressed in the Holiness Union of the South, it was feared that the Holiness Movement would be decimated by a lesser than catholic and international outlook.[239] Fowler had come to favor a more coordinated relation and action among the "holiness people" to save them from more personal, local, sectional, or organizational ends.[240]

For over a quarter of a century Fowler led the National Association in its expanding ministries and influences. In 1910 he helped organize at University Park, Iowa, the National Holiness Missionary Society as the foreign-missionary auxiliary of the National Association.[241] Other independent-holiness "faith missions" developed during the same period, such as the Peniel Missions and the Oriental Missionary Society, which have since received support from the holiness-camp constituencies across America.[242]

Because of the initiative of local holiness leaders, there

opened in various states academies, Bible institutes, colleges, and "universities" to train the youth of holiness homes in the holiness tradition under a controlled environment.[243] Holiness periodicals were begun in nearly every quarter of the nation, only a few of which have survived to the present time.[244]

While many left Methodism to form the "independent" instead of "interdenominational" holiness associations—some of which were later merged into the Church of the Nazarene and the Pilgrim Holiness Church—the majority of the older leading evangelists, teachers, and pastors associated with the National Association continued to speak out against "come-out-ism" and encouraged the people won to the holiness profession to remain and become a "leavening" influence within their respective denominations.[245]

After Fowler's death in 1919, the following men served as president of the National Association for the Promotion of Holiness: Will H. Huff, 1920–21; George J. Kunz, 1921–24; Joseph H. Smith, 1925–28; A. L. Whitcomb, 1928;[246] C. W. Butler, 1928–42; C. I. Armstrong, 1942–46; H. M. Couchenour, 1946–50; and P. F. Elliott, 1950–52. The dominance of Methodist leadership within the movement from Inskip on has manifested itself by the fact that all presidents of the Association have been Methodist ministers, with the exception of A. L. Whitcomb, a Free Methodist, of C. I. Armstrong, a Wesleyan Methodist, and of P. F. Elliott, a Pilgrim Holiness minister.[247]

In his presidential address before the National Holiness Assembly in Chicago, May 11, 1927, Joseph H. Smith recognized the National Association as only one product of the Holiness Movement. Desiring to preserve the genius of the movement begun in 1867, Smith approvingly quoted Inskip on the following words:

> We are not a Church, but are parts and parcels of many churches. We are not an Association, for we have not even a constitution or a by-law to our name. We appear before you as a simple Committee, and as such

> we represent a Movement... to carry tidings of a full salvation in peace and with power, as far as Christianity has gone, and wherever the doors of churches and the hearts of men may be opened to receive.[248]

Smith claimed that even though the "Committee" had developed into an "Association," it was as far from the thought of the early committee that churches should rise out of it as was the institution of a Methodist church from the mind of John Wesley when he organized the "classes" and "societies."[249] Of the various schools, holiness denominations, annual camp meetings, missionary societies, holiness associations, publishing establishments, and traveling evangelists, Smith wrote:

> Now it happens that but one of these Missions and none at all of these Churches, Colleges, Schools or Publishing Houses are federated in any official, organic or dependent way with the National Association, nor are they federated with one another. Each is its own separate and individual unit. Self-founded, self-administered and self-sustained, yet they are all integral parts of the great, growing Holiness Movement. And as such they are all closely affiliated. One in doctrine; one in purpose; and, to a very large extent, one in method. Their patrons, their constituencies, and their beneficiaries very largely overlap. So that, instead of carnal rivalry and business competition, a true and sincere spirit of fraternity pervades them all.[250]

Under the presidency of C. W. Butler, however, the National Association entered a new era. Through his leadership a closer cooperation between the educational institutions was established, and greater friendliness between the holiness denominations and the National Association developed.[251] Under the leadership of C. I. Armstrong and H. M. Couchenour, the constitution and by-laws of the National Association have been changed so as to admit whole denominations and individual churches as auxiliaries of the national organization.[252]

While the movement has maintained a strong evangelistic emphasis through evangelism's decline in the major wings of American Protestantism and its members have sponsored several educational institutions and fostered missionary enterprises, yet at times its weaknesses have hindered its progress in different areas. Confessing that they have often blundered as people, thereby evoking unnecessary opposition, the office editor of *The Pentecostal Herald*, the Reverend John Paul, concluded in 1904 that the following barriers to progress had arisen sporadically within the movement: (1) lack of courage; (2) earthly mindedness; (3) lack of tact and wisdom; (4) legalism—because of the movement's reaction against worldliness—gaining a foothold through views on Sabbath-keeping, diet, and dress; (5) looseness of conscience at some points, such as business matters and social behavior; (6) lack of study; (7) waste of time in worthless activities; and (8) lack of touch with humanity and its practical needs.[253]

As it was in Wesley's day, so it has been in the contemporary movement; not all movement has been forward and upward.[254] Retrogressions and embarrassments as well as successes and advances have marked the course of this modern Wesleyan emphasis within Methodism and her family of small denominational and undenominational offspring.

CHAPTER THREE

Joseph H. Smith, 1855-1946

EARLY LIFE

Into the "greene countrie towne" of William Penn there came, in the early nineteenth century, another family by the name of Smith. Although bearing the rather anonymous yet famous appelation of John Smith, this particular Irishman, with his wife, Eliza, reared a family which, finally, was a credit to the ideal of the founder of "the City of Brotherly Love." John and Eliza Smith were adherents of the Presbyterian tradition which had been first introduced into their thriving city by the Reverend Francis Makemie one hundred and fifty years before.[255] Staunch Scotch Presbyterianism was fully established in their home life, and under the influence of that faith their six children were reared.

The birthplace of the nation was the birthplace of Joseph H. Smith—one of the five sons born to John and Eliza Smith—who has been the subject of research for this paper. Joseph was born June 4, 1855, and was educated in the public schools of the "Quaker City." Although a precocious child, Joseph was not always minded to apply his superior abilities to the assigned lessons at school. Consequently, his mother had to employ a special tutor for him beyond the regular school sessions.

Young Smith displayed his intellectual endowment, however, by finishing his "high-school" studies the very month he turned fifteen. This attainment had provoked such repeated comment and praise from his friends that soon Smith also found several reasons for thinking highly of himself. Speaking at a later date of his attitude in youth, he said, "I was so very haughty and proud!" [256]

In order to secure immediate employment and status for himself in the business and social world, he falsified his age and was soon moving in society far in advance of his years. He early obtained a position in a large mercantile firm in Philadelphia and rapidly won promotion to the position of bookkeeper and cashier for the company. Within a matter of a few months he was drawing an enviably large salary for a "teen-ager" in that period.[257] Of this position in that business world, he wrote: "I handled hundreds of thousands of dollars right along, and practically had the power of attorney in all matters of business." [258]

Socially, Smith was a good mixer. His physical build, his ready Irish wit, and his prankster ways easily placed him as a leader within his social circle. He was described thus by a young man who sat under his ministry some twenty-five years later:

> He is a man you would look at twice if you met him on the street a stranger. Massive, masculine head, noble forehead, blue eyes, grave yet genial face, rather slight graceful figure.[259]

Religiously, Smith was a failure. Although reared on the Westminster catechism and Bible, he had become irreverent and ungodly in attitude and action. Still eating and sleeping under the parental roof, he had thrown off, to all outward appearances, the pious training of home and church. Those devout Presbyterian parents had named their son Joseph, after the Joseph of Genesis, doubtless hoping thereby to challenge him, by the noble traits of that Bible character, to the highest type of Christian manhood. Nevertheless, of all the Smith children, Joseph came the closest to falling into "outbroken wickedness." [260]

After a year or more of disinterest in religion, Smith was attracted to the Sunday evening services of the nearby Central Methodist Episcopal Church on Arch Street. He was drawn to this congregation of a different denomination by virtue of the large crowds, the many young people, and "a sort of magnetic attraction in the presence and power of the Spirit."[261] But the revivalistic pastor of Central Church, the Reverend E. I. D. Pepper, found Smith a disturber. During the church services Smith played mischievous pranks and instigated disturbances of various kinds through the assistance of his young associates. Those Methodistic Christians often came to him, inviting him "to come to Christ," but he would scoff or joke or argue with them, according to his mood.[262] So obnoxious did he shortly become that the worshippers would rebuke him, and on one occasion they put him out of the church building. But Smith would always return—yet not to worship.

Conversion and Call

At one midweek service Smith was at his worst. The pastor, Mr. Pepper, could stand it no longer. Leaving the pulpit, he walked back to where the disturber was sitting and demanded that Smith never return to that church. The scene which followed was exciting. Smith jumped to his feet, used language and threats which caused some young men of the church to accompany the pastor home that evening after the services and older men to demand a hurried, unscheduled meeting of the official board of the church. As the officials were about to get out a warrant for Smith's arrest, one of the board members arose and said,

> Brethren, this action disappoints me. I have had my eye on that young man for two years. I covet him for Christ. I believe, brethren, that prayer will be better than police for that boy, and I move you, Sirs, that we do reconsider this action, and that we band ourselves together in a secret conclave of prayer, and never let up until we see him converted at our altar.[263]

The motion carried and thoughts of legal action were dismissed, but unceasing prayer followed. As Smith had not known of the prayer-covenant among the board members of Central Church, neither did the latter know what was taking place in the private life of Smith. But they were praying. So was he.

For eight weeks Smith privately sought God, sometimes spending much of the night in prayer. Finally, after having publicly presented himself at the Central Church's altar for prayer, Smith arose and requested the Methodists to sing *with* him and *for* him the gospel song he had heard that congregation sing many times before, but now for the first time with meaning and significance for himself:

> O happy day that fixed my choice,
>   On Thee, my Saviour and my God;
> Well may this glowing heart rejoice,
>   And tell its raptures all abroad.[264]

Smith had come to his Aldersgate. He had experienced what the Methodists called conversion.

While Smith's conversion occasioned great rejoicing in the Central Methodist Episcopal Church, Philadelphia, at ten minutes after nine in the evening, January 29, 1874, it called forth no great emotional outburst from Smith. But he did experience great calm and peace filling his soul.[265]

That evening a friend placed in Smith's hand J. A. Wood's book *Perfect Love*. Smith had no desire to retire that night until he had read more than half of Wood's book and recorded the following in his diary: "I am converted, my sins are forgiven. I am justified, and now I am after something else. I guess that is what they call being sanctified." [266] From that hour forward he was in earnest pursuit of heart purity.

At the office the next morning a new problem arose. Having deceived his employer about his age in order to gain his position, he was confronted with the decision as to whether he should confess his deception or live a lie. He faced the possibility of losing his lucrative position if he should confess his falsehood, since his employer was not especially interested in his employees becoming religious.

JOSEPH H. SMITH

Counting the cost, Smith promptly approached the man and said,

> I have taken to religion. I got converted last night, and it is my duty to tell you that you are under a misapprehension about my age. I am only between eighteen and nineteen years old, and not twenty-three.[267]

Without hesitancy his employer forgave him and retained him in the firm's employ.

For Smith bookkeeping had been only a means to an end. His scholastic attainments and personal traits had won for him compliments and encouragement from some attorneys in Philadelphia to become a lawyer. To prepare himself to enter the legal profession, he had made an arrangement with his employer that, when the business of the firm was cared for, any spare minutes within office hours could be used in studying law.[268]

About ten o'clock that first morning after Smith's conversion there was a lull in business. To properly utilize his time Smith reached as usual for his copy of Blackstone's commentary on law, and began to study. Soon he felt an inner disturbance.

> ...the same Spirit that had prompted me and taught me to testify to Father and Mother began to gently deal with me about my occupation, about my profession, about my calling, and I looked up, oh, I must confess, with feeling of disappointment.[269]

Immediately Smith knew which way things were heading in his life. For that was not the first time he had faced this problem. During childhood and youth, and even in that irreligious period of his life, he had often been haunted with the thought that if he ever did become a professing Christian he would have to preach. Shrinking again from the thought of preaching, he bowed his head over his desk and prayed, "Lord, can't a man serve Thee and be a lawyer?" To his inmost soul the answer was inescapable.

He spoke to me in the exact words I will now quote to you. He said, "My son... wilt thou serve me as I plan for thee, and not as thou choosest for Me?" I said, "I will, Lord!" And I threw the Commentary on the floor and never picked it up, and from that minute to this, Beloved, everything in my life has had to bend, and if need be, break, to my call to preach the Gospel.[270]

Entire Sanctification

Smith attributed the radical changes and the spiritual progress he made during his early Christian life to the fact that from the night of his conversion he was in constant pursuit of holiness of heart or entire sanctification. Every day he seemed to be advancing in faith as he prayed, studied the Scriptures, read John Wesley's *Plain Account of Christian Perfection* and *Sermons,* and sang from the *Methodist Hymnal.*

> My conversion was amidst circumstances most favorable to my early acquaintance with and interest in this experience. "Old Central" Methodist Episcopal Church in the city of Philadelphia was outstanding in its fidelity and devotion to the doctrine of Perfect Love as a second distinct experience, definitely and instantaneously wrought in the heart of a believer. Its pastors were chosen with consideration of efficiency in this line of evangelism. Its fourteen class leaders were all alike true as teachers and witnesses to the blessing. Every Sabbath afternoon a distinctive Holiness meeting was conducted by the pastor himself. This was also attended by many witnesses and seekers from other churches; and together with the continuous revival ever in progress in the church there was a constant pressure and precipitation of this grace upon the people. The young folk as well as the older were alike led and helped on full salvation lines.[271]

Having clearly grasped from the start that there was something "more to follow," Smith declared that "it is safe for me to say that there was not a single day between my conversion and my entire sanctification but what I made progress in the divine life."[272]

Having attended all six meetings at Central Church on Sunday, March 1, 1874, expecting that any moment he would be entirely sanctified, he was still outside the coveted experience when he left for work Monday morning.

> *But I was looking up!* Monday I reached the store earlier than usual. None of the clerks or sales ladies had come up. I got my books and cash all out in order. Then I knelt beside my desk and said, "Lord, wilt thou lift me up now?" And He said, "I will, my child." And then and there, at between eight and nine a.m. on the 2nd of March, 1874, I entered into the soul's rest of faith as a second, definite experience of grace.
>
> I remember well the first open testimony I gave to this experience. It was on that Monday night. The pastor had omitted preaching and threw the meeting open for testimony. I was the first to rise and said, "This morning down at the store where I work at 928 Chestnut Street, the Lord truly sanctified my soul. And the joys I have had today are much greater than the joys I have had and have witnessed to among you for the past five weeks, and those were greater and higher than the pleasures I had all the while I was in the world." [273]

When Smith related his testimony some fifty-eight years later, he affirmed that he believed the secret back of his constancy in the experience of heart purity had been due very largely to the place he had given that teaching in his ministry, and the "definiteness and positiveness" with which he had borne testimony to it in his own experience.[274]

His First Sermon

The evangelistically minded pastors of Philadelphia *early* recognized a peculiar effectiveness in Smith's ability to relate his experiences of conversion and entire sanctification. During their revival services, he was called from church to church for the specific purpose of relating *the steps to and in* his Christian pilgrimage. These invitations he gladly accepted. On one occasion he was invited to one of the largest Methodist Episcopal churches in the city, and the pastor added these words to the invitation: "And I don't care, Brother Smith, if you *take a text*." Those last three words were like "joy bells" to him, for he had already felt "the call to preach" and was restlessly waiting to begin.[275]

As he formerly had had the privilege of studying law at the office during the slack moments, so now he used his free time to study the Scriptures. Accepting the invitation to "take a text," he was spurred in his study to construct a "skeleton" (as he had heard it called) for his sermon. The Tuesday arrived on which he was to preach his first sermon. Business having been heavier than usual, he hurried home, with the "skeleton" in his pocket, partook of the evening meal and made final preparation for his first preaching service. Following the hastily eaten meal, he ascended the stairs to "pray some more" and to change suits. Upon arriving at the church, he found the building crowded with people and the pastor anxious to usher him to a chair behind the pulpit. He described his first experience behind the pulpit as follows:

> Sometime before, when I was yet a sinner, I would sit in the gallery and could see right down over the pulpit, and I noticed that pretty generally, the preacher would wait until they were *singing the second hymn,* then he would slip his "skeleton" out of his coat pocket and put it into the Bible. So I supposed that was the orthodox time to do it and I waited. Pretty soon, the pastor introduced me but LO! as I put my hand into my pocket, I discovered that *I had left my "skeleton" in the other coat.* I ... came the closest to taking my seat when the *blessed* Holy Spirit brought to my mind these words of the Saviour, "But the Comforter, which is the Holy Ghost ... shall teach you all things, and bring all things to your remembrance, whatsoever I have said unto you" (John 14:26). I calmly rested upon that promise. Whether the Comforter erased from my mind any thing that was irrelevant or inappropriate I never knew. There simply flowed from my lips streams of applicable thought and truth, pointed and direct application with much earnestness; and with *confidence that God* was both guiding and helping; and that He,

> too, was addressing hearts through the message. *I was trusting Him entirely as to the message and the result.* ... I think it was nineteen seekers that knelt at the altar of prayer and if not all—nearly all "got through." [276]

That first preaching experience did two things for the "boy preacher" as he was soon called. First, those seekers who bowed at the altar at the close of his first sermon were to him *a seal* to his divinely given call to preach; and second, that service set a precedent and determined an important practice for the rest of Smith's long pulpit ministry. Ever after that hour when Smith was expected to preach, he would "search the Scriptures," "pray much for light and love," do his best to work out a "skeleton" of what he was to preach, and then always "buried" it before going to the pulpit. Once on his feet before the people he depended fully on the promise of John 14:26.

> ... I do no more depend upon my feet to keep me standing, nor upon my lips to keep me speaking, than *I depend upon the Holy Spirit to direct and enable memory and mind and voice in uttering the message of God for the hour.* (... I want to preach as if I were but a voice of another, and to appear as a telegram carrier, bringing a message from a person other than myself.) [277]

In 1941, he declared that after having finished more than threescore years in the active ministry, he had never had occasion "to carry manuscript or written notes to the pulpit." [278]

The Preacher's License

Following that first preaching experience Smith expected soon to be in the ministry. But it did not come so quickly as his own mind craved it. However, just about a year from the night that the official board of Central Methodist Episcopal Church on Arch Street had met to get out a warrant for his arrest, they met in official session and unanimously voted him a license to preach the gospel. At their quarterly conference a short time later they passed and issued another paper to Smith which through the years caused increasing marvel to his mind. Said he,

> There is no authority for it in the canons of Methodism; there is no precedent for it; I know of no parallel to it. This paper, given me with my license, signed by the president and secretary of our meetings, read, "We commend Joseph H. Smith to the Church of the Lord Jesus Christ, with our commission and charge that he do spread Scriptural Holiness over these lands." Beloved, I have been under, not only the direct call of the Spirit, but I have been under the commission of my church thus to speard Scriptural Holiness over these lands.[279]

A striking conversion, a definite experience of entire sanctification, a call to preach and the first sermon sealed with seekers, a license and peculiar charge in his hands to preach the full gospel—all these forced Smith to his next major step in life. Should he go immediately into the work of preaching, or should he take time to further his educational qualifications for the ministry? With his intellectual thirst and ability for learning as evidenced by his public school record and his personal effort to prepare himself for the legal profession, Smith faced one of the biggest crises thus far in his life.

Some with whom he counselled about the matter urged him to take time out for "the sharpening process" of formal education, assuring him that he would achieve more with less effort in the years to come. Knowing that Smith did not have the necessary funds to enter college, two members of the Central Methodist Church assured him they were ready to underwrite the cost of his college education.[280] Others with whom he counselled, sensing his "burning zeal for souls" and natural talents, encouraged him to enter directly the preaching ministry.

About that time a presiding elder from the South came to Philadelphia seeking funds and home missionaries to work among the "poor whites" of the southland. The need presented an inescapable challenge to Smith. With his counsellors evenly divided as to the course he should follow, Smith could not easily decide whether to take up gospel work immediately or to enter college for a ministerial education. Although having prayed for guidance for some time, he could not satisfactorily settle the latter through either his own reasoning or that of his friends.

> Finally, the morning came that I must decide, and give this presiding elder my conclusion; and I waited on the Lord that morning, in the garret, of my parents' humble home. People had told me, you know, how, through the culture and the advantages of college, and the degrees... I would have access into the higher classes of society, and among the learned... that, of course had weight; but while I was at the feet of the Lord, asking the Captain of my salvation directly for guidance, He sealed to me this Scripture that settled the matter for me: "Mind not high things, but condescend to men of low estate." [281]

Arising from his knees he sent word to the Methodist "presiding elder" that he would return with him as a home missionary to the state of Georgia.

Without putting a premium upon ignorance or deprecating a limited formal training, after fifty-two years in the ministry Smith declared his reason for neither regarding himself misled nor regretting the way the Lord had led him:

> But it is my glory that I am not a College man in this that it was not because I could not have been, but because GOD ASKED ME NOT TO BE.... I OBEYED. And if my ministry has not been wholly emotional, if it has been expository rather than altogether hortatory... and if today I am learning more still than ever before ... this I say is my glory, that not the College but Christ Himself shall have the glory for all of my life and ministry.[282]

Home Missionary Labors

In 1860, Georgia had more churches of the various denominations than were to be found in any other southern state, excepting Virginia. Ten years after the close of the Civil War found Georgia still desperately striving to rehabilitate herself as the once-famed "Empire State of the South." So deplorable had social and economic conditions become during the war and the period of reconstruction afterward that "the penalty for horse-stealing was again made death—the unfailing sign of a primitive condition."[283]

Challenged by the heroic missionary labors of William Taylor (later bishop), Smith began his first ministerial labors in 1875 (before his twentieth year), along with the 168 other Smiths who were listed as Methodist Episcopal ministers that year.[284] Taking with him to Georgia his young wife,[285] the former Miss Sallie A. Markle, Smith struggled through his first year of service on fifty-five dollars of cash salary, five dollars of which he gave away to a "poor preacher" at the first conference session. Unable to afford a horse, Smith had walked three thousand miles on his circuit in order to preach his two hundred sermons and otherwise minister to his people.[286]

While the South, and especially Georgia, welcomed northern gifts and capital with which to recover her own economy, her people were none too receptive to northerners, not even preachers. Although Smith was not too well received by his southern neighbors among whom he so sacrificially labored, he nevertheless won some converts to Christ. Those years of missionary service around Dalton, Whitfield County, Georgia, were perhaps the least popular of his whole ministerial life.[287]

However, he gratefully celebrated his golden anniversary in the Christian ministry by accepting an invitation to hold "a season of meetings" in the Methodist Episcopal Conference in Georgia where he had begun his ministry in 1875. He was privileged to lead into the grace of Christian holiness grandchildren of some who had been helped under his ministry a half century earlier.[288]

Conference Membership

The year 1881 found Smith back in eastern Pennsylvania, serving as a pastoral supply on the South Media Methodist Episcopal Charge. The next year he was admitted by Bishop Edward G. Andrews as a Preacher-on-Trial in the Philadelphia Conference and began his four-year ministerial course of study prescribed by his denomination as prerequisite to full ordination in the Annual Conference.[289] Taking his place with eleven other young men, candidates for the ministry in the same Conference, Smith earnestly pursued his ministerial studies along with his pastoral duties. All of those young men except Smith had gone to college, as he might have done had he not felt led to go to Georgia as a home missionary. When the four years' study course was completed Smith had maintained the highest average of the whole class. He took no personal credit for this honor but attributed it to the Holy Spirit's quickening and illuminating ministry upon his mind. Since he believed that he had honored the Holy Spirit in answering the call to the southland, he believed he could then depend upon that same Spirit for more than natural aid in his studies.[290]

From the very first sermon Smith preached in the large church in Philadelphia, he was a "winner of souls." His missionary labors in Georgia and his service within the Philadelphia Conference heightened his effectiveness in persuading men to seek Christ. In rapid succession he served the Methodist circuits at Raubsville (1882–83), at Cherry Valley (1884), at Lahaska and Lumberville (1885), and at Marshallton (1886).[291] (Inskip's conversion had occurred at the latter circuit fifty-four years earlier.) So successful was Smith as an evangelistic pastor that he won the attention of the foremost leaders of the National Camp-meeting Association for the Promotion of Holiness. Having been rejected twice before that year on account of his lack of years, in 1883 Smith was elected a member of the National

Camp-meeting Association, a movement which he was ever after to promote with untiring zeal.[292]

Full-time Evangelist

During those few years in the pastorate Smith had had a premonition—he called it a "spiritual presentiment"—that he would some day devote full time to evangelistic work. Fearing this recurrent impression upon his mind might be but an escape from "the irksomeness of the details of the routine of the pastorate," he devoted a day to "fasting and prayer" in order to settle the problem. There in his prayer closet he concluded that God, and not he himself, was calling him into evangelistic service.[293]

Encouraged by unusual revivalistic manifestations under his preaching, Smith plunged more zealously into his regular pastoral duties and to calls for evangelistic services in other churches as he had the time. Soon he exhausted his energies and had a serious break in health. Before finishing his assignment on the Marshallton circuit in 1886, the doctors ordered him to a sanitarium at Ocean Grove, New Jersey, where he spent part of a year. Upon his return home the physicians demanded that "he must never be in excitement again; he must never be in any public service again." But Smith knew better. First, he had had a call to preach, and, second, he had had a call to enter the field of evangelism. The Spirit had whispered to him, declared he, that he was to be led into a larger ministry.[294]

Physically unable to preach, Smith was forced to rest for a whole year and a half, thereby cutting off his salary and means of family support. During this trial of his faith he neither borrowed nor asked for anything from his friends. Yet, in answer to prayer, all his material needs were supplied for himself, his wife and three children.[295] He was being schooled in financial matters for "the life of faith" which he was subsequently to live for the rest of his ministry.

One day in 1887 he received "an illumination" and announced to his closest friends that he believed the Lord was going to let him attend the Mountain Lake Park Camp Meeting, in Garret County, Maryland, during that summer. From two standpoints that plan seemed impossible. In the first place, he was without finances adequate for the trip, since his whole family needed all that came to them for daily necessities; and secondly, doctors had demanded his absence from religious services where any excitement might be manifested.

Finally, just the night before the camp meeting was to begin, a telegram came from Philadelphia with this message: "You are to join the party for Mountain Lake Park tomorrow morning. All expenses paid." That was just the outward providence for which he had been looking to confirm him in believing his "inner illumination" had been of God.[296]

Knowing the doctor's orders and fearing that something fatal might befall him while away at the camp meeting, Smith's closest friends greeted him reluctantly. After two or three days' stay on the camp grounds, Smith himself had a startling surprise.

> ...the Lord gave me...a sweet assurance that He was going to let me preach at that camp meeting. Now that was beyond any thought of mine, but I just kept it all to myself.... The next day David Updegraff, the leading agent in the camp meeting came to me and said, "Joseph, if thee wanted to preach would thee come and ask me?" I said, "No, sir." He said: "Joseph, what is the matter? Thee's not going to backslide on our hands, is thee?" I said, "No David, but at a time like this, as critical as this, all inward leadings... should be checked and proved by some outward providence that we have got nothing to do with." He said, "Joseph, I am thy outward providence. Thee will preach tonight."[297]

As Smith preached that night, he was divinely healed in body, without either anointing or special prayer for it.[298] The principle of divine guidance upon which he had begun acting at the opening of his Christian pilgrimage (and continued to follow thereafter) had been confirmed again: "All inward leadings should be checked and proved by some outward providences that we have got nothing to do with."

Speaking some years later of that evening's service (in 1887) at Mountain Lake Park Camp Meeting, he said:

> Not only did He help me preach that night, but that is thirty-seven years ago, and from that day to this I have preached five hundred times every year. I have traveled twenty-five thousand miles each year to do it, for my evangelistic mission began that night. God took that way to the opening of my way from the pastorate into the wide, general evangelistic work.... There has been no place in those thirty-seven years where He has not manifest the savor of His knowledge in the saving and sanctifying of souls. He has made us triumph in every place.[299]

Because of his illness Smith had been given a supernumerary relation to his Annual Conference in the spring of 1887. It was that which released him, after his remarkable healing at the Mountain Lake Park Camp Meeting the following summer, to answer his "divine call" to continuous evangelism. The next fourteen years found Smith serving in camp meetings during the summer months and holding revival services in various churches the balance of each year. However, it was not until 1901 that his Annual Conference appointed him as conference evangelist, which office he held until given retirement status in 1923.

Smith's rise in the esteem of Methodist ministers and others in the interdenominational Holiness Movement was very rapid. Had he stayed within the regular channels of his Annual Conference, he might have been one of its most eminent pastors. According to Smith, that was markedly illustrated by a conversation which occurred and the sequel which followed it.

> One day my dear presiding elder came to me, and said: "Brother Smith, if you can see your way clear to keep away from those meetings (he did not say what kind, but everyone knew what kind I was going to), I see your way to the leading appointments in the conference." I said, "Beloved, do you charge the same high

price to those who go to lecturing Chautauquas, or only to those of us who go to holiness camp meetings?" [300]

To Smith that was evidence enough that the Wesleyan message which he preached might carry with it at times some ecclesiastical liabilities. But he would not be dissuaded. The sequel to that conversation however was reassuring to Smith.

> I never have gone to the leading appointments of the Philadelphia Conference; but I will tell you something that did happen.... A few years passed and I was preaching one Sabbath morning to 11,000 people at Ocean Grove, New Jersey. There were as many as 400 Methodist preachers there, and many other preachers. God was graciously with us, and was wonderfully blessing me. (I was at that camp meeting for ten consecutive years.) This presiding elder was sitting right behind me. Tears were running down his cheeks, and he... turned around to another, and said, "Brother, I started him." [301]

Following his induction into full-time evangelism, at Mountain Lake Park Camp, Smith held meetings in rapid succession at Mt. Pleasant, Ohio; Jacksonville, Illinois; St. Louis, Missouri; McKeesport, Pennsylvania; New York City; Greencastle, Indiana; Philadelphia; Minneapolis, Minnesota; Des Moines, Iowa; and Carthage, Illinois. In order to be more centrally located in his expanding field of evangelism he moved to Indiana in 1888 and accepted calls for ten-day "Pentecostal meetings" so as to move rapidly from one place to another.

The first five years were eminently successful. Arising in a testimony meeting at the Mountain Lake Park Camp Meeting in the summer of 1892 he bore testimony in the presence of hundreds who had occasion to know by personal observation and religious-journal reports just what he had been doing. He said,

> I feel that I must testify this morning. This is a memorial place to me. Five years ago from this pulpit

there began a new chapter of my life's history. I came here first under a vigorous protest from my friends, because of my physical condition. But here I was given, as it were, a new lease on life, and went out from that meeting more thoroughly consecrated to God for the work of the promotion of holiness, than ever before. Since then I have been in the field, i.e., evangelism almost continuously. I have had five abounding, triumphant years, preaching holiness through these lands. I am here now by the grace of God, and for the glory of God, and I know I love Him with all the powers of a purified heart. Glory! [302]

As men observed his labors and reported them in the holiness periodicals such expressions as the following appeared in print:

Bro. Smith, a young old-fashioned Methodist, of the most pronounced type, full of the gospel of Jesus Christ, which he loves to tell to saint and sinner; and he has it in such fullness in himself, that it is as a river of living water, flowing forth into the hearts of others, causing sinners to surrender to Jesus, and believers to present themselves before the Lord for the fullness of his salvation.[303]

Smith's "spiritual father," Dr. E. I. D. Pepper, spoke of him as an eminently successful evangelist; and David Updegraff, a foremost Friends' minister, wrote of him as "our beloved brother... who is, under God, without a *superior,* in our judgment, as a preacher and a leader of the people." [304] Updegraff was himself getting the "headlines" in the largest holiness camp meetings of that period—Pitman Grove, Mountain Lake Park, Ocean Grove, Eaton Rapids, and others. Smith was at that time working side by side with the Reverend William McDonald, the Reverend J. A. Wood, Dr. G. D. Watson, Dr. S. A. Keen, and bishops of the Methodist Church. Yet, he was ranked at the very top of those leading Methodist bishops and pastors who had become evangelists in behalf of the Holiness Movement through church, conference, and camp-meeting channels.

Without naming Smith as one of its promoters, Gaddis

made special reference to the rapid growth and numerical strength of the Holiness Movement in the state of Indiana.

> Indiana is the real leader, sociologically speaking, as it stands at the head (on this percentage basis) of all the states of average size and varied rural-urban population, and contains more than its share of the places of origin, present headquarters sites, camp meeting grounds, etc., of the present-day holiness groups.[305]

Gaddis' conclusion harmonized with that of the editor of *The Christian Witness* in 1899:

> Indiana is one of the hopeful fields for holiness work today. No state has made greater progress in holiness evangelism during the past five years. It is notable, too, as the residence of some very aggressive evangelists. Here reside the masterly exegete, Rev. Joseph Smith, the scholarly E. F. Walker, the versatile and vivacious C. W. Ruth, the successful Joseph Dempster, and the Boangeres, J. T. Hatfield, known as the "Hoosier Evangelist."[306]

Smith was frequently in the "first churches" of Methodism, holding Pentecostal meetings. In 1897, he was at the First Methodist Episcopal Church, Los Angeles, and following his ministry there holiness meetings were held regularly in the church.[307] In the fall of 1899, Smith was invited to hold Pentecostal meetings at the First Methodist Episcopal Church at Evanston, Illinois, the home of Northwestern University and Garrett Biblical Institute.[308] But Smith accepted calls to the smaller churches as well. *People, not place*, seem to have motivated him in entering the field of evangelism. No church was too humble or congregation too small for him to give less than his best in Christian service.[309]

The largest national and state camp meeting associations early and repeatedly demanded his services, such as: Mountain Lake Park, Maryland; Sebring Camp and Camp Sychar, Ohio; Pitman Grove, New Jersey; Des Plaines and Urbana, Illinois; Eaton Rapids, Michigan; and Des Moines (later at University Park), Iowa.[310]

The Evangelistic Institute

To Smith camp meetings were also schools of evangelism for himself and others who attended. From the Scriptures, observation, and personal experience he was convinced that a successful evangelistic ministry called "for *fellowship* and training" in such institutions as the camp meeting. He readily acknowledged his own indebtedness to the founding fathers of the National Camp-meeting Association for the Promotion of Holiness.

> ...the earlier leaders of this present Holiness Movement—Inskip, McDonald, Wood, Pepper, Updegraff, Keen and such men—made up the Faculty under which we were first proved and then trained for the teaching unto others of the same things which we had heard of these men and their colleagues among many witnesses. Of a National Camp meeting in those days, Bishop William Taylor said that 10 days spent by a young preacher amidst such influences and under such preaching was equal to a year's course in a Theological Seminary in his preparation for the work of the Lord. But besides many such camp meeting privileges, the writer was much under the direct tutorage of some of these men, notably E. I. D. Pepper and John Inskip, and then later in the closest fellowship with such succeeding leaders as David B. Updegraff and Samuel A. Keen.[311]

However exaggerated were Smith's views on the educational value of the camp meeting, he seemed to have played a leading role in making the holiness camp meeting a "training post" as well as a "soul-saving institution." From the best evidence available to this investigator, Smith was the first to introduce "the school" or "institute" feature into the holiness camp-meeting movement. His vision was to train men as evangelists just as Sunday school teachers were appropriately trained through Chautauqua channels and through the Northfield Bible Conference instituted by D. L. Moody.[312]

In analyzing the condition of the church in the last decade of the nineteenth century, Smith declared two facts were easily apparent: first, "the regular pastor is not as evangelistic as he was in the days of old"; and second, "providence is raising up supplementary agencies in the line of special evangelists, cooperating with the pastors in the salvation of souls." These trends forced him to devise some kind of schooling that would *"increase and intensify the evangelistic force of the regular pastorate, and also... develop and train those called to special evangelistic work."* [313]

He further observed that the theological seminaries of that period were not, generally speaking, developing the evangelistic vision and skills requisite to a sustained evangelism in the churches. Believing that the theological seminaries were emphasizing Christian scholarship more than Christian evangelism, Smith was convinced that something comparable needed to be done for evangelism—not as a *substitute for* but as a *supplement to* scholarship. Declared he:

> Many of us are thrust out into evangelistic fields without any training for it, other than what we can gather up by the way. This is the experience of most of the evangelists now in the field. There is a growing demand on the part of those in the field—pastors and evangelists everywhere—for some kind of simple Pentecostal training that will develop us in skill, aptness, and fruitfulness in this work of getting souls saved and sanctified. In the absence of such schools along truly Pentecostal lines, such as do not compromise our own doctrines and experiences, it has occurred to us to supplement our great camp meeting work with an Itinerant Institute as a forerunner, we trust, of bigger and better things.[314]

At the very first session of his Itinerant Institute on evangelism in 1897 at Mountain Lake Park Camp Meeting, Smith expressed the hope that in the future colleges would be established to train evangelists. He believed that right training would both intensify ardor and make for greater fruitfulness in that work. Until such time as the colleges were established, he hoped that either through correspondence courses or Chautauqua-like assemblies the ends for which he was striving could be achieved.[315]

Little did Smith realize that one of the young ladies who stenographically recorded the first Itinerant Institute in 1897 would found two such schools within the not-too-distant future. That stenographer, Miss Iva Durham, a Methodist deaconness, founded Epworth Evangelistic Institute in St. Louis, Missouri, in 1902, under the direction and endorsement of Bishop Fitzgerald of the Methodist Episcopal Church. Smith was called to assist in Miss Durham's school as a convocation speaker, evangelist, and counsellor. When a reactionary attitude developed toward the holiness doctrine within the St. Louis area of Methodism, Miss Durham (Mrs. Iva Durham Vennard after June 8, 1904), with the fullest support from Smith, founded Chicago Evangelistic Institute in 1910. From 1913 until near the end of his life, Smith served as part-time instructor on the faculty of this interdenominational, coeducational "evangelistic institute" in Chicago. It became his base of operations for his midwest and eastern evangelistic ministry, since his permanent home had been established in Redlands, California, shortly after the turn of the century. In Chicago Evangelistic Institute Smith realized most fully what he had hoped for since the early days of his itinerant evangelism. He promoted its interests financially, numerically and academically, and served as one of the most trusted counsellors its founder, Mrs. Iva Durham Vennard, ever had.[316]

With Dr. C. J. Fowler, then president of the National Holiness Association, the Reverend Seth C. Rees, and Dr. E. I. D. Pepper as his evangelist associates at the 1897 session of the Mountain Lake Park Camp Meeting, Smith opened his first Itinerant Institute with a period of prayer for the help of the divine Spirit upon their minds. He then declared that those in attendance would learn from three sources— the Holy Spirit, the Holy Scriptures, and holy men and women.[317]

The sessions of the Institute from day to day were conducted so as to both understand the nature of evangelism and develop those arts and techniques adaptable to the individual minister's personality in "winning souls." But basically and primarily, a Pentecostal training in evangelism meant to Smith and his colleagues a proper conditioning of the minister's own spiritual life. He *must* be filled with the perfect love of Jesus toward others.[318]

Smith studiously avoided the stereotyped professional approach in evangelism, both in himself and in instructing others. "Imitation is disastrous to the evangelist. Let God reproduce His power and efficiency in your own personality," he declared.[319] So firmly did he believe that the living Spirit of God made for a wholesome variety and adaptability to the needs of the hour that he later declared that if men ever observed him conducting any two or three meetings in just the same way or preaching the same sermon again and again, word for word, following the same manner or intonations, they were to consider him "not fully in the Spirit."[320]

Following Wesley's pattern of examining witnesses, Smith inquired of the evangelists, pastors, missionaries, and religious editors present and discovered that some had possessed the "evangelistic gift" before being baptized with the Holy Spirit, others received it at the time they were filled with the Spirit, and still others after that crisis experience. But to all, the baptism with the Spirit greatly augmented their effectiveness in soul winning.

Instructing his audience in New Testament evangelism, Smith showed from Acts 6 and 8 that "evangelism is not an office, *but a gift*" within the church. His lifelong attitude was expressed when he said,

> Nothing has pained me more than the observation of some specialists who sink into evangelism as a business or profession. We must have it as a passion.... Our passion will take us beyond caste and social privileges; it will take us to "Samaria." [321]

Smith also expressed his concern for those whose "passion for souls" was not complete, by which he meant that they were zealous for conversions, for philanthropies, for benevolences, but had only a passive consent toward holiness. For him New Testament evangelism meant "the successful propagation of salvation in each and all of its distinctive stages." That of course included leading believers into holiness of heart. "We need a passion for a perfect spirituality." [322]

Smith stressed not only the necessity of staying in "a practical, close contact with the needy" if a passion for souls is to be sustained, but also of keeping the evangelistic message "Biblical." For him the evangelist was "an interpreter of the Scriptures," who trusted the Word of God, not stories or entertainment, to win men.[323]

But all those present at Smith's first Institute did not agree with him that expository preaching was best for evangelistic work. Even Dr. Fowler, himself an expository preacher, demurred in the matter. Fowler recognized that many had proved themselves successful evangelists who had neither the education nor the mental traits to be expository preachers. Whereas Smith emphasized the primacy of the Scriptures in evangelism—as the Spirit's instrument in "precipitating" salvation—Fowler without minimizing the force and function of the Scriptures stressed the "unction of the Spirit." Affirmed Fowler, "Let me emphasize it: *unction, unction unction!* You and I must have unction. People will put up with bad gesture, poor rhetoric, broken English, almost anything, in fact, if we have the unction of the Spirit." [324] Smith's first Itinerant Institute had covered the wide range of problems integral to the evangelistic task of the church. They studied sermonizing for revival work, altar calls and altar methods, the Holy Spirit's gifts, anointings and guidance, the passion for souls and the evangelistic gift, the raising of money for an evangelistic campaign, the evangelist's relation to the pastor and to fellow evangelists, and the pastor's relation to the task of sustained evangelism.

Smith considered his venture a success for himself and others. Pastors in attendance prayed for the evangelistic gift and for revival results in their churches to which they were to return. Evangelists shared their experiences as to successful and failing methods and prayed for greater "unction" to promote their work. Some settled the matter of a call to full-time evangelism, while others entered into their "Pentecost," either during the class sessions or at the altar-call period. Smith's Itinerant Institute had been a "school in holiness," a "school in methods," all in one.[325]

Smith set forth in his Itinerant Institute the principles or ideals which he had practiced and many of which he continued to follow through his long life as an evangelist. As to his financial policy, he felt himself led by the Spirit of God to refuse to set terms for his services, even when asked for them. He left the matter of his support "wholly with the Lord," trusting the people to give as prompted by the Spirit. In his thirty-third year in the evangelistic ministry, he affirmed

> ...I have never made a contract that I had to have so and so before I came, and I never made a complaint that I did not get so and so after I got there.... I have brought up five children. They all but one have college diplomas, and two... of them have professional diplomas besides, and are in professional life. I have met all these family obligations, and all else; and, beloved, to God's glory I say it, I never had an obligation to meet that I was not able to meet.[326]

Smith sought carefully to avoid everything that would savor of the "mercenary" in his evangelistic labors.

As to his methods, they were distinctly his own. He believed that each revival or camp-meeting campaign, as well as each service in each campaign, was a success only as he discovered the "divine strategy" for each. By prayer and dependence upon the Holy Spirit, he believed himself led by the Spirit in each message and method.[327] Smith became noted among his associates for his success in encouraging people to believe in Christ for forgiveness or perfect cleansing even while he was preaching. On one occasion at the Mountain Lake Park Camp, Smith asked those to stand who had found Christ during the sermon, and fourteen men and women arose and witnessed in a few words to their deliverance. He did not strive for numbers at the altar but for the establishing of a vital relationship between human souls and Christ.[328]

As to his preaching style, he was in harmony with the Methodist ideal and original emphasis at Drew Theological Seminary.[329] He stressed the necessity of full preparation of a sermon in advance of a service, but then trusted the Holy Spirit to stimulate his memory, without the aid of notes, in its delivery. Directness and spontaneity were essential, he affirmed.

> Preach from the fulness of your heart in your natural tone. Cultivate extemporaneous address. Dependence upon the Holy Ghost, naturalness and supernaturalness, are the elements of true evangelistic preaching.[330]

So profitable had been the school of evangelism at Mountain Lake Park Camp that it was repeated the following year, and then gradually extended to other camps where Smith was called to minister. While his procedures did not always remain the same, he always aimed at winning souls to their heritage in Christ. He not only sought to help ministers in the exposition of the Scriptures and the precipitation of salvation at all its distinctive stages, but he endeavored to assist the laity in making the most of their opportunities for evangelism through the Sunday school and other organizations of the church.[331]

The "School of the Prophets," as the Itinerant Institute came to be known across the country (sometimes called "The School of Pentecostal Methods," or "Evangelistic Institute"), incorporated within it some of those principles which have proved helpful in modern education. It was empirical, adapted to the individual's problems, open to individual participation, and conducted by one recognized as an expert in the field of evangelism and scriptural exposition. The public evangelistic services were occasions for demonstrating the principles taught in the "School of the Prophets," although they were not merely conducted for that purpose.

Smith's name became synonymous with the "School of the Prophets" as he conducted them in the National Holiness Camp meetings, in the state holiness camps, in denominational camps, in conventions and conferences, and in churches large and small from coast to coast. He took his school to the people rather than ministering mainly to the people who could leave their stations in life to attend some institution in which he taught. He was more than an itinerant evangelist; he was an itinerant educator in the field of scriptural exposition and evangelism. By 1939 Smith could write:

> Now for fifty years the greater part of the summer season has been spent in camp meetings. Twenty-six at Mountain Lake, thirty-six at Eaton Rapids, twenty-five at Sebring, ten at Des Plaines, sixteen at Sychar, six at Indian Springs, and numberless others for shorter or longer ministeries [sic]. A few sessions back, Brother H. C. Morrison and I figured and found that we had each spent ten solid years (night and day) of our lifetime on *camp grounds.*
>
> I have come to view the best of these camps not simply as products and memorials of the great National Holiness Movement; but rather as ARMY POSTS for the great Onward Movement into which this ministry is soon to advance in its recovery of *Evangelism to the churches of our day, and the spread of Sanctifying Truth in those churches whose erring philosophy as to indwelling sin has made them slow* to accept it....[332]

Dr. H. C. Morrison, founder of *The Pentecostal Herald* (1888) and of Asbury Theological Seminary (1923), and for nearly a quarter of a century president of Asbury College, had opportunity to know Smith as few others of the latter's contemporaries. After having sat through several sessions of Smith's "School of the Prophets," he wrote, "We do not believe that in all the summer schools in the country for ministers of the gospel, there can be delivered a better series of lectures than those delivered by Rev. Joseph H. Smith."[333] Morrison had been invited occasionally as a guest lecturer at summer schools for ministers, such as at Duke University and other places in the south, at which both bishops and professors of the well-known theological schools were the co-speakers. He esteemed Smith's work equal to the best of its kind he had found anywhere in Methodism.[334]

Evangelizing Methodism

Central Methodist Episcopal Church, Philadelphia, of which Smith became a member in 1874, had had a sustained evangelistic emphasis. In addition to the "protracted meetings" or special revivals, the regular weekly services in that church had netted revival results for fifteen consecutive years. For Smith, that had been close to being an ideal New Testament church. He longed to see the same pattern in all of Methodism.[335]

His own Christian life and public ministry were begun with the purpose of promoting Christianity as he had found it in his home congregation. Both in his Georgia and Philadelphia Conference assignments he had been successful as an evangelistic pastor. His larger, full-time evangelistic ministry was with the view of carrying into action the slogan of early Methodism—"to spread scriptural holiness over these lands." While Smith did not receive appointment as Conference Evangelist until 1901, he was constantly in demand, both before and after that time, by various Methodist preachers across the country.

By the time Dr. S. A. Keen (Smith's close associate in evangelism) died in 1895, he had been called by the bishops to seventy-six sessions of annual conferences in Methodism to hold Pentecostal services for the ministers and others attending the conference sessions.[336] Keen was succeeded in this holiness ministry to Methodism by Smith and Dr. E. S. Dunham. The latter, an Ohio Methodist and assistant editor of the *Christian Standard* of Philadelphia, had conducted evangelistic and Pentecostal meetings at nearly a hundred sessions of annual conferences by 1908.[337] Smith believed that Keen had been raised up of God "to show that his work could be made a success," and at the Mountain Lake Park Camp in 1896, he called upon the people to pray that the work of evangelizing Methodism for holiness would be not only carried on but given a new impetus.[338]

The following year some of the bishops of Methodism chose Smith as Keen's successor and employed his services for Pentecostal meetings at the Detroit and Northwest Iowa Conferences. Some of these services became like camp meetings in the results which were witnessed at the altars in conversions, restorations, and baptisms with the Holy Spirit.[339]

So successful was Smith in presenting the message of Christian holiness to ministry and laity alike that when the General Conference of the Methodist Episcopal Church convened in Los Angeles in 1904, Bishops Mallalieu, Joyce, and McCabe invited him to conduct Pentecostal meetings during the General Conference. Having obtained the Central Baptist Church in the city for these daily services, Smith preached to the hundreds of ministers and laymen who crowded into the auditorium, with many finding only standing room. When the "altar call" was given seekers filled the altar space, for either pardon or purity.[340]

Dr. Morrison, who shared the preaching with Smith in four of these Pentecostal services, wrote thus of Smith's General Conference ministry:

> Joseph Smith is a great preacher of the Word. He is always forceful and clear, never excited, harsh or dictatorial. He convinces, and draws men to the truth. He puts in the sword, not as the smiting of an angry foe, but with the careful-kindness of a determined surgeon, who will cut out the disease to save the patient....[341]

So acceptable were the Pentecostal meetings of Smith

and Morrison at the 1904 General Conference that they were engaged by Bishop Mallalieu, chairman of the General Commission on Evangelism for the Methodist Episcopal Church, for the General Conference four years later at Baltimore, Maryland. The fruitfulness of those 1908 services opened several calls to both Smith and Morrison for further revival work within Methodist circles.[342]

No one of the leaders or promoters of the National Holiness Association was more widely accepted or highly esteemed for so long a time after Methodism had sought to sluff off its holiness doctrine than was Smith.[343] He had become the successor of the Palmers, Inskip and McDonald, and S. A. Keen as *the* holiness evangelist to the General Church.

But all was not going well for holiness preachers (or the holiness doctrine) within Methodism. According to Smith many of them were discredited by some officials of the denomination and often given lesser churches than their non-holiness, though no more capable, ministerial brethren. In 1925 Smith wrote, "For the past 16 years, few that have aspired or been elevated to the Methodist episcopacy have been holiness men and more of them hold the modern Holiness Movement in disrepute."[344] Smith still felt duty-bound to remain and minister within the denomination and pray and labor for a change of viewpoint and direction for Methodism.

While Gaddis has made much,[345] as has Dr. Elmer T. Clark in his book *The Small Sects in America,*[346] of the growth of holiness sects after 1893 because of the withdrawal of large numbers of holiness people from Methodism to "set up housekeeping for themselves," yet neither of them has given equal attention to the number and work of these Methodists who did not leave the parent denomination. Smith's constant and nationwide contact with Methodism, as well as with Wesleyan bodies formed outside the parent denomination, gave him firsthand knowledge of the contemporary situation.

In 1912, Smith wrote his findings and views on the Holiness Movement and Methodism, affirming that

> Till this present time, notwithstanding the independent and interdenominational extensions of the Movement, a large majority of all those who enjoy the experience and of those who are engaged in the work of Holiness, belong to Methodist churches. And a big percentage of these are of the ministry and membership of the M.E. Church. The subscription lists, too, of our distinctive holiness papers... are largely made up of the names of Methodists.[347]

While affirming that the general drift of Methodism, officially and educationally, was away from her original genius and mission, he nevertheless held that historically the Holiness Movement owed a debt to the denomination. Writing as a Methodist, he declared:

> Holiness is the crown of our doctrine. Evangelism is the glory of our history. The spread of these throughout the world is plainly our mission and our stewardship, and to stimulate and sustain these in Methodism is the chief business of the Holiness Movement.[348]

Smith then asked the leaders of the church for a better opportunity to do the work which he believed was providentially given to the movement. But in spite of losses and trends away from holiness and evangelism, he was still convinced that Methodism afforded the greatest opportunity for carrying out the mission of the Holiness Movement.[349]

As late as 1925, Smith was asked, "Has the Methodist Church repudiated the doctrine of entire sanctification?" His reply was that "of all the persons now attending and sustaining our inter-denominational holiness camp meetings, fully three-fourths are members of Methodist Churches."[350] He affirmed that any repudiation of the doctrine was purely administrative and not by the legislative action of the General Church. The "standards remain inviolable," he declared, and "We who are in the church and help press Holiness are really the loyal Methodists."[351]

He was somewhat encouraged in his faith for Methodism's return to the holiness doctrine after he had attended the 1933 Ocean Grove Camp Meeting sessions.

> I have just spent a week of days listening to (E.) Stanley Jones in the mornings and Bishop Moore in the evenings at one of the greatest and most telling meetings I have yet been privileged to attend. This unique and phenomenal Ocean Grove with...its 70 years of history is itself a direct product of the National Holiness Movement. So also are Stanley Jones and Bishop Moore!
>
> And I may say of these two beloved brethren, that in all their messages at this session they sounded clearly the note of a second definite work of grace. Upon one occasion Bishop Moore's message itself was specifically upon Christian Perfection and this from an expository and an experiential standpoint. His testimony was definite, positive, and unequivocal to Christian Perfection.[352]

The holiness camp meetings, the circulation of holiness periodicals, the flow of graduates from holiness Bible institutes and colleges into the ministry and missionary fields of Methodism, along with those already preaching and witnessing to holiness within the church, gave Smith hope for a "great Holy Ghost revival along all lines of Christian experience" which would "recall Methodism once more to her own true standards of faith." [353]

Had Smith lived to witness Methodism's revived evangelistic emphasis as evidenced by its Philadelphia crusade in November 1949 (which added about seven thousand new members to the denomination in that area),[354] in its Board of Evangelism's action in establishing "an 'old-fashioned' camp meeting at Lake Junaluska in the summer of 1951," [355] its "evangelistic mission" at Washington, D.C., in March, 1952, following the "five-week preaching revival by Dr. Billy Graham in the huge Washington armory" [356] and its General Conference action in May, 1952, doubtless he would have felt that the revival for which he had labored so long was about to break.

The general conference voted to participate in a united evangelistic effort on the part of world-wide Methodism in 1953. The general conference also recommended that a Chair of Evangelism be established in connection with each of the theological seminaries of the church and that theological students be given effective training in all types of evangelism. This decided trend in a return to evangelism marks one of the most significant developments in Methodism within the past decade.[357]

Smith's faith would have been further rewarded by learning that the leading college of the Holiness Movement had been credited by some outstanding Methodist leaders with having helped to save evangelism for the Methodist Church.[358]

NATIONAL HOLINESS ASSOCIATION WORK

Spiritually reared under the ministry of E. I. D. Pepper, John S. Inskip, and others who were members of the National Camp-meeting Association for the Promotion of Holiness, Smith early became identified in spirit and service with the movement and continued with unabated interest in its work until his death.

His principal contributions were to serve as the called evangelist and Bible teacher at the camp meetings and holiness conferences or conventions, to write for the leading holiness periodicals, and to teach and preach at the holiness schools of the movement.

Having repeatedly and insistently declined any official position in the Association, contrary to his preference he was elected as its sixth president in 1925, and served in that office for three years.[359] While his field reports during that period were encouraging to the constituency and his personal labors at an all-time high in behalf of the holiness cause, nevertheless he doubtless came the closest to failure as an administrator of the national conventions of the movement as in anything he had undertaken in public life.[360]

Smith's election to the presidency of the National Association had provoked great hope in many members for the future of the organization. But in spite of Smith's best efforts the national convention under his leadership reached an all-time low in its Cleveland session in May, 1928.[361]

When Smith was relieved of the presidency by the election of the Reverend A. L. Whitcomb, who declined the office, and Dr. C. W. Butler took his place, no one seemed more assured than Smith that God had led in the Association's selection of Butler. He believed Butler to be the "Joshua" who would bring in the "second rise of the Holiness Movement," an objective for which he had been specifically laboring as its president from 1925 to 1928.[362]

In 1925 Smith wrote an article on "The Second Rise of the Holiness Movement," in which he appraised the task of the movement in its first rise under Inskip and others and the needed revival of it over half a century after its beginning.

> At the first rise of the Movement, the doctrine of holiness had become almost dormant in the church which had been entrusted with it as its chief doctrinal depositum, but Regeneration and the Witness of the Spirit were dominant. Now the New Birth and the knowledge of sins forgiven are as far in the background in the large church as Holiness was then. At the First Rise none of our preachers questioned the Inspiration, the Authenticity or the Authority of the Bible. At the time of this Second Rise men draw salaries from and reach office in the Christian church for destroying the faith of the fathers, in schools, publications, and pulpits of the Church.... At this time... those are suppressed who stand for the "old-time religion."
>
> But Holiness and Holiness alone has the solution to these problems.... In this her Second Rise the Holiness Movement advances to withstand this whole apostasy and maintain a pure gospel in the earth.[363]

From 1928 until his death, Smith was listed and affectionately referred to as the honorary president of the Association. Butler's high esteem for Smith was manifested by featuring the latter's "School of the Prophets" sessions at the annual conventions of the Association as long as Smith was physically able to attend. While a zealous and valuable supporter, Smith, unlike Wesley, was not an organizer and parliamentarian.

Author

Smith's literary work began about the time that he entered the field of evangelism. His earliest writings were expositional and devotional. Having been closely associated with Dr. Pepper, William McDonald, and David B. Updegraff, he was naturally one to whom they turned as a contributor to the holiness periodicals which they edited. Pepper edited the *Christian Standard,* McDonald *The Christian Witness,* and Updegraff the *Friends' Expositor.* After the *Friends' Expositor* and the *Christian Standard* had been discontinued, Smith continued until his ninetieth year to send contributions to *The Christian Witness.* In 1913 he became a member of the editorial staff of the *Heart and Life Magazine,* for which he wrote until about 1945. In 1923 he became a regular contributor to *God's Revivalist,* for which he wrote during the rest of his active life. His contributions to *The Pentecostal Herald,* edited by Morrison, his long-time camp-meeting associate and co-worker, began at the turn of the century and continued rather sporadically until about 1944. Other lesser holiness periodicals also used his articles. The holiness denominations occasionally featured Smith's writings in their official organs, among which were the *Herald of Holiness, The Free Methodist* and *The Wesleyan Methodist.* Through both the interdenominational and the denominational holiness periodicals, he was more nearly ministering to the whole of the Holiness Movement in America than perhaps any other one writer.

Perhaps no one of the holiness journals or magazines received as much from his pen as did *The Christian Witness,* which was generally looked upon as the official voice for the National Holiness Association. Besides devotional, doctrinal, and expositional studies, Smith also wrote a weekly commentary on the International Sunday School Lessons under the caption "Spiritual Life Suggestions." Another distinctive feature in his *Witness* writings and also later in the *Heart and Life Magazine* was his "Question Box." As people faced problems of doctrine, of Christian experience, of ethical living, or of Scripture exposition relative to Christian perfection, Smith opened his "Question Box" column in those publications to assist them with a solution.

Smith did not take time to write out a systematic treatise of his theology, even as Wesley had not done before him. But like Wesley he had a "system" within the framework of which he thought and wrote and preached.[364] His system of thought, however, can be discovered as one reads his articles and the few books which he wrote. The two most significant of Smith's books were *From Glory to Glory* and *Pauline Perfection*. In the former, his purpose was to present " 'the glory of the Lord' as the standard and as the source of the glory of man." His procedure was to analyze the Scripture text found in II Corinthians 3:18 (which he affirmed contained the philosophy of man's chief end), and then to set forth "the leading steps or stages of a glorious life."[365]

In his book on *Pauline Perfection*, he sought to expound the teaching of Paul upon "this richest and rarest of all themes," Christian perfection, of which Paul himself was the Christians' pattern.[366]

It would be difficult to estimate how extensive in terms of bound volumes were the writings of Smith. Had all his writings been published in book form he would easily have averaged a modest volume a year for over sixty years. Since much of his writing was done for periodicals which have been or will be lost to the reading public, some have regretted that more was not put into more permanent form. But Smith viewed his ministry as that adapted to meet the immediate needs of the Holiness Movement, which was perhaps more largely reached through its periodicals than through its books.

More of Smith's writings would doubtless have appeared

in book form had he not been so constantly changing his location and place of writing, because of his itinerant evangelism.[367] In keeping with his "Pentecostal circuit" and to meet the immediate needs of the holiness people, his longer or shorter articles were more conveniently produced for publication in holiness periodicals than were books.

Smith's style was his own. He abhorred imitation or affectation in all the work of the ministry. A mere reading of the titles under which he wrote, all with the view of promoting Christian holiness in some one of its stages, individually or corporately, discloses his versatility of mind.[368] He overworked no set of terms to the exclusion of other equally meaningful words in his expressing of the gospel. However, the earliest writings of Smith reflect to this investigator a greater discipline of thought and style than his later writings do. His zeal to excel in soul-winning seems to have detracted from his excelling as a writer.

Smith had no set of proof texts from which he could not depart and still impart his message. He felt that the whole underlying strata of the Scriptures, at their deepest levels, were permeated with the thought of "holiness unto the Lord." While recognizing that certain Biblical texts taught some phases of holiness more explicitly than others, yet to Smith all parts of the New Testament, and most of the Old Testament, were throbbing with that central idea of Christianity—holiness.[369]

While relatively free from allegorizing the Scriptures, Smith's writings nevertheless abounded with figures and analogies with which to elucidate the gospel.[370] Much of nature was vocal to him and afforded him media through which to convey the divine and invisible realm with which he dealt. He found analogies for teaching purposes in the fields of transportation, communication, merchandizing, warfare, government, medicine and surgery, athletics, and family life.

According to Smith, the supernatural realm works best *with* and *through* the natural order of things. Therefore, to him all life teemed with possible channels of making the supernatural message understandable within the range of the experience of each and every man.[371]

BIBLE-EXPOSITOR EVANGELIST

Usually students of revivalism have not associated "the study" with the camp meeting, nor the scholarly aptitude with the soul-winning art. In Smith they seem to have been closely related.

Dean of Holiness Expositors

In the eyes of his colleagues, Smith excelled in the exposition of the Scriptures. This was evidenced by the way he was repeatedly called to the same campgrounds year after year, a record unparalleled by any other in the Holiness Movement.[372] His "School of the Prophets" became popular because of his ability to make the Scriptures luminous for both laymen and ministers with their varying levels of educational background.

Dr. Gross Alexander—for many years professor of New Testament at Vanderbilt University and editor for some years of *The Methodist Review*—rated Smith as "one of the greatest expositors of the English Bible in all the world."[373] Dr. J. C. McPheeters, the successor of Dr. Morrison both as editor of *The Pentecostal Herald* (now called *The Herald*) and as president of Asbury Theological Seminary, called Smith "the dean of holiness expositors." Dr. J. A. Huffman, president of Winona Lake School of Theology, wrote of Smith as one of America's greatest New Testament expositors.[374] "Bud" Robinson, after extensive contact with the holiness preachers of his day, "set out Joseph H. Smith as the greatest Bible teacher in the holiness movement."[375]

Remembering that Smith was a self-taught man, these estimates of his ability and achievements have been the more remarkable. Having foregone the advantages of both a college and a seminary education, he was forced to develop his own techniques of study and expression while busily engaged in ministerial tasks.

Unlike some others of his colleagues in the Holiness Movement, Smith did not feel it sufficiently advantageous for his mastery of scriptural exposition to study either Hebrew or Greek.[376] While a student of other translations of the Scriptures, especially the American Standard Version, he was an incessant admirer and user of the Authorized Version of the English Bible.

Expository Principles

When asked to define expository preaching, Smith replied that

> Briefly stated, Expository Preaching is the exposing of the heart-meaning of God's revealed word, to communicate it to others, and to enforce its requirements and to encourage the appropriation of its blessing.[377]

When further questioned as to the procedure to follow in acquiring this method of preaching, Smith enumerated the following as having been formative in his own ministry: (1) "The Spirit's illumination upon the otherwise hidden mysteries of God's Word";[378] (2) the mastery of English grammar for exegesis and of the appropriate diction for expressing to the people the meaning of Scripture; (3) the adequate use of the context as "the best introduction to, and commentary upon, the text"; (4) a reasonable independence of commentaries and other men's writings; (5) the elucidation of Scripture with application and example; (6) the measuring of the intellectual and spiritual calibre of the congregation that is to hear the sermon; (7) dependence upon the Holy Spirit in the pulpit "for *recollection, utterance,* and *demonstration*"; and (8) the straightforward utterance of "the word of truth," backed by a "thus saith the Lord."[379]

With incidental differences in their points of view regarding the approach to the Scriptures, Smith and Dr. Wilbert W. White, founder of the Biblical Seminary in

New York, were one in aim. White described his own life work thus: "It has been to demonstrate the practicability of actually making the study of the Bible in the mother tongue the organizing, dominating discipline in a school of preparation for Christian leadership."[380] Smith and White were agreed that the interpreter of the Scriptures must be kept "face to face with the writings themselves."[381] With White, Smith believed that for many readers the Bible had been buried under a debris of commentaries and wrested by preconceived philosophies, and that what was needed was an open-eyed, open-minded, and open-hearted facing of the Scripture for oneself.[382]

Smith's stress upon the expositor's reasonable independence of others' books and comments did not mean to him an "uncharted subjectivism" or a careless license with the text of Scripture. The true expositor must both *abide by* what is written and *depend upon* the inspiring Spirit to illuminate his mind for the work of interpretation. For Smith "spiritual illumination" did not "suspend the necessity of study in things of the spiritual life and the Scriptures." Said he, "... *the use of all of our faculties and that to their utmost ability*, is required of us with regard to things of God, and the vital things of spiritual life."[383]

According to some interpreters of Protestantism, Smith's principles and practice have been the fountainhead of the cults and isms of the times. But he would have replied with Dr. Abdel Ross Wentz that

> It is a mistaken opinion that the Bible as a religious authority has produced the unstabilizing extremists and the super-individualistic cultists that give such lurid color to the pages of Protestant history. Not the Bible itself, but the segmentation of the Bible, its use only in parts and sections, has produced this unlovely confusion of tongues. Taken as a whole the Bible is the soundest stablizer [sic] of religious experience that is known to Church History. Permitted to exercise its full power it ... acts as a veritable balance wheel against tangential explosion.[384]

Had they met and compared notes, Smith and White would doubtless have had much in common as interpreters of the Word. While White acquired a thorough academic training which contributed much to his development and application of the "inductive method" in Bible study, Smith arrived at the same method through self-direction and self-discipline. Whereas White built an institution which incarnated his aims and ideals,[385] to which students *came* from the various denominations, Smith on the other hand *took* his "School of the Prophets" to the ministry and the laity in the camp meetings, conventions, and revivals which he held, as well as to the student groups attending the holiness colleges and institutes where he taught and preached.

Expository Aims

While Smith and White employed many of the same principles in Bible study and exposition, they shared the benefits of their discovery and labor in dissimilar ways. White labored to develop his method of study on a scientific basis so that he could impart the *method* to others; Smith employed his method in his own study and labored primarily to impart the *fruits* of his study to others with a view to effecting immediate changes in his hearers.[386]

Smith was quick to discriminate between evangelism and evangelicalism. To him the latter meant a simple statement, declaration, or defense of Christian doctrine; but to him evangelism meant the precipitation of "its acceptance, appropriation and application" to one's own heart and life. Evangelism then is impossible without involving both psychological and spiritual exercises, without enlisting the whole personality in life-decision.[387]

Emotional Appeals

Having served much of his public ministry during a period in which the emotional in religion was decried, Smith carefully distinguished between mere emotionalism and evangelism.

Now the truth is that while Evangelism will frequently, perhaps always, engage the emotions, it will also enlist the intelligence and all the reasoning powers of the mind; and it has never succeeded until it has likewise engaged the will, and that, both of the evangelist and of those, or the one, evangelized, and the faith of both alike.[388]

He held that the Holy Spirit should no more be excluded from one's emotional life than from one's volitional or intellectual life. True spirituality is achieved by the Holy Spirit's operation upon and manifestation through the entire human personality. In seeking for the scriptural standard for Christian experience, he was impressed with the apostles' emphasis upon fervor and zeal in the believer's life.[389] To him any conventionality which repressed proper religious feeling in either pulpit or pew was "traitorous."[390]

Evangelism's Field of Operation

For those who would limit evangelism to the conversion of sinners, Smith had a word.

...evangelism is not confined (as many seem to suppose) to the single epoch of conversion. It applies and may obtain along the whole range of the gamut of truth and the blessings of the gospel. Paul applied it to particular virtues or graces like that of giving, and Methodism has proven its equal application to Sanctification or to Justification. "Do the work of an evangelist," is as appropriate to all stages and phases of preaching as is either the work of a teacher or an herald of the truth.[391]

Such a view of evangelism doubtlessly accounted for Smith's repeated calls to the same camp meetings, churches, and schools year after year. He recognized four distinct classes of people which could be found in the average public congregation—sinners, backsliders, unsanctified believers, and those entirely sanctified. Upon the first three classes he ever sought to "precipitate" conversion, reclamation, and entire sanctification, respectively. But among the believers he always followed the scriptural distinctions between the "lambs" and "sheep," between "children" and "young men" and "fathers," and endeavored to foster those conditions of faith and obedience by which all stages of Christians might advance in the Christian life.[392]

A second limiting view of evangelism which Smith sought to overthrow was the view that the work of evangelism is to be carried on only by a special class. He enforced the necessity of both lay and ministerial activity in world evangelism, but directed his efforts more particularly to arousing *all* ministers to their duty of functioning as evangelists. Smith recognized that some had a peculiar gift in that direction and were providentially set apart by God for that work, but held that the pastor's responsibility was in no wise diminished by the work of "specialists."[393] He insisted that the pastor's evangelistic activity should be as much in evidence as his social, financial, ecclesiastical, or intellectual activity, if not more so.

> For we are bidden to be "instant in season and out of season." Paul was evangelistic in the Philippian jail, at Mar's [sic] Hill, and in every synagogue and by the way. With him as with the Saviour, personal and public evangelism were conjunctive rather than either in substitution for the other. We lay it down as a rule that real, faithful personal evangelism of the pastor will issue, sooner or later, in a larger public evangelism.[394]

Evangelism Threatened

By the second decade of the twentieth century, Smith was increasingly convinced that the need of the hour was evangelistic preaching. After liberally trained ministers had brought vast areas of Protestantism under their power, Smith claimed that the first place they generally evidenced the effects of their education was in their loss of "evangelistic function, force and fruit." Undaunted by "the spirit of the times" which he regarded as the greatest threat which evangelism faced, Smith declared that "evangelism is the only fitting work for the times that are upon us; and the right sort of evangelism is needed.... Not a reverie, but a call to battle is the duty of the hour."[395] Recalling that history recorded the fall of nations, the corruption of institutions, the degeneration of churches, and the apostasy of schools, but also that Christian revivals rejuvenated and originated new channels of operation, Smith called upon the youth of the Holiness Movement to join the ranks of the evangelists in order to help promote the Christian faith.[396]

Against the odds and obstacles he faced in evangelism in the second and third decades of the twentieth century, Smith firmly maintained his life-long views on evangelism, being sustained in them by his eschatological convictions which spurred him on to greater activity. The "signs of the times" spoke to him of the imminence of the Lord's return, the end of the age, a change in divine economies, and a closing of "the day of salvation."[397]

In the light of the Scriptures, Smith believed that Christ had

> ...pronounced mankind now ripe for such immediate Evangelism as He...demonstrated in the case of this Samaritan woman.... Lands as heathen or as religiously hybrid as Samaria must not have educationalism or Americanism thrust upon them as a substitute or a necessary prerequisite for salvation. All such betterments of society and to civilization have come as sequel to and as result of Evangelism rather than as a forerunner or a surety of it....[398]

According to his understanding of the Scriptures, the itinerancy of evangelists was to continue until the world had been evangelized. There is the ceaseless "Go" for the gospel minister. He believed and proved for himself that there is "no more certainty in any business than this of Biblical, Spirit-led and loving evangelism...."[399] Whereever he went, though with diminishing returns at certain periods, Smith "saved some."

To those of the young generation whom he called to join him in an all-out evangelistic thrust, he pointed out the reproaches they must be prepared to bear in fulfilling the Pauline exhortation, "Do the work of an evangelist," [400] and Christ's command, "Go ye therefore, and teach all nations." [401] They would doubtless be labeled "irregulars," "illiterates," "insignificant," and "fanatics." [402] But he consoled and encouraged himself and others with the thought that God has had "irregulars" all through history whom He has used to carry out His purposes, such as Enoch, Melchisedec, the judges in Israel, and the Old Testament prophets, whom he believed portrayed and prefigured the evangelists of these latter days. Convinced that he had Biblical grounds for his faith, the rise or fall of evangelism's popularity could not change him.

> In the New Testament, Evangelism has priority and precedence over Ecclesiasticism. John the Baptist may have instituted a school of piety among his disciples; but he never organized a church; and represents at once an Old Testament prophet at his zenith, and a New Testament Evangelist at his dawning.
>
> Christ's commissioned twelve and seventy were sent forth on missions purely evangelistic.... They were only to minister the truth together with the immediate blessings and benefits of the Kingdom. *And this is Evangelism.*
>
> Christ Himself was an Itinerant Evangelist. If He taught philosophy, this was but incidental to the urgency with which He pressed immediate salvation. If at length, He instituted a Church, this was to build an arsenal for the Truth and establish footing for the forces that were to save men. He crowns His own ministry as prophet upon earth with a commission to His followers to go forth and evangelize the world. Any use or abuse of the Church that excludes or hinders direct evangelism in season and out of season; or any exercise of ecclesiastical power that discredits or deters evangelists is a manifest corruption and perversion of the Church.
>
> Stephen turns the more temporal office of a deacon into an enlarged occasion for evangelist's work. An evangelist's passion will make use of official position.
>
> Philip so sets things afire wherever the Spirit sends him, or Providence takes him, or persecution drives him that he honors the designation of Philip the Evangelist....[403]

The other reproaches of illiteracy, insignificance, and fanaticism can easily be endured if the evangelist remembers that Jesus was spurned by many because He was not of the Rabbinical schools, and that He was only regarded as a carpenter's son—and that from the despised "city of Nazareth." Jesus too was accused of being "beside himself" and of casting out demons by the prince of demons.[404]

Even though holiness evangelism might be largely discredited by church and school, the "end of all things" drew Smith on in a relentless quest for the souls of men. Until "the end," holiness evangelism must be carried to "*all* churches, denominations and sects of Christendom the world over."[405]

Such an evangelistic crusade did not mean the creation of another church organization or denomination. Smith held that an advanced and aggressive Holiness Movement could be carried on in which there would be no changing of the modes or ordinances or views upon various secondary matters of the several communions. With the tolerance enjoined by Paul in Romans, chapter 14, Smith believed that the various churches could steadily recognize and maintain the fact that "the kingdom of God is not meat and drink; but righteousness, and peace, and joy in the Holy Ghost."[406]

After having spent more than sixty years in "preaching a free and full salvation," Smith testified that he had never told one person that he would have to leave the church of his choice and join the Methodists in order to enjoy what Smith enjoyed in divine grace.[407] He spent the last two decades of his long ministry laboring, praying for and thinking of ways to launch a "super evangelism" which he believed would precede the closing of the gospel age.[408]

Missions and Schools

His Missionary Outreach

Along with his predecessors and contemporaries in the

Holiness Movement, Smith maintained that the holiness camp meetings had mothered both extensive home and foreign missionary enterprises and numerous educational institutions. The missionary outreach of the movement early had been expressed in the world-tour of Inskip, McDonald, and Wood, and the large support they gave to the faith missions established by Bishop William Taylor in India, South America, and Africa. Wrote Smith,

> As early as the first few decades of this Modern Holiness Movement... it contributed (directly or indirectly) millions of dollars, and scores of men and women, to the Foreign Missionary work of the various churches (particularly the Methodist Episcopal Church and the M. E. Church South), and had stimulated the Missionary spirit in the homeland many degrees.[409]

Smith had displayed his interest in missions by giving the earliest years of his ministry to the "poor whites" of Georgia instead of going to college, and in supporting the mission projects of Bishop Taylor, of the Oriental Missionary Society, of the National Holiness Missionary Society (World Gospel Mission), of the Bethel Mission of Shanghai, China, and of his own denomination, to which he also gave his daughter, Grace, as a missionary to India. From his theological viewpoint holiness and world-wide evangelism were inseparable. "This is established in Scripture, by the Lord's promise concerning the gift of the Holy Ghost, by the acts of the apostles and by their examples, exhortations and epistles."[410]

His own ministry abroad began in 1895 with a short visit to the Hawaiian Islands where, along with others, a Japanese liquor dealer was converted. Eighteen years later Smith and his wife went on an evangelistic tour of Japan, Korea, and China, and to Smith's surprise the converted liquor dealer was his appointed interpreter before the Japanese Methodist Conference to which Smith ministered in Japan. The interpreter told his experience to Smith in these words:

> I was a liquor dealer in Honolulu. I represented a Japanese liquor firm...but when Kihara (one of our Japanese Methodist preachers in Honolulu) came into my liquor store he said, "...Come and hear the American evangelist preach tonight in the Methodist church." I went and...gave my heart to Christ. The next day I empty out all the liquor. The next night I stand on the streets of Honolulu and preach Jesus.[411]

Smith's ministry in the Orient was fruitful even as it had been in the States and Canada.[412] His passion for missions never abated as is evidenced by his contemplated evangelistic tour in China as late as 1938, when war conditions forced him to cancel travel plans.[413]

His Educational Concern

Smith's Itinerant Institute, early incorporated into his camp meeting work, was an outward expression of his inner convictions on Christian education. Himself without professional training within academic halls, he had nevertheless so disciplined his own mind and developed his theological knowledge that by 1907 he was called to Meridian, Mississippi, which was at that time the largest holiness educational center in the world. While the range of courses of the two "colleges" extended from the primary through the secondary to the liberal arts and theological level of instruction, Smith devoted his energies to the theological and evangelistic side of the institutions' program.[414]

As director of the School of Theology within the Male College, and as pastor, along with his wife, of the whole college community, Smith was imparting his views to students who came from many different states of the union and some foreign countries. Here as elsewhere Smith's philosophy of Christian education was evident. He stressed a balance between the intellectual and the practical, the spiritual and the natural in education. All educational advantages and advances, however, were to augment the evangelistic effectiveness of the church in general and the ministry in particular.[415] It was at Meridian that Smith left his lasting imprint upon some of the present-day promoters of the Holiness Movement, including Dr. John Paul and Dr. J. C. McPheeters. As an ideal for the future preachers in his classes, Smith exhorted, "Young men, when your passion for learning outruns your passion for souls, it is time to call a halt until your passion for souls outruns your passion for learning." [416]

A special committee, reporting to the Board of Trustees of the Meridian Women's College and the Meridian Male College in their annual joint meeting, May 25, 1909, described the spiritual aspect of the schools as follows:

> Sectarianism is unknown. The historic doctrines of Christianity are diligently taught. Irreverent criticism and modern speculation keep their distance.... The condition of every individual soul is looked after...is seen in the fact that the schools having enrolled nearly 1000 the past year, are closing without more than a dozen or two unconverted, besides many have been cleansed and led into the riches of grace. The diligent work of Rev. and Mrs. Jos. H. Smith, the College pastors, deserves mention here as having contributed ...to...the promotion of a type of religion which is practical and enduring....[417]

Smith served the Meridian Schools from 1907 to 1912 when he took his leave for an evangelistic tour in the Orient.

Following an evangelistic campaign in Whittier, California, Smith was one of several who launched the Training School which has become known as Pacific Bible College, located at Azusa, California.[418] This west coast institution was similar to those founded in St. Louis and Chicago by Iva Durham Vennard to whom Smith also had been an inspiration and a close counsellor.

While Smith's ministry in exposition and evangelism extended to practically every holiness school (denominational and interdenominational) in the nation, it was at Chicago Evangelistic Institute that he gave the most consecutive and intensive instruction.[419] At the Chicago school he delivered lectures on evangelism, Bible exposition, missionary preaching, hermeneutics, and life and service problems. There he stressed education for the glory of God and the service of men, maintaining that the greatest service is that of bringing men to Christ in personal salvation, which in turn stimulates learning and produces those reforms and social progress which are the by-products of experiential Christianity.[420]

Smith held before the constituency of the movement the reminder that they were under a specific "educational limitation" because of their mission, which was *evangelism*. That for Smith necessitated the leaving of much of general education to the state- and church-sponsored colleges, while the Holiness Movement was to major on that which produces evangelists. Recognizing the independent holiness academy, college, or university as legitimate and helpful by-products of the movement, Smith nevertheless declared at Cleveland Bible Institute in 1922 that

> The real memorial of the Holiness Movement to this time is the holiness camp meeting and the holiness evangelist and the holiness evangelists' training school. Those are the real and true monuments thus far building in the progress of the holiness movement.[421]

As a reactionary against certain trends in the educational world, he wanted to see the holiness institutes brought to such a standard of efficiency that their graduates would go out equipped for Christian evangelism without dependence upon other institutions as "finishing" schools.[422]

> It is one thing to know and it is another thing to be able to show. One thing to have the experience, another thing to be able to teach.... One thing to understand His truth, it is another thing to speak it in their tongue and to acquire ability to teach and preach under the unction of the Spirit with the view of getting people immediately sanctified. This is the genius of the holiness ministry and that is the boundary line of our ambition in the educational field, that we may have sufficient auxiliary educational equipment for this special training....[423]

That not all holiness educators agreed with Smith as to the educational boundary of the Holiness Movement was manifested by the number of holiness academies and colleges, and attempted holiness "universities," and theological seminaries which sprang up in the Holiness Movement.[424]

Memorabilia

Those who associated with Smith over half a century or more of his public life have indicated that he adorned his theology by the life he lived. Dr. H. C. Morrison, one of Smith's closest observers and associates, chose to write of Smith in terms of highest confidence.

> It has been my happy privilege for many years to labor in camp meetings, conventions and revival meetings with Rev. Joseph H. Smith, a member of the Philadelphia Conference of the M.E. Church. He is a great New Testament teacher. I have known of no man who could state the fundamental doctrines of the gospel of Christ more clearly and make them more inviting, give them finer emphasis, and gather from them larger fruitfulness, than this beloved and honored brother, Joseph H. Smith. He, like myself, has grown old in this blessed service of spreading scriptural holiness over these lands. He has been a man of great courage, of remarkable calm under trying circumstances, a wise counselor, and I have associated with no man that was more free from adverse criticism, or unkindly remarks about his fellowmen, friend or foe, than this same beloved Joseph H. Smith.[425]

Smith bore frequent testimony to a clear-cut, radical experience of conversion and to a definite, second-crisis experience, which he believed perfectly cleansed his heart from all unrighteousness and conditioned him to progressively perfect holiness by growth in the grace and knowledge of Christ. On his seventieth birthday anniversary, June 4, 1925, Smith was laboring in a camp meeting in Cincinnati. Instead of his usual sermon that day he narrated the facts and events surrounding his conversion, entire sanctification, and progress in the Christian life. Said he, "I humbly bear witness that since God saved my soul He and I have never had a break." [426]

Certain that he had been sovereignly chosen, through no merit of his own, to be a preacher of the gospel, Smith never set a price on his ministry, but from his first "hard scrabble circuit" to his closing years of evangelistic itineracy, he trusted God to supply all his needs—physical, material, and spiritual. He committed the matter of his income to the Lord and those for whom he ministered, accepting without complaint whatever he received. Although living by faith during his half-century of evangelistic labors, he had been so prospered and had so wisely managed his private affairs as to leave in his estate sufficient funds to amply care for his surviving widow, and an orange grove in Southern California—the proceeds of which were to go entirely to the "work of the Lord." [427] Nor had his family gone without its needs. Without academic degrees for himself, he provided college training for his five children, four of whom received a college degree and two advanced to professional degrees. [428]

All through his Christian life he had lived frugally, and a few thought stingily. But for some years before his death he annually gave half of his income to Christian causes, with not a few young people receiving his friendly and financial support in their academic preparation for life's service. [429]

While away from his first wife and their five children for months in succession, he endured the separation cheerfully because of his unmistakable "call" to evangelize wherever the doors of service were providentially opened. As each of his children turned twenty-one, he asked him or her "to write a personal letter as to what he or she thought of father." [430] He wanted so to live his religious profession that those who knew him best might have confidence in him and the Christ he served.

While away from home he lived under all sorts of conditions. From the tents and poorly constructed and furnished cabins of the early camp-meeting grounds to the finest hotels in the heart of the great cities, from the homes of the humblest laymen to the residences of the wealthy, Smith learned the art of adjustment without complaint.[431]

In spite of constantly changing living conditions, continuous travel and service in all kinds of weather and through periods of exhaustion or injury, Smith was remarkably preserved in vitality for his work. Not less than three times it seemed that his ministry had come to an end, first in 1886, then in 1895, and again in 1929. But Smith prayed and was assured by the Lord that he had a wider ministry yet to perform. Soon after an unexpected recovery from a skull fracture due to a fall during an ice storm in an Indiana city in 1929, he declared:

> Some years ago the Lord wired to me this promise, "With long life will I satisfy him, and show him my salvation." Now He has added this postscript, "I will renew his youth like the eagle's." I am enjoying my ministry more than ever before.[432]

While he never emphasized divine healing as did some in their public ministry, Smith nevertheless believed in and had experienced both instantaneous and gradual divine healings by faith. To these, along with healthful practices, Smith attributed his long life and ministry.

Smith ever reflected buoyancy and great confidence about his future ministry. He never looked forward to retirement, but to ever larger fields of service and fruitfulness. In 1927 he wrote,

> Not a thing in my life has caused me to be out of the sound of God's call; nothing personal, business, marital, educational, or physical has hindered the sound of His voice. God and I have some secrets about my rejuvenation of my mind and body. I do not think of myself as being called fifty-four years ago but as being called now ... it is the joy of my life to believe and be assured by God that the best and biggest things of my ministry are all ahead....[433]

Like Wesley he was an early riser who devoted his earliest morning hours to prayer and study of the Scriptures. The irregular hours of travel and late hours at public services did not deter him from his morning vigils. From those early hours of prayer and meditation came his devotional articles, his Sunday school lesson commentaries, and his sermonic insights. He never ceased to apply himself in study, and at seventy-five felt himself still a freshman in learning.[434]

While the life of unceasing prayer yielded for Smith many remarkable answers to prayer for bodily healing, for the conversion of individuals known as difficult cases, for church revivals and financial necessities, one of the chief marks of his life was the "guidance of the Holy Spirit."[435] Smith both preached and professed to practice the Spirit-led life. One of the more unmistakable instances of divine guidance occurred thus: Smith was at Camp Sychar in Ohio when he felt a strong desire to go to Ocean Grove Camp in New Jersey, in the Mecca of Methodism in that day. Knowing that he had an appointment in Indiana following the Sychar Camp, he at once discarded the impression to go to Ocean Grove. But in prayer it returned. Convinced that God was guiding him to go, he secured by wire his release from the Indiana meeting, recommending that another minister be called to fill his place. Then, without a call from that Ocean Grove Camp and paying his own expenses, he started eastward.

> I started to Ocean Grove and as I drew near there I thought, perhaps the Lord is sending me here to rest. It was the Saturday before the last Sunday of the camp, and it was hard to obtain a room. I went down back streets and alleys so that no one would see me. I finally succeeded in getting a room on the second floor of a boarding house. I prepared for rest and went to bed. In a little while someone knocked on the door. I said, "Come in," and it was Bishop Fitzgerald. He said, "Brother Smith, when they brought me word you had arrived on the grounds it settled a question that has

been in my mind all the week. Bishop ———— failed me—he was to have had the service tomorrow morning. There is any one of a hundred men I could call upon, but the Lord has not led me to do it. I could preach myself, but have had no leading to do so. The Lord has sent you; you will preach tomorrow morning."

Later I learned the act behind the scenes. Some women...had been praying that God would send a holiness message before the camp closed.... The result was that they not only took care of my expenses but from that morning issued ten years of evangelistic work—they held evangelistic pentecostal meetings every year. Thousands of people, preachers, etc., from Washington, Baltimore, etc., came and hundreds were saved and sanctified....

. . . .

They had a great meeting down in southern Indiana. You see why I am desirous of acquainting you with the leading of the Holy Spirit.... I want us all to be taught of God.[436]

Smith ever depended upon the Holy Spirit in everything he was called upon or found necessary to do.

For as God's child and Christ's servant, I am to eat and drink, and walk and talk and all else that I do *as unto the Lord.* Having the Holy Spirit with me always and dwelling within me, I dare depend upon *Him* to guide, and guard and enable me to please Him and glorify Him in all things.[437]

After having attained the place of the foremost Bible expositor in the Holiness Movement and having acceptance as a sensible, scriptural teacher of holiness by some of the highest officials of his own denomination, Smith still seemed to manifest the same self-abnegating attitude which characterized his early ministry. This was evidenced by what he refused. In 1914 he published his reasons for turning down for the third time the offer of honorary degrees. While appreciating the good will and high esteem such offers represented, he declined the honor, for he wanted nothing by way of title that would seem in any measure to put him above the majority of his brethren. He cited the famed Albert Barnes as his example of one who refused the degree of the Doctor of Divinity upon "scriptural grounds." When even the title "Reverend" was used with his name it was not to his liking. He preferred to be known as just Joseph H. Smith. He further believed that he was following the spirit of the original leaders of the National Holiness Movement, such as Inskip, Cookman, McDonald, and others who wore no title of "Doctor." [438]

Another mark of his refusal to seek or take honor to himself was his unwillingness to keep statistical records of his success as a soul-winner. He would not claim and record the scores of thousands who had been seekers at his altars, since he believed that very few, if any, individuals won through the evangelist's ministry were converted apart from the prayers and direct efforts of pastors, parents, Sunday school teachers, and fellow Christians.[439] If "Bud" Robinson, an associate and co-worker in holiness evangelism with Smith, saw one hundred thousand people seek the Lord in meetings where he preached, it is safe to say that Smith equalled that number himself.[440] Between 1874 and 1932 Smith had traveled over one million miles on railroads to perform his service—with no estimate included as to the number by horse and buggy, or by auto and boat—and had preached about thirty-two thousand times.[441] No estimate of the miles traveled or the sermons preached the last fourteen years of his life has been discovered.

Controversial as the doctrine of sanctification has been through the years and opposed as it was by several within the Methodist Church, by some in the bishopric, and several in its ministry and laity, Smith claimed to have kept himself free from the spirit and practice of controversy.

> No headway is ever made by controversy and by contention.... It may surprise you if I tell you that I have been on this big circuit for thirty years and set especially to spread Scriptural holiness over these lands. I don't remember ever once to have been in a controversy on the subject of holiness.
> I don't allow myself to be drawn into contention.

> God has not retained many of us as lawyers. He has subpeoned the whole of us as witnesses.... Nobody has ever been argued into holiness. Some have argued themselves out by getting into a contentious controversial spirit. Just enjoy the luxury of letting the other fellow have the last word when you know he is wrong....[442]

Such was the spirit of Smith. With humility and a conciliatory spirit he moved among his ministerial brethren, but never to compromise *his deepest convictions* concerning God, His Word, or the gracious possibilities of Christian experience.

Never did Smith feel that he had arrived at perfection of either character or service. Nor did he regard himself as one who had attained unto a state of grace from which he could not fall or within which he did not need that same diligent watchfulness which characterized his earliest years as a Christian and minister. In his eighty-fourth year he wrote:

> And think you, beloved, that I myself have any leeward to relax my vigilance in these afternoon hours of my Christian life and ministry when I can stand here and see through tears as many as eight if not ten fellow workmen that with me have stood—or with whom I have stood—in somewhat of front ranks of this very ministry, that have fallen—some by lust, some by covetousness—none of them to ever regain a like place in the ministry and some two or three of them to never give sure evidence of having regained the peace and favor with God? Nay, I will not relax, but with our pattern Paul, "I will watch and pray that I enter not into temptation," and "will keep my body under, lest having preached to others I myself should be a castaway."[443]

CHAPTER FOUR

The Gospel of Grace and Glory

In this chapter the writer has treated the underlying assumptions in Smith's theological thought and developed his doctrine of revelation, which is basic to all that follows in his system. Smith accepted the Methodistic formulation of Biblical teaching as most nearly representing New Testament Christianity; he believed the Bible to be the only revealed authority for Christian faith; he accepted as valid Paul's claim to be the pattern Christian for all generations of believers; he claimed that a New Testament ministry must be evangelistic and that all Biblical doctrines are directly or indirectly related to experiential Christianity.

Smith's doctrine of revelation centered in "the gospel of grace and glory," dimly etched in nature, but clearly unfolded in New Testament Scripture. Therefore both the created world and the inspired Word are revelations from God.

THE STARTING POINT

His Theology Methodistic

The point of vision from which Smith viewed all theology was identical with that expressed by Dr. John McClintock at the centenary celebration of American Methodism held in New York City, January 25, 1866. On that occasion McClintock,[444] later the first president of Drew Theological Seminary, in speaking on "The Distinctive Features of Methodism," declared:

> ... Methodism ... takes the old theology of the Christian Church, but it takes one element which no other Christian Church has dared to put forward as a prom-

inent feature of theology. In ours it is the very point from which we view all theology.... Knowing exactly what I say and taking the full responsibility of it, I repeat, we are the only church in history from the apostles' time until now that has put forward as its very elemental thought—the great central pervading idea of the whole book of God from beginning to the end—the holiness of the human soul, heart, mind, and will. Go through all the confessions of all the churches; you will find this in no other. You will find even some of them that blame us in their books and writings. It may be called fanaticism, but dear friends, that is our mission. If we keep to that, the next century is ours; if we keep to that, the triumphs of the next century shall throw those that are past far in the shade. Our work is a moral work—that is to say, the work of making men holy. Our preaching is to that, our church agencies are for that, our schools, colleges, universities, and our theological seminaries are for that. There is our mission—there is our glory—there is our power and there shall be the ground of our triumph.[445]

His Authority Biblical

While Smith was in accord with Methodistic theology, he claimed not to have based his beliefs upon the theology of the church or the writings of Wesley. Recognizing the debt to them for leading him into a Christian experience, he claimed to have returned to the Bible itself for his mature theological views. Within five weeks after his conversion at a Methodist altar, he claimed by faith the state of "perfect love," and thereafter ever sought to understand better the Biblical teaching concerning it. Thus, the sources of his doctrinal position seem to have been in the following chronological order: the church, individual Christian experience and the Scriptures. The latter soon assumed the place of final authority, with personal experience and the historical testimony of the Methodist Episcopal Church corroborating for him the witness of the written Word.[446]

His Pattern Pauline

Claiming the Scriptures as his authority, Smith regarded Paul as the "master builder," both in doctrine and in life. As Moses had been sovereignly chosen for a unique position in the Old Testament dispensation, so Paul had been divinely set before the Christian ministry and before the whole church as a pattern experient of "Christian perfection" or perfect love, as well as an authoritative apostle in formulating it as a doctrine. Paul then was to be emulated by all Christians throughout the history of the Church.[447]

Interpretating Paul as the pattern Christian and gospel minister for all time, Smith aimed at conforming his ministry to the Pauline standard. He thought of Paul thus:

> *He was a minister of Jesus Christ.* His "system of doctrine" was as well articulated as any skeleton could be; but it was so covered with flesh and skin, so clothed with the comely attire of common homespun, and so vitalized with warm, divine love, that it might come close to men to touch them and make them whole, rather than appear as a stalking skeleton to frighten them off from afar.[448]

His Ministry Evangelistic

Although a teacher and a preacher, Smith considered himself above all else a *minister* of the gospel of Jesus Christ. According to his thought, the teacher imparts truths or principles, and the preacher proclaims the "good news" that these truths are personally and corporately realizable through Christ, but the minister does not stop until his hearers have become actual recipients or experients of that which he explains and urges upon them.[449] That accounts for Smith's interest in theology as a science as secondary to his possession and "precipitation" of it as an experience.

His Doctrine Experiential

Convinced that the *knowledge of God* is "personal and experimental rather than theoretical or philosophical," his life passion was to become *personally acquainted* with God so as to minister that experiential knowledge to others.[450] Having chosen to be a "Biblical" rather than a "philosophical" or a "systematic" theologian, Smith always treated metaphysical aspects of theology Biblically and experientially. His chief objective was to translate the theology of the Bible into his own life and the lives of others. Inwardly and outwardly, he unceasingly sought to incorporate his whole life into his ministry which was always evangelistic.[451]

Standing within the circle of the perfect love or holiness concept as he found it in Scripture and claimed it in experience, Smith oriented all phases of Biblical theology to that central, controlling idea. That concept covered for him, as no other, the central idea of the gospel of grace and glory, both on its divine and its human side, both in its origin and its objective.[452]

THE GLORY AND GRACE MEDIATED: REVELATION TO MAN

Smith regarded the nineteenth Psalm as one of the theological treasures of the Bible. In verses 1–6 he found the "theology of nature" which antedated and is more universal than the "theology of Scripture." In verses 7–14 he believed the "theology of Scripture" is epitomized.

The World As Revelational

The Psalmist saw the glory of God in His creative handiwork in nature and regarded it as a mode of divine revelation. Likewise Paul taught that the heathen world has not been without revelation since through the medium of nature God's eternal power and Godhead and goodness have been discernable in every nation to all generations, so that they are without excuse if they know Him not in certain of His attributes revealed through nature.[453]

Having schooled himself in the Conference Course of Study for Ministers, prescribed and required by his denomination in the 1880's, Smith had early studied Bishop Butler's *Analogy of Religion*. To him it must have served as a strong apologetic for general revelation or the revelatory value of all nature. He saw in the heavenly expanse as well as in the growing lily that which was analogous to the moral and spiritual realm. With Wesley he believed that the divine natural government of the universe held forth much to teach man of the divine moral government under which he must accountably conduct himself.[454]

However, all the evidences in creation of God's eternal power and Godhead, and in the "tickings of his moral law in the voice of conscience," are at best, thought Smith, but a preface and introduction to the revelation of truth in Christ by the Holy Spirit.[455]

Smith believed that "all creation and all providence preach the gospel if men could but interpret the undertones of their voices." For him the message of redemption was written in the remedial properties of much of nature, but, because of intellectual pride and sensuality, man is blinded to God's revelation through the natural order.[456] The "vicarious" element in nature bodied forth for Smith an analogy to the atonement of Christ. Thought he,

> ... it has evidently been God's design that the world about us and the constitution of the human mind and race should furnish both pictures and shadowed outlines of all this glory which was to be brought to light in the face of Christ Jesus, through the Gospel.[457]

The Written Word As Revelation

To Smith the written word of Scripture was "special" or "supernatural revelation," "the true and sure and full record of what *God hath spoken.*"[458] While the outer natural world and man's rational and moral nature have been God's voice to all, the Scriptures are His authoritative Word to all generations that have had them within their reach.

Following Paul's thought in Romans, chapter 1, and in II Corinthians, chapter 3, Smith found three distinct and successive levels of revelation: nature, the law, and the gospel. Each level was a disclosure of the divine glory but with ever-increasing brightness. While the natural order revealed certain aspects of God's glory, the legal code heightened that revelation, and the gospel climaxed it. On the other hand, nature also veiled some aspects which the supernatural revelation unveiled. "... and the law but dimly showed the crowning glory of the Lord, which was reserved for the Gospel to unfold." [459]

Scholarship and the Scriptures

Smith's approach to the Scriptures was that of the conventional, nineteenth-century, orthodox scholar who could not accept modern Biblical criticism's evolutionary and naturalistic presuppositions and consequent conclusions.[460] While somewhat informed concerning the methods and conclusions of the "liberal" scholars, he spent little time constructing an apologetic against their views. In that position he followed Wesley who did not defend Christianity on a rationalistic basis against the intellectual attacks of deism.

> The surest way to bring deists to Christianity, thought Wesley, was not by argument but by living example, by the positive affirmation of the principles of the Bible in character and in life. The aim of the Wesleyan revival, therefore, was to establish biblical Christianity over the land.[461]

For him, as for Wesley, supernatural revelation was the starting point for Christians; and his duty was not to enter into a rationalistic controversy about the Bible, feeling little could be accomplished through argument, but to preach vigorously "plain, old Bible Christianity." [462]

Smith felt that "the tendency to elevate reason above revelation, to rate scholarship above spirituality, to follow professors, philosophers, and 'authorities' rather than the Bible," obtained always and everywhere when the doctrine of Christian perfection was neglected.[463] According to his estimate, "The bulk of Christian scholarship ends in knowledge about Christ and about the Gospel, rather than knowledge of the Gospel and of Christ." [464]

In the account of the Wise Men coming from the east to worship the Christ-child, Smith found illustrated the right relationship between scholarship and the Scriptures.

> It shows that when scholars are rightly adjusted by faith in Christ to the Scriptures God will use their scholarship to further their way and bless the world. In fact, the chief key-stone lesson of this whole incident is the rightful co-relation between revelation and science. True learning in the right spirit tends towards the Christ, but needs the Scriptures to complete it; and the faith of Christ, with the light of the Scriptures, subserves such learning to Gospel ends. Reason needs faith to supplement it, and faith employs reason to establish it.[465]

True science and philosophy by making right connection with the Scriptures, as illustrated in Matthew, chapter 2, thought Smith, can fulfill the will of God; otherwise they may frustrate His purpose and end in "uncertainty and ignorance concerning 'the beginning' and 'the ending of things'; concerning the meaning and purpose of life; and concerning God Himself." [466]

The Scriptural Doctrine of Scripture

Since for Smith the seat of authority for the Christian faith was the Bible, the Scripture's teaching concerning itself was of utmost importance to him. He could not allow the Scripture's testimony to itself to be questioned and still retain as valid what it had said about God, man, sin, Christ and salvation.[467]

Citing Jesus' and the apostles' attitude toward the Old Testament as exemplary, Smith felt scripturally bound to hold "the written Word" and "the spoken Word" of God as inseparable. He found a basis in Christ's and the apostles' teachings for esteeming the New Testament as sacred, inviolable and authoritative as they had regarded the Old Testament.[468] Of the whole Bible he affirmed: "We need *no other authority or proof for what we declare, than that it is plainly taught in the Bible. If it is there, God hath spoken it.*"[469]

Two passages clearly voiced for him the basic doctrine of Scripture: "All scripture is given by inspiration of God, and is profitable for doctrine, for reproof, for correction, for instruction in righteousness: that the man of God may be perfect...."[470] "... no prophecy of the scripture is of any private interpretation. For the prophecy came not in old time by the will of man: but holy men of God spake as they were moved by the Holy Ghost."[471]

Revelation and Inspiration

According to Smith's view, the divine will and plan for all time has been supernaturally revealed, objectively recorded, and providentially preserved in the Holy Bible for the salvation of all mankind. In that sense revelation has ceased and is final.

But the appropriation and application of that revealed salvation in each individual's life and service in unrevealed and unrecorded until personally received by faith in each believer's life. In that sense "revelation" may be said to be continual to each individual through the Holy Spirit's illuminating and teaching ministry.

> ... revelation is for the whole Christian world and deals with the things of the kingdom in general, while illumination is for the individual Christian, in the interpretation and application of revelation and in the discovery of one's own place and the direction of his own path in the way and in the work of the kingdom here.[472]

While there was repeated and progressive revelation within the Old Testament Scriptures for Israel, yet for both Israel and the Church, revelation reached its perfection in Christ and the apostles, and then ceased (with the death of the last apostle) for this gospel era or dispensation. *Continuous* revelation was not even known in Israel, for there were periods, such as the inter-testamental era, when no *new* revelation was given.

In all the progress of the Christian centuries, neither theologians, philosophers, nor scientists have either added or changed a single doctrine of Biblical theology as the apostles knew it. The apostles and prophets had scaled, by supernatural assistance, the mountain peaks of spiritual truth, and what they saw they set forth in the Scriptures. The history of Christianity is evidence that the recovery of lost truth, rather than "revelation" or the "discovery" of any new truth, has produced and marked the revivalistic and fruitful periods within the church.[473]

Smith cautiously distinguished between the Word of God and the Scriptures. The Word of God existed prior to and in some instances apart from the Scripture for centuries, and even Jesus' words—the very words of life—were not in written form at first. Even many Israelites, not understanding the meaning and application of their own written Scriptures, were still without the Word of God. The same principle obtains in this New Testament era, for "many persons have Bibles and have Biblical scholarship that do not know what God has said." Nevertheless, Christians this side of the primitive church have not had "the Word of God against or apart from the Scriptures," even though many may have had the Scriptures without having the Word of God. Having the *body* of Scripture without the Spirit who inspired them is to be without the Word of God. To have the Word of God one must have both the letter of Scripture and the living Spirit illuminating that letter to the believing mind.[474]

Smith held that "special" or "supernatural" revelation brings to man what God has not revealed or that which is undiscoverable by man elsewhere. "In the Bible is revealed everything that is necessary to salvation, and *what God has revealed elsewhere is not enough to save men's souls.*"[475] Revelation itself, however, is not salvation, although necessary for it. For without this revelation to man's faith, he is left at Mars' hill with a "forestry of interrogation points as to deity and eternity," and in Athens before the altar to the unknown god.[476]

Smith rejected any rigidly mechanical theory of inspiration by which special revelation was brought to men. "In the main," he held to a "plenary and protective view of inspiration" by which the Holy Spirit so supernaturally supplemented the limitations and frailties of the prophets and apostles, without destroying their individuality, as to produce an accurate record of precisely what God wanted permanently preserved in Scriptures.[477] However, within the framework of the fully inspired Word there are instances of "verbal" inspiration as in the specifically prophetic deliverances found in "the Magnificat of Mary, the record of Christ's priestly prayer, the Annunciation of the Angels. . . ."

> Inspiration is that movement of God's Spirit upon the memory, perception and imagination of men's minds whereby His revealed Truth is communicated to man, and that movement upon his language by tongue whereby it is transmitted from His chosen agents to the people to whom it is addressed. This is the Word. And when this transmission was by His wisdom, carried from direct speech and from tradition to writing under divine guidance, help and control, this gave us the Scriptures. And again, God's message to men, thus in Scripture is the Word of God.[478]

At least six things were sufficient proof for Smith of the inspiration and, therefore, of the reliability and divine authority of the Scriptures: (1) their enduring universality;[479] (2) their inherent, superhuman content; (3) the "unlettered" authors, such as Peter and John, who wrote such epistles as the epistles of John and the epistles of Peter;[480] (4) the effects of the Scriptures upon the morals and spirits of men; (5) the testimony of such enduring, superhuman, and effective writings to their own origin and nature;[481] and (6) the literal fulfillment of the Old Testament Scriptures concerning the birth, life, ministry, death and resurrection of Christ.[482]

Inspiration and Illumination

While revelation became final in Christ's spoken words and the elucidation and confirmation of them by miraculously credentialed apostles, the Spirit who brought the revelation and inspired its recording has had a continuous ministry throughout this church age (or dispensation).[483] His ministry of *illumination,* upon the inspired revelation, unto its proper interpretation, unto its rightful application in producing salvation, has been promised to all seekers after "saving truth."

The Holy Spirit is the one source of both divine inspiration and of spiritual illumination, whose objective in each is to produce salvation. The illumination, which the Spirit imparts, differs mainly in degree from the inspiration given to the prophets and apostles. There is no new revelation (either in germ or norm) given, but only the assistance necessary to understand and apply that which has been revealed for salvation in this dispensation.

> We fully believe that God's mind was revealed to the writers of the Bible, so that the internal revelation might be handed down to us, but we further believe that God will so quicken our spiritual and mental powers by His blessed Holy Spirit that we will first appropriate the same, and then in turn, reproduce these ideas and transmit them to the minds of others. This may be termed either "direct illumination," or rather, "the revelation of God."
> ... while the Holy Ghost does neither substitute nor supercede [sic] Scripture by His direct illuminations, He does open the secrets of the same, apply the principles thereof, and inspire and authorize timely and personal applications of the same in living messages of faith. The Bible is not a casket in which the Spirit of revelation is buried; it is a jewel box from the gems of which the living Spirit of Light radiates.[484]

Just as inspiration, reserved alone for the prophets and apostles, brought them knowledge which neither genius nor progress in learning could attain, so illumination, falling upon that which has been revealed through uniquely inspired men, brings the Christian knowledge unattainable by the highest intellectual reach of unillumined minds. As it required "inspiration" for the prophets to receive and show these things to others, so it requires "illumination" for men to receive and understand these revealed truths today. "Both are divine. But they are not equal." Yet both are necessary, if God is to be known.[485] Since "the world by wisdom knew not God," that which brings the knowledge of God to man—namely, divine inspiration and illumination—correspondingly transcend human intelligence as the latter transcends animal instinct.[486]

Illumination and Interpretation

The Spirit's illumination of the human mind is requisite to grasping the Word of God. While Biblical scholarship brings to light interesting facts *about* the Scriptures, only by spiritual discernment, immediately given by the Holy Spirit, can men apprehend that "saving truth" as it is in Jesus which alone brings eternal life. Nor is this illumination securable to any but penitent souls who are seeking the light.[487]

> ... as Inspiration was needed to give us a correct and completed Revelation of God, so Illumination is necessary to give us a correct and complete understanding of the will and way of God and also of God Himself. And Jesus has come to give us such an understanding. In nature man was in darkness and in ignorance of God.... By Grace we are made capable of knowing God. And by the Spirit's Illumination "we behold as in a glass the glory of the Lord"...[488]

While following the Protestant principle in stressing individual study of the Scriptures, Smith warned against "private interpretations" which violated any plain teaching of the Bible or substituted one's own opinions or supposed "illuminations" for the best light of sanctified, scholarly study of the Bible.[489] Remembering that considerable of the Biblical message is presented in the form of sign and symbol, Smith cautioned against personal fancy, or hasty, superficial treatment governing the reader in his interpretation of the Scriptures. "The diligence of a student and the devotion of a worshipper are required to decipher God's sign language aright." [490]

For Smith one of the plainest and most valid of all rules of interpretation—of Scripture or any other book—was that literature should be "understood as bearing its plain and primary literal sense, unless a good reason can be given why it should be understood otherwise." [491] His "qualified literalism" displayed itself in his treatment of the Book of Revelation, "the most pictorial in the whole Bible."

> And as in other instances of Scriptural rhetoric—as the description of the holy city on the one hand, and the fiery torments of hell upon the other, we must penetrate into their higher and deeper significance than of anything merely material and physical, so must we pray for anointed eyes to see through the angel's "signs" for that which is infinitely more glorious or even more terrible that may be signified thereby.[492]

Believing that all the truths, principles, and laws underlying *all* Scripture are applicable to every day and age, Smith held that "the *application* of them under the differences of the Spirit's administration (see I Cor. 12:5) will vary ... with the differences in the days and the times." [493] For example, "the harlotry stigma of a women's shaven or shorn head in Paul's day" may pass away with the "change in society or in women" which causes it to mean less in this day.[494] Consequently Smith enjoined Bible students thus: "Study the customs of the times in the light of what is written and see what abiding principle is in the midst of that particular custom." [495]

He laid down five rules which he himself had followed in interpreting the English Bible: first, the right understanding and use of the English language; second, the rule of a holy purpose in studying the Scriptures; third, the right key to unlock its treasures, both in the Old and New

Testaments, which is Christ; fourth, the proper aim of finding out the things God has not revealed elsewhere; and fifth, the rule of dependence upon the Holy Spirit, who inspired the Word, to bring illumination to the reader's heart and mind.[496] Following those rules Smith found an inner unity of theme and harmony of objective and progression of movement within the Scriptures which led him to believe there were no contradictions within the Bible, but that if seeming contradictions appeared they existed in the Bible reader, due to lack of scholarly information or spiritual illumination, rather than in the Bible itself.

The Central Figure in Scripture. All revelation for Smith was Christo-centric and all illumination rested upon what had been revealed of Christ in the Scriptures. At no time, he affirmed, is the personal Christ lost sight of when believers are under the illumination of the Spirit.[497]

> Christ is the all absorbing doctrine of truth of the Scriptures. All other truths end in or emanate from Him. He is the Truth. And inspired writers are so imbued with this truth that they refer all preaching and prophesying found in the Bible to Christ.... So that the doctrine of not a part but of the whole Bible is the doctrine of Christ.[498]

But the Christo-centricity of Smith's theology was not without its inseparable anthropological reference. For it was not in Christ in creation, or in providence, or in incarnation, or in suffering, or in regal honor, or in judgment alone, but in *Christ indwelling His people* that Smith found His supreme glory manifested. "Christ in you, the hope of glory," whether in time or in eternity, was to him the crowning glory of the gospel.[499]

In thus understanding the Scriptures, Smith the Methodist was one with his older contemporary Baptist theologian, Augustus Hopkins Strong, who addressing theological students said: "... I believe that the doctrine of union with Christ is the central truth of all theology and of all religion." [500]

CHAPTER FIVE

The Gospel of Grace and Glory—*Cont.*

This chapter contains a treatment of the God of glory, the author of the gospel of grace and glory, in His nature, attributes and tri-personal being. It has set forth Smith's view on the glory of God as manifested in creation and providence, and as marred in the fall of angels and man from their first estate in holiness. The ruinous fall of man and its effects upon himself and the earth have received primary consideration in this section.

THE GOD OF GLORY

Without arguing the existence of God, Smith followed the scriptural approach of assuming God's existence and proceeded to set forth what he believed God had revealed concerning himself in the Scriptures, a portion of which was a reaffirmation of what He had already disclosed of himself in nature.

His Nature

To Smith the divine nature was that something behind God's attributes and activities, "investing them and determining their course," yet being distinct if not inseparable from them. God's "nature is changeless and exhaustless," too great to be self-contained. His is therefore an "outgoing and an outgiving nature," which overflows the bounds of His own selfhood.[501] He is "lovingly social; He talks." [502] The divine nature is intense, it burns with "meridian heat," it is vanquishing of all unlike itself, best expressing itself in fervent love of righteousness and burning hatred for iniquity.[503]

His Attributes

Smith did not think it profitable to study the divine attributes abstractly. He looked rather for them as they were manifested through the incarnate Christ and through concrete divine activities in nature, history and the church. Looking chiefly to Christ, Smith found there "God translated in human life" and the divine attributes integrally related to human life and destiny. Christ "came not only to tell us of God. He came, likewise, to show us God. 'He that hath seen me hath seen the Father also. I and the Father are one.'"[504]

Smith believed that God had revealed himself as the infinite, eternal, holy, personal Being whose perfect wisdom and self-sufficiency render Him equal to all He sovereignly wills or permits. The deepest fact and highest glory of the divine nature, expressed through His attributes, is that He is holy- (righteous) love. Four major features of that divine holiness are: (1) inflexible and invariable justice, equity and righteousness; (2) unfailing goodness in mercy, kindness, helpfulness, patience and forbearance; (3) spirituality, or existence apart from and superior to matter; and (4) infinite abhorrence of evil. It is the latter which constitutes the "wrath of God." The love of God includes all these phases of His holiness.[505] Smith would have agreed with his younger colleague in the Holiness Movement, H. Orton Wiley, who analyzed holy-love in God as the uniting in himself of self-affirmation and self-communication—holiness being the self-affirming aspect of the divine nature, and love the self-communicating aspect.[506]

His Tri-Personal Being

The existence of the Godhead in one nature but three persons was, for Smith, the most profound problem of theology. The doctrine of the Trinity, although a divine mystery and therefore not apprehensible by rational speculations, was experimentally knowable to the Christian through the baptism with the Holy Spirit. In expounding John 14–17, Smith found that "the Savior conjoins the highest spiritual experience with the highest illumination on the deepest problem of theology." The soul coming into union with God through the Son and the Spirit "may know the Trinity as no other soul can." For Smith, true theology in its deepest reaches is not known through books or formal instruction in the schools, but through the soul's reception of the Comforter, the Holy Spirit, who reveals God the Father and God the Son to the heart. According to John 14:16, 20, 23, the whole Trinity is promised to the Christian as a love revelation when the Christian enters fully into divine union. The soul thus baptized with the divine fulness comes to "a knowledge of a true theology."[507]

Smith's claim of an experimental grasp of the Trinity in unity and a unity in Trinity was scripturally grounded, but historically in keeping with the claims of some early Methodists whom Wesley had commended.[508] For him the modal view of the Trinity, not to mention Arianism or tritheism, did not answer the demands of Scripture or meet the test of experience. In Smith's thinking nothing short of an ontological Trinity, a tri-personal Being, satisfied the claims of revelation and of Christian testimony.

While each of the three persons in the Godhead majored in some aspect of the planning, providing and administering of creation redemption, the second person, the Son, is "the central magnet of the triune God." From Him all saving truth radiates and to Him all gravitates in the Spirit's administration of His kingdom's affairs here on earth.[509]

The Glory of God Manifested: Creation and Providence

In Heaven and Earth

Smith accepted the Genesis account of creation as necessary to and sufficient for a sound and stable faith. For him that excluded such theories as the eternity of the world, or an eternally creating deity, or theistic evolution, or an impersonal creative process. According to the New Testament commentary upon Genesis, chapter 1, God created by His Word—He spoke and it was done.

Were the creative days of Genesis twenty-four-hour periods or millennial eras? Smith's reply was that that question was doubtless beyond a satisfactory answer, either to himself or others. However, merely expressing his own *opinion, he* preferred to think that those days represented twenty-four-hour periods inasmuch as Paul drew an analogy between the creation of the world and the salvation of the soul.[510] Reasoning from his own and others' experiences of salvation—both in conversion and entire sanctification—he was inclined to hold to an instantaneity in creation. A further factor inclining Smith to hold to a suddenness rather than a gradualism in creation was the suddenness with which the second coming of Christ and the resurrection of the saints at His appearing will occur.[511]

He refused to speculate about the possible eras and orders of being antedating man's advent upon the earth. From the Genesis creation account he derived the destiny or purpose for which the heaven and earth were made: "Two things in this Creation are plain: Everything was made for man, and man was made for everything." [512] He continued to keep man at the apex of all creation even though believing that the earth was but a fraction of the created universe.

While God is transcendent to His creation, He is immanently present in it as sustainer, preserver and moral ruler. "He is not only life in Himself, but He is also the life of the world." [513] He is ever interested in the minutia of His works even to noting the falling sparrow and to numbering the hairs upon the heads of men.

> .... God alone controls and holds and moves.... But more silent is He in the universe than the heart within our bosom which by some hundreds of thousand strokes in a day sends life to our farthest extremity and our tiniest eyelash, as well as strength to our

strongest arm. Yet for the most of the time we are *unconscious* of its presence.[514]

Smith found mental and soul rest in confiding in the divine sufficiency which sustains all things and is equal to all exigencies arising in a universe containing other free wills. "His power is infinite and our security is in the fact that *His motive power is love.* This is as unchangeable as His might."[515]

Thus, Smith held that the divine motive in creation was not merely to exhibit sovereign wisdom and power, but rather to express the "divine love of the Father and the Son." While creation was a sovereign choice of God, He made place within that creation for other wills—angelic and human. God's will is absolute in the sense that He is conditioned by nothing outside His own volition, but not so absolute that He disregards wills that He has made.

> It has pleased him to sovereignly will certain habitations and bounds for angels, and for nations, and for each man. Within these bounds, His will may be fulfilled or frustrated by the creature. Yet his sovereignty appears again in that obedience is rewarded with an honored place and part in His own greater plans; and disobedience punished with a loss of liberty. Moreover, the fractions and defaults of such as have not fulfilled His will are overruled to the accomplishment of His own purposes in different ways; and this without credit to the account of His first chosen agent. Man has neither responsibility nor right outside the bounds of his own habitation; and usurpation of power beyond what Nature or Grace has allowed for us is punished as anarchy and rebellion.[516]

In Angels

Smith firmly believed in the existence of an angelic order of beings, especially created by God, free spirits in nature, superhuman in power and wisdom, proved by probationary tests, and now probably "fixed" in their eternal character and destiny. These spirit beings differ in rank and office, some known as angels, others as archangels, as cherubim and as seraphim. They move freely between the earthly and heavenly realms of existence and are in touch with laws which are as much higher than those man can operate as those physical laws man can control are "beyond the apprehension or application of the brute creation." [517]

Adjoining Deity in all phases of redemptive work, angels have filled a leading role in revelation, as instanced by the giving of the law to Moses, announcing the "miraculous conception" to the Virgin Mary, heralding the incarnation of the Son of God on the first Christmas, guarding Christ in His earthly life lest at any time He "bruise his foot against a stone," strengthening Christ in the wilderness of temptation and in the Garden of Gethsemane, declaring the resurrection of the Son of man on the first Easter morning, and, at the hour of His ascension into heaven, His coming again. They are now "loftily sounding His praises in the courts of glory," and shall return with Him in a flaming manifestation of divine glory.[518]

"Angels are ministering spirits sent forth to minister for them who shall be heirs of salvation." They are of service to Christians in all stages of their salvation—temporal and spiritual. Smith believed that they might "operate laws to avert accidents or death to the servants of the Lord before their time," and hold an intimacy of fellowship with the "blood-washed saints in heaven that we scarcely can dream of now." [519]

As part of the unfathomed creations of God, the angels who have remained holy add to the glory of the God of creation and redemption. They perfectly fulfill the divine will for them in character and service, serving both in heaven and on earth.[520]

In Man

The origin, nature and destiny of man, as given in Genesis, was to Smith authentic and inseparable from the central theme of redemption in the rest of the Scripture. By a special creative act God formed man's body out of the dust of the earth (which He had previously created) and into that body breathed the breath of life which made man a living soul in His own divine image.[521]

The image of God in man constituted him the crowning specimen of divine creativity. Not only a sentient and an intelligent being, man was also "a moral being, capable of being right or wrong, able to know good or evil, made in the image of God, but capacitated to acquire the likeness or nature of demons."[522] Created thus, man was given a large, yet limited, freedom which made him "the most active and responsible agent in selecting and shaping the course" of his own life.[523]

Created with a nature positively holy and with power to choose to remain that way, Adam was placed on probation within time (history) for a fixed state of character. By continued right choices Adam could have retained the holiness of nature with which he was created and have entered into a state of "inadmissable" holiness such as the angels in heaven now know.[524] By wrong choice, he could change himself into a corrupt and corrupting creature, unfit and unsafe as an inhabitant of God's moral universe.[525]

In his original holiness Adam knew God directly and had no need for the prophet or priest to mediate the knowledge of God to him. Undying in nature, Adam could have successfully passed his probation and entered his eternal state without tasting physical death.[526]

Believing that intense, infinite love moved God to create all, Smith held that God expressed His love in the twofold fact that man was made in the divine image and that everything was made *for* man. Man's likeness to God not only capacitated him to be a companion for Him, but also to receive the divine commission to serve as God's vicegerent over the earth. As an under-sovereign, man was to develop and have dominion over the empire of nature which was originally free from the decay and dissolution, the defeats and deaths, characterizing it today.[527]

Early catechized in the Westminster Catechism, Smith

had always believed that "man's chief end is to glorify God," but he did not stop there. He further held that "somehow, somewhere, the glory of God and the true glory of man converge into one—that they are some way identical." [528] Recognizing the seeming impossibility and incredibility of such a view, due to the metaphysical differences between divine infinitude and human finiteness, nevertheless the *original* ethical oneness of divine holiness and human nature (made in the divine image) convinced him that as God had shared everything else with man in creation, He would likewise share His glory too.

> But man—God's miniature counterpart—cannot glory but in righteousness, in holiness, in the Divine image, in the Divine environments; for God is man's element....
>
> And as man's glory is in God, so God's glory is in man. No other creature represents so much of His wisdom. None but human nature is capable of so much of himself.[529]

Destined to an ever-expanding knowledge of and participation in the everlastingly, inexhaustible nature of God, man was ever to ascend in God, yet never cease to be man. Sharing in the eternal felicities of the divine glory, as the bride shares in the glories of her husband, or the son in the honors of his father, so man was to enjoy the fulness of God forever.[530]

The Glory Marred: The Ruin of Man

According to His own divine estimate, God's created world, including both nature and man, was *good* as it came from His creative hand. Its goodness was soon marred through the manifestation of evil, first from without and then in and through man. Man's fall is inextricably tied up with an extra-human origin of evil.

Origin of Evil

Smith's doctrine of evil centered in an evil personality,

called in the Scriptures "that old serpent, which is the Devil and Satan," "the tempter," or "that wicked one."[531] Originally a holy being (perhaps an archangel), endowed with great beauty and wisdom and power, this spirit-creature sought to lift himself in pride above dependence upon the Creator and to assume prerogatives of Deity. His choice to rebel was final, irreversible, and therefore his "fall" was fatal.[532] Having corrupted his originally holy nature, he thereafter became the arch-deceiver, *the* liar and father of lies, whose avowed aim was the defeat of God and all His purposes in the world, especially His purposes in and through man.[533] Satan evidently was not alone in his rebellion since other "holy angels, while serving their probation, fell from their first estate," and became the demonic forces organized under Satan, bent on human injury and defeat.[534]

Original Sin

While man's fall was occasioned by the evil suggestion of the tempter, through the instrumentality of the serpent in Eden, it was by no means necessary or inevitable. Created with an inner positive holiness, Adam was capable of triumphing over the temptation to wrongdoing. As a finitely free agent, he deliberately chose contrary to the divinely set but beneficient bounds of the all-wise and all-good Creator. That rebellion merited punishment and brought the human family and its Edenic home under the curse of Almighty God.[535] The disobedience meant depravity and death within man's nature, and upon his earthly home a destructiveness which defeated the good ends of much that God had in mind for man when He made the world. Man's polluted nature involved him in "an affinity, a similarity and a relationship with satan" from which only God could deliver him.[536]

The fall of man was an unspeakable sorrow to God but not a surprise to Him. God foreknew, but did not foreordain, the apostasy of Adam, nor any disobedience since—

not even Judas's. Since God's foreknowledge is not causative, man stood condemned, fully responsible and accountable for his sin. As in the case of Pilate and the crucifixion of Christ, the Scriptures ever hold in balance the twofold truth of God's foreknowledge and man's accountability.[537]

Smith viewed the first man as having stood as the natural and respresentative or "federal" head of the race. His acts while deeply personal were also official. What he did not only affected himself but implicated his posterity. The first transgression severed the spiritual union between man and God, deeply marred the moral likeness to God, and so *deprived* man of his original holiness, that his nature was *depraved*—set in perversity against its Maker. Thereafter, all descendants of the first human pair were begotten in the image of a fallen humanity. This depravity, self-originated in Adam and Eve, was transmitted by hereditary processes to all their offspring so that in the latter it was "inherited" or "inbred." [538]

While Scripture showed unmistakably to Smith that "we are by nature very far gone from original righteousness and of ourselves inclined only to evil, and that continually," the universal experience of the race confirmed him in his belief.

> We presume that evidence so cumulative, so complete and so demonstrative, could not be adduced upon any other subject as that which history, experience and Scripture furnish in proof of the universality, totality and incorrigibility of human corruption.[539]

No one thing to Smith was greater proof that man had lost the divine image than universal selfishness. Since *God is love* in whose image man was made, and whose nature "pours itself out, all out, for others, and for all others," man's selfishness indisputably exposes humanity's depraved moral state.[540]

Some traces of the divine image in fallen man could be found, thought Smith, in "wifely devotion and maternal love" which speak of a nature "that lives and that is for others." Tribal instinct, patriotism and philanthropy are "hints at a nature greater than the individual." [541]

To Smith, therefore, total depravity did not mean that all souls born into the world are as corrupt from the hereditary evil passed on from Adam as they are capable of becoming. He rather taught that no person since Adam (except Christ) has escaped this iniquitous inheritance and that no part of any man's personality was without its corrupting taint. He held to an *extensive* rather than to an *intensive* total depravity.[542]

Although the Creator of moral agents who were capable of originating evil but not of eradicating it, God cannot be charged with evil or responsibility for it. Smith readily admitted that all the meaning of evil, or its extent in enduring consequences and penalties, could not be known in this life, "for here as elsewhere 'we know in part.'"[543] However, rather than furnishing men with a mere intellectual answer to the problem of evil, the Scriptures have given them a "correct knowledge of sin sufficient to move them to abhor it, deplore it, and to cry with all their heart... to find a Saviour from it."[544]

By the permission of evil—satanic and human—within divinely set limits, the sovereign supremacy of God in His world has not been destroyed. While never the author of evil, He *uses* it and that "without either compromise of righteousness and truth or conflict with man's free moral agency and responsibility." The natural afflictions of mankind in the world, while generally penal, through God's redemptive program may become disciplinary and be overruled to the Christian's eternal welfare, as well as his present good.[545]

Twofold Nature of Sin

Foundational in Smith's view was a necessary distinction between sin as an act and sin as a state or condition of the moral nature of the transgressor. While Adam was pure in nature when he first voluntarily transgressed and corrupted himself, his posterity began probation with a corrupted nature and were stimulated to acts of sin by an inherited corruption. Thus, sin has existed as a reigning force in the world, with all men (except Christ) having come under its power.[546]

Smith held that such scriptural terms or figures as "the sin," "the body of sin," "our old man," "this body of death," "flesh," "the body of sin and death," and "the carnal mind" designate the inherited sin. From the usage of these terms, Smith derived the view that inherited sin or depravity in a man is "unitary in nature," but manifold in its manifestations. "In the Epistle to the Galatians, nearly a score of the 'works' of the flesh are named, but the 'flesh' itself is mentioned in the singular number and stands for a unit (Gal. 5:19-21)."[547] Christ likewise mentioned thirteen "evil things" which come from within, out of *the heart* of man. "This is the single fountainhead of the many streams of wickedness which defile mankind."[548] While aggravated by the evil around them, "men's hearts are not defiled by this evil world, but this world is defiled by the output of men's evil hearts."[549] The "inbred sin," a universal and inevitable inheritance, has left the human family not only morally impure, but also impotent.[550]

The *acts* of sin—both Adam's and mankind's—incurred guilt and merited punishment in penalty. The *sinful* state of Adam and his posterity merited the condemnation of God. Whereas Adam was guilty for both his act and his state, his posterity in the beginning of their probation are guilty only for their acts of sin. The sinful state lying behind their acts only merits for them personal condemnation as they refuse the divine salvation which has been provided for its removal.[551]

While all since Adam have begun their probation with an *inherited* pollution or *depravity,* their acts of sinning have also brought upon them an acquired depravity for which they are personally responsible and feel condemned.[552]

THE GOSPEL OF GRACE AND GLORY   163

Penalty and Effects of Sin

Smith taught that sin is fatal from two sources: first as a penalty, and second as an effect or consequence in the race. The divine penalty pronounced upon sin was death—death spiritually, physically, and eternally. "Death is the consequence of the disease of sin. 'To be carnally minded is death.' That is, it will surely kill the soul." [553]

For Smith, death could never be interpreted to mean annihilation for man.[554] Rather it is a *separation* at every level at which it works. "Judicial" or spiritual death began the moment of Adam's sin and issued in the severing of the spiritual union existing between his spirit and his Maker. "Natural" or physical death issued in the separation of the body and spirit, a dissolution of the union of matter and spirit which made man *man*. "Everlasting" or "the second death" is the fixed and final separation of the spirit from God who is the source of all holiness and happiness.[555]

While the death penalty was stayed and its final execution postponed until the great judgment day, there were devastating effects upon the whole of the human family, four of which immediately appeared. First, man lost fellowship with and the true knowledge of God; second, he lost the moral likeness of God; third, he lost his place as under-sovereign over the created earth; and fourth, he lost bodily and blessed immortality.[556]

As those effects manifested themselves in man's personality, his understanding became darkened, his emotions and affections degraded, and his volitions degenerate.[557] His bodily appetites were distorted, his physical frame diseased, greatly depleted, at times deformed, and finally doomed to dissolution.[558] Man's fall was the "forfeiture of the glory of man's being." All of his existence became somewhat awry.

> ... man's industry is turned into labor, and woman's bliss of motherhood is trammeled with travail, as she goes into the jaws of death for every one that she would bring into life. Both toil and travail are the toll that

must be paid by every generation of the race on the transgressor's way to the tomb.[559]

The Extended Probation

While God would have been just in immediately executing the total penalty upon the first human pair, He lovingly chose to extend their probation and offer them redemption from their sin. Typifying the coming Redeemer, animals were slain in Eden to cover the shame and nakedness of the sinning forebearers of the race. With faith in the promised coming One, they could look forward to "redemption through His blood."[560]

It was evident to Smith that since the fall "God's government and dealings with mankind on earth must be as with a depraved and incorrigible carnality," as well as with the deceitful rivalry of Satan who ever seeks to divert man's worship to himself.[561]

Therefore, not only by a "kingdom" of spiritual evil under the strategy of Satan (a more-than-human wisdom and energy), but by his own depravity and its corresponding defeats in nature, man must face his probation on earth.

The Cursed Earth

As part of the judgment upon man, his earthly home was "cursed" and shared in the penalty upon man's sin. It was the *moral* evil to which man consented which brought him the *natural* evils with which he has struggled in himself and his world ever since. Error, disease, and death in his own person, along with earthquakes, destructive storms, pestilences, decay, barrenness, and the like in the earth have continued to plague man's pathway and dissipate his capacity for progress.[562] Whatever has brought suffering to the animal kingdom, an impoverishment to the plant kingdom, and destructiveness in the movements of natural forces, can be accounted for by the divine judgment upon an originally perfect and perfectly harmonized world.[563] "We ourselves are living in the debris of a primal and possible universe.... Not only man himself but man's abode on earth was ruined by the Fall." [564]

> Hence the underlying doctrine of the Bible is the doctrine of the *Fall of Man*. All that is said about creation is God's acquittal of any charge of having made the earth as we now find it, or having made man as he is, or having incorporated either death or disaster into the economy of His administration over the creatures He had made in holiness and planned to live forever with Himself in the government of the universe.[565]

When the sentence of death, which fell upon mankind, has worked itself out through the whole creation, the present "heaven and earth shall pass away" to give place to "a new heaven and a new earth wherein dwelleth righteousness." [566]

CHAPTER SIX

The Gospel of Grace and Glory—*Cont.*

In this chapter the manifestations of the Son and the Spirit for redemptive ends are set forth. The person and work of Christ, the Lord of glory, have been developed under the headings of the God-Man and the perfect mediator; the person and work of the Holy Spirit, the Spirit of grace and glory, have been studied in the light of His ministry to men in conviction, in illumination, in regeneration, in sanctification, in bearing witness, in guidance, in endowment with spiritual gifts, in unifying of believers, in intercession for and through believers, and in supplying grace to believers in every time of need.

THE GOD OF GRACE MANIFESTED: REDEMPTION FOR MAN

The Person and Work of Christ: The Lord of Glory

What theologians have called Christology, thought Smith, really unites in inseparable relation the fall and the restoration of man. He held that the *underlying* doctrine of the Bible is the doctrine of sin, and the *crowning* doctrine is the doctrine of salvation; they are the two hemispheres of truth which find their union in the central doctrine of the Bible, the Saviourhood of Christ.[567]

The Law of God. The Fall left mankind under a twofold darkness concerning God "which must be recognized by the seeker after spiritual light." In the first place, the natural heart of the whole race is carnal; that is, antagonistic to God and in that state cannot receive the spiritual knowledge of Him. Further, man is under the displeasure of God because of his personal sinning, and consequently is under a judicial darkness which conceals from the unaided human reason the knowledge of the glory of God.[568]

Into that *natural* and *judicial* darkness resting upon the race, God let shine the light of the law. While the light of nature was universally distributed, God chose to build a nation which would receive anew the true light of himself and be the bearer of that light to all nations.[569]

God, therefore, called (and overruled in its development) the nation Israel, through whose life and leaders He could give again to mankind the knowledge of himself. The law given to Moses for that purpose was twofold—ceremonial and moral. The ceremonial law was styled "the law of commandments contained in ordinances" (Eph. 2:15). It foreshadowed the atoning work of Christ, which He was to fulfill in himself *for* men—thereby releasing men from the yoke of the law.[570]

The moral law or decalogue was that law which "mankind has ever been under... and will be not only for all time but for eternity as well, since its obedience or transgressions now fixes his estate forever." [571] This law "Christ came not to destroy [nor annul or suspend] ... but to *fulfill*" *in men*.[572] It is as binding in the moral world forever as "the law of gravitation is binding in the natural world for time. It was not simply enacted because of man's fall, it is in the nature of things." [573]

The moral law in itself gave no hope or help to man under sin, but only disclosed sin as "a racial, universal, and perpetual fact," both in "its manifoldness, its unchangeableness, and its issue in doom and destruction and death." The only suggested escape from and cure for man's malady was in the ceremonial law, with its types and shadows, which pointed to Christ.[574]

While the darkness of man's natural condition was somewhat relieved by the giving of the law, it still left him in a "dispensational darkness," which meant that "the revelation of God's glory by the Law was partial, not intended to be permanent, on account of the more glorious revelation which was to supercede [sic] it." [575]

The Gospel of Grace. For Smith, it was the assured purpose of the gospel not only to reveal the glory of the Lord but to change men into the divine image.[576] The gospel made no change in God's moral law, but it did provide a way for men to keep it. While the law may have begotten in men's minds "the throbbings of holy purpose," the gospel brings to them the power to accomplish that desire for righteousness.[577] Three things are clearly taught in this gospel: (1) man needs a change; (2) by gospel grace and power he can be changed; and (3) this change is into His image.[578]

While all men need this change, grace comes to no one as an irresistible force. Each decides his place among the elect by meeting the foreordained conditions to become and remain Christian. Having voluntarily qualified for the elect, believers are divinely predestinated to a "state of salvation from all sin in this life, and from 'the wrath to come' in the next life. . . . God predestinates their relationship with himself and their eternal abode and inheritance." [579]

The Gracious Redeemer. Having interpreted *doctrinal* Christianity as issuing from and resolvable into the personality of Christ who said, "I am the way, the truth, and the life," Smith laid great stress upon the scriptural teaching concerning the *person* and *work* of Christ as the one and only redeemer from sin.[580]

With the Athanasian symbol, Smith virtually affirmed four distinguishable yet inseparable concepts in the *incarnation* of Christ: His absolute deity, His perfect humanity, the unity of His person, and the diversity of His two natures.[581] Smith regarded Christ as very God of very God inasmuch as the Holy Spirit who inspired the New Testament called Him "the Son of God." He believed Him to be very man of very man because Christ repeatedly called himself "the Son of man." Smith found no difficulty in accepting the miraculous conception and virgin birth of Christ through which deity and humanity were united in the one person, Jesus of Nazareth. By means of that supernatural birth Christ came into the world free from the moral taint inherited by all other descendants of the first Adam, and, therefore, entered upon His earthly existence as pure and perfect in His human nature as was unfallen Adam in Eden.[582]

Jesus' humanity veiled His deity as He "made himself of no reputation" and condescended to the form of a servant. The lowliness of His birth, of His home surroundings, of His early life, and of His irregular, itinerant ministry involved a humiliation unfathomable to men's reason.[583]

Lacking no truly human faculty or affection, emotion or appetite, the humanity of Jesus was continually manifested by His entrance into the "fellowships" of men. While He did not enter some human relationships, such as marriage and parentage, He ever exemplified a sociability, highly honored the marriage relation, and commended parental instinct and affection.[584]

Without effacing His humanity, the Godhead of Christ was likewise manifested to those who believed. He was "God translated in human life," and therefore, man's "primer" in the study of God's righteousness, mercy and spirituality.[585]

> *His Inflexible Righteousness.* As the man Jesus would suffer rather than sin; and as He would uphold the moral law till all be fulfilled;... He is revealing God's unchanging holiness....
>
> *His Unwearying Mercy.* Christ's compassion upon the poor, His pity for the leper, His sympathy for the blind, His succor for the widow in distress, His forgiveness of the penitent, and His patience and forbearance with His erring, blundering, forgetting disciples, these things do not only prove to us what a good man He was. They show us how God feels and acts toward men suffering and sorrowing upon earth....
>
> *His spirituality*... our Lord showed that all material things are transient, but that God is eternal.... He laid down His own natural body, and took up a spiritual body that would die no more. Thus while

Holiness is pure spirituality, it is nevertheless capable of incarnation and possible on earth.

Thus He came to show us God.... He announces that He will still declare the Father unto us.[586]

Smith refused to hold to a metaphysical impeccability in Christ and yet declined to speculate as to the consequences of a peccable Christ failing under temptation during an earthly probation. He preferred to believe that Jesus' temptations were *real* and that He *suffered* being tempted, thereby qualifying Him to enter sympathetically into the moral tests of all mortals on probation, but that He met His temptations "as a man" and overcame them by means of prayer and the Word of God, which are available to other men.[587]

Smith regarded the post-resurrection appearances and ministries of the Lord Jesus Christ as especially revelatory of the latter's full nature and mission. On the road to Emmaus, He disclosed himself as the *Christ* of prophecy and, therefore, the Messiah for the world; in Jerusalem, He manifested himself to the apostles on two different occasions, demonstrating His humanity to them as *Jesus* who had been crucified; and at the Sea of Tiberias, His *Lordship* (or deity) over His own people and servants here and now clearly appeared. Thus, Smith had set forth the redeemer as God and man, two natures united in one perfect personality forever.[588]

Smith interpreted Christ's messianic work under three different offices: prophet, priest, and king.[589] Extending from His baptism to the eve of His crucifixion, Christ's public prophetic ministry bore the following characteristics: (1) the keynote of repentance as sounded by John the Baptist; (2) the appeal to reason as well as faithful reproof and rebuke; (3) the stress upon individual choice and moral responsibility in accepting and acting upon His claims; (4) the emphasis upon the deadliness of sin, even in professing disciples; (5) the frequent presentation of a coming day of judgment; and (6) the universal appeal for sinners to find salvation in Him.[590]

During that prophetic period of His ministry, He was both a teacher and lesson. He was God as well as the teacher about God. He was God close enough for man "to see Him and handle Him."[591] "His incarnation was not an assumption for the time but an exhibition of the way God is, and the way God feels, and the way God will do for us for all time. 'He that hath seen me hath seen the Father.'"[592] He both declared and demonstrated God's nature before men.

As demonstrations of His deity to the faltering minds of men, Jesus wrought and cited His own "miracles as proofs" of His origin and mission in the world. "None but God only could show such mercy, grace and goodness as were exhibited in these works," claimed Smith.[593] By both His person and His words and works, Jesus as *prophet* was the mediator of truth concerning God, the revealer of the Father. He came to earth to bring God back to man.[594]

The priestly office of Christ was assumed at the close of His prophetic ministry as He submitted to the death of the cross. Smith took up the words of John the Baptist concerning Christ, "Behold, the Lamb of God, which taketh away the sin of the world," and read the whole New Testament in the light of Christ as both sacrifice and priest, as both the offering for man's sin and the voluntary offerer of himself as man's atoning lamb.[595]

Smith observed that Christ sought to keep a balance in man's thinking between His person and His mission. "It was the Lord's custom when any circumstances had brought His divine Sonship into notice to immediately counterbalance it by reference to His humanity and to His humility and His pending death."[596] Although having made "the great confession," not even Peter was ready to receive Christ's full word as to His mission in the world.

> It was thus before the cross...Peter...rejects the suffering and the shame—doubtless for himself as well as for his Lord. He is among the first to voice a protest against a "Sanguinary" religion. He would fain proclaim

the royal claims of Christ, but deny or conceal his humiliation.[597]

Christ's priestly work was twofold: His work on the cross outside old Jerusalem; and His work on His mediatorial throne in the heavenly Jerusalem—"the holiest of all," or the immediate presence of God. The former work was completed with His death and resurrection; the latter began at His ascension and will continue until He comes again.[598]

In the "cross work" of Christ, Smith centered his doctrine of the atonement. Thought he,

> The Blood, too, is a marvel and a mystery to us. Its divine merit and its cleansing efficiency are evidently meant to baffle the understanding of men and of angels. So that, no matter how much theologians may yet advance in reasoning about Atonement, the Atonement itself will ever be the ground of faith rather than grasp of reason.[599]

Beholding God as the moral lawgiver and ruler of the universe, and men as transgressors of the divine law under condemnation, Smith held to a fourfold necessity for the atoning death of Christ. In that death he saw (1) a *revelation* of the infinite love and righteousness of God, (2) a *propitiation* of the divine wrath against sin, (3) a *reconciliation* by substitution between God and men, and (4) a *redemption* of human nature through a release from its enemies and a renewal of divine righteousness within believing hearts.[600]

As a *revelation* the cross of Christ was "the sublimist [sic] exhibition of devotion in history," and became throughout time and eternity the "concluding and crowning credential of God's love for man."[601] While the incarnate Word, during His prophetic ministry, was a manifestation of "the glory as of the only begotten of the Father, full of grace and truth," He surpassed all previous expression of human sentiment, sympathy, and service by the supreme sacrifice of himself—"the climactic revelation of the glory of the Lord." He gave "his life a ranson for many."[602]

As the cross revealed the love of God, it also was "the exhibition of the glory of His righteousness" from both the divine and the human side.

> From its Divine side (for His death was voluntary in Him, though necessary for us) it glorifies God's righteousness in that it countenances no abrogation nor suspension of the righteous law nor any nullification of righteous penalty, but sustains and enforces righteous government by providing pardon only in the sacrifice of a substitute. Could sinful man have escaped without penitence, penalty or propitiation, then the power of God's righteousness would have been wrecked and the prospect of man's righteousness ruined.... But we, "being now justified by the blood of Christ," our honor of God's law is enhanced beyond measure, the enormity of our sins appears to us in deepest dye; so that, concomitant with our acceptance of the Lord our righteousness, we experience a most violent hatred of sin and a most intense love of holiness. Thus is the righteousness of the Lord glorified in our hearts, and crowned before the universe as well.... This is the glory of the Lord, that He can be "just and yet the justifier of the ungodly." [603]

The human side of the exhibition of the Lord's righteousness appeared when Christ "accepted aversion, abuse, assault and murder at men's hands, rather than to consent to evasion, compromise, surrender or sacrifice of righteousness." [604] Dying in the agonies of Calvary, Christ's glory shone in a "righteousness that would meekly die rather than live to condone sin." [605]

Smith's atonement doctrine savored somewhat of the patristic theories as developed by Irenaeus, Origen, and Augustine.[606] He held that one of the redemptive aspects of the atonement was its victory over the powers of evil. Thus viewed, Christ's death was the ransom price paid for the release of humanity from "the bandits" who had seized humanity—namely, Satan, carnality, and the world.

> We will look only at the three bandits as they appear at the crucifixion of Jesus: a) When Satan entered the heart of Judas; b) carnality enthroned in

Judaism with the malice of Scribes and Pharisees crying, "Crucify Him"; and c) the world's darkness and cowardice on moral issues as seen in Pilate. These... have bound humanity and have held us for a price. Nothing else but death would satisfy.[607]

Since Satan is bent on man's damnation to death, since "to be carnally minded is death," and since "the world is turning constantly to death," Christ's death was a sacrifice offered, a price paid, a satisfaction rendered, to the world, the flesh (carnality), and the devil to meet their demands of death for humanity. To conquer these three foes, Christ gave himself for us.[608] Standing in a representative or federal relation to the race, Christ the new and last Adam could meet "the bandits' demand" for all mankind. As the sin of Adam the first had brought all under the power of Satan, carnality, and the world, so the obedience of righteousness unto death of the new Adam could defeat death and cause all to be made alive.[609]

When asked *how* the blood of Jesus Christ cleanses human nature from sin, Smith replied that it was not by any "corporeal touch of literal blood," cleansing as by chemical action, or by "the life-flow of Jesus' blood" in believers, causing them to live as He lived; rather, thought Smith, the blood of Christ has a "meritorious efficacy" in securing for believers "those energetic and effective operations of the Holy Ghost whereby sin is destroyed and expelled from the soul." By trusting in the merit of that shed blood, the believer obtains both the forgiving act of the Father and the sanctifying act of the Spirit.[610]

Since "the life is in the blood" of humans, Smith believed God had shown that His highest estimate of all things earthly is placed upon *life* by the exalted esteem given to human blood.

> So exalted is God's esteem of human blood, that notwithstanding He designed and in the former dispensations He planned to portray in symbol and type the shedding of the blood of His Son, He never once allowed the use of human blood for this purpose. He stooped

rather to let the blood of bulls and calves, of goats... be employed for this sacred purpose rather than that the blood of a man should be spilled with His sanction.[611]

Smith found in Scripture an "infinite preciousness attached to the Blood of Calvary's Cross, because it was the blood of the incarnate Son of God." "Human flesh attained new and added value when it became the investment of God's own Son."[612] Since Smith held Christ as both sinless in nature and conduct, he could find "no accounting for the death of Jesus by anything whatever in Himself."

> He had power to exempt Himself from accidental death; He could have called for legions of angels to protect Him from tragic death. A governor could find nothing in Him worthy of death. "And in his mouth was no guile." "He had done nothing by reason of the righteous character of Him whose blood was shed." His blood is *intrinsically* precious, because it is the blood of the Son of God in vestment of human flesh; and it is the blood of a righteous man.[613]

Therefore, because of who and what He was in himself, *"His Blood alone has redeeming value."*[614] By His blood, He is a *covering* of men's sins "from the sight and wrath of God." By that blood, Christ is a *ransom* "from the bandits into whose hands men have fallen captive," and by that blood Christ *cleanses* away the vileness of human nature—that "corruption that is in the world through lust."[615]

Redemption by the blood of Christ was made the more central for Smith when He discovered that of the more than one hundred names to be found in Scripture for the Lord Jesus Christ, the one that is perpetuated in heaven and throughout eternity is *the Lamb*. "The Lamb that was slain and lives again."[616] The redeemed in heaven are those who have washed their robes and made them white "in the blood of the Lamb." "Surely," concluded Smith, "the most 'precious thing in the earth and Heaven is the Blood of Jesus Christ.'"[617]

The *extent* of the atoning work, Smith thought, was *universal* in merit, provision and invitation, but *conditional* in its appropriation and realization by morally responsible individuals.[618] Christ's death rendered all men salvable, but in itself saved no one unless the "unconditional salvation" of infants and other non-responsible humans be included in the "finished work." [619] Smith always presented the "double efficacy" of Christ's blood in effecting man's redemption. Christ gave himself a ransom for all men, but in a very special way He at the same time gave himself *for the church*, that He might sanctify and cleanse her.[620] Thus, the death of Christ, God's sacrificial lamb, was an atoning provision for the complete recovery of all men from sin inherent and actual, racial and personal.

The *mediatorial* work of Christ at the Father's right hand engaged much of the thought and ministry of Smith. Beginning with His ascension, Christ entered His high priestly office and ever since has carried on a ceaseless ministry of intercession in "the holiest of all," in behalf of both His own disciples and the world of trangressors.[621]

For Smith, the Christian could find his highest joy in remembering not only what Christ had done *for him on the Cross*, but *what He is now doing* for the believer at the Father's right hand. He held that all "the office work of the Holy Spirit as Comforter, that the whole of the Spirit's operations and administrations in this dispensation, issue from the intercession of the high priesthood of Jesus Christ." [622] "We are truly as dependent upon the priesthood of Christ as we were upon the sacrificial office of Christ, and upon the prophetic ministry of Christ, and as we will be upon the royal kingly appearance of Christ." [623]

Having given himself unto death on the cross for the justification of sinners and the entire sanctification of believers, Christ now gives His risen life as the great high priest in intercession for their preservation in grace unto eternal life.[624] Finally, at the last judgment, the priestly mediation of Christ will entitle believers to a place at His side at "the marriage supper of the Lamb."[625]

As prophet, Christ was the mediator of revelation; as priest, He has become the mediator of righteousness; and as king, He is and shall be the mediator of redemption in both its retributive and rewarding aspects. The kingly office work of Christ, thought Smith, should be viewed thus:

> Now, there is a threefold aspect of the kingdom of God. There is the kingdom of God to be manifested at the appearing of the Lord Jesus Christ; and there is the kingdom of God to be extended by the Holy Spirit, through the ministrations of the Church throughout the world; and there is the kingdom of God within you, that "cometh not with observation."[626]

At the ascension of Christ, He entered upon a "mediatorial reign"; and from the heavenly throne at His Father's right hand, He is *administering* the affairs of His kingdom on earth" by the personal Holy Spirit. But His present kingdom is altogether a "kingdom of redemption" to save men from sin itself rather than from the mere consequences of sin. Smith asserted that

> All the physical, material and social blessings of Christianity in the life that now is—and they are many—are but *earnests* and can never be final *fulfilments* of the inheritance that is incorruptible and undefiled and that fadeth not away.... These blessings of Christianity are no more truly the Kingdom itself than the best of physical health is the same as a resurrected body. No, the Kingdom is supremely a subject of hope—and that hope not some world product of the progress of a (so-called) Christian civilization, but rather the revealed hope of the Gospel which ever centers in the coming of our Lord Jesus Christ.[627]

Until the ultimate phase of the kingdom appears, at the bringing in of a "new heaven and earth wherein dwelleth righteousness," Smith did not offer more than an individual realization of the kingdom of God through the personal indwelling presence of the Holy Spirit, with its resultant beneficient influences upon all social institutions and relationships.[628] Until the last day, urged Smith, "We are to look for the Kingdom of God . . . in our own heart rather than in the nations of the world, or in our own land, or in the federation of churches, or in our own church, or in our own home. The Kingdom of God is within you." [629]

At the appearing of Christ and His eternal kingdom,[630] He shall *reward* those who have exhibited *from within* both the holiness and happiness of the kingdom of God here, and shall visit *retribution* upon those who have resisted the call to enter the kingdom of righteousness, peace and joy in the Holy Spirit.[631]

The Person and Work of the Holy Spirit:
The Spirit of Grace and Glory

Co-equal with the Father and the Son in wisdom and power, in holiness and love, in grace and glory, the Holy Spirit is the vicegerent of Christ the Son here on earth as He heralds and administers the salvation of Christ to the souls of men. His supreme work in this dispensation, thought Smith, was doubtless disclosed in the New Testament's repeated use of the adjective "holy" in the name *Holy* Spirit (Ghost). Since in the holy trinity the Spirit is co-equal with the Father and the Son in holiness, the former's distinctive mission is evidently to make men holy. Just as the Spirit is the "source of inspiration and fountain of revealed truth to the church," so *"the Spirit is the source and fountain of holiness"* in believers.[632]

Nothing is known of the Spirit's ministry to the angelic order but much has been revealed concerning His relation to men. Although active in creation and in providence, and "the chief in Inspiration and Revelation," the Holy Spirit's greatest, most glorious work is that of transforming fallen men into the image of God—of making saints out of sinners.[633] He is the Spirit *of grace* and *of glory* which He imparts to men.[634]

Mankind has been living under the dispensation of the Holy Spirit, which is called in Scripture "the day of salvation," ever since its inauguration on the day of Pentecost (following Christ's ascension). But just as the Spirit's "day" or dispensation has had a definite dawning, so also it will have an end, or nightfall. "This dispensation of the Holy Spirit will end 'when that great and notable day of the Lord shall come.'" But until then, the gospel promise is that "whosoever shall call upon the name of the Lord shall be saved." [635] In this dispensation, the Spirit is to be recognized as the supreme authority over all aspects of the church, as well as the abiding comforter and guide in the hearts of individual Christians.[636]

In fulfilling His office, the Holy Spirit's chief instrument in administering saving truth and grace to men is the Word of Scripture. When subservient to His operation in and among men, other human and natural agencies may also be channels for His workings. Smith thought there were some *direct* shinings and strivings of the Spirit upon the hearts of men, beyond the medium of the Word.[637]

The Spirit has been given to bring man back to the true glory of his being. Since there are degrees in the recovery of that lost glory, consequently the Spirit's work is different at those various levels. Recognized by Jesus, the apostles, and many Christians of all ages, the basic difference in the Spirit's ministry lies between that directed toward the world of unregenerate men and that in behalf of the regenerate believer in Christ.[638]

The Strivings of the Spirit. The Spirit's first administrative work in recovering lost men is that of *arresting* and *awakening* them to their hopeless condition outside of divine grace. It is more than convincing the mind of a few religious principles and evoking human resolutions to do better. It is a reproving of the conscience, a "stinging of the heart with a sense of guilt," a calling for immediate attention to moral responsibility and to the eternal consequences of moral carelessness.[639]

Smith designated this phase of the Spirit's work as "strivings" inasmuch as the Spirit encounters the human will and seeks to bring it to right decision and action. Since the human will is "held by passion, by prejudice, by habit, by association, and by that strange fascination of sin which none can describe but all have felt," the Spirit strives to awaken and alert the soul until that soul willingly surrenders to the divine will for his life. This operation of the Spirit is often called *conviction*, and is "the greatest mercy that can come to an unconverted man." [640]

The Spirit's convicting ministry is world-wide and from generation to generation. While universal in extent, the intensity of it is not uniform inasmuch as conditions are not uniformly conducive to the Spirit's work of striving with men. God's people, individually and collectively, are to cooperate with the Spirit through prayer, preaching, and persuasive witnessing and living to furnish Him with channels for an effective convicting ministry upon all men. [641]

His strivings with the individual and the race are not uniform throughout life. There are times and seasons of special conviction which when repeatedly resisted ends probation, and the Spirit gives men, individually and collectively, over to themselves. "His Spirit shall not always strive with man." [642]

The Illumination of the Spirit. When the Spirit's strivings have won a yielding response in the human soul, the Spirit then reveals the "wretchedness and helplessness of man to himself," and causes him to cry out for mercy, confessing his sins. Following this disclosure of the self, Christ is then "revealed as the propitiation for his sin as the present Saviour of his soul." [643]

Without this illuminating ministry of the Spirit, man's soul is deceived by self, sin, and Satan, and is unaware of its real state and standing before God. This natural ignorance cannot be removed by human culture or volitions; it is a spiritual defect which only the Spirit of God can correct. The pre-Christian ignorance and conversion of Saul of Tarsus has demonstrated this truth. [644]

Having fulfilled the Pauline Scripture, "For God, who

commandeth the light to shine out of darkness, hath shined in our hearts, to give the light of the knowledge of the glory of God in the face of Jesus Christ," the Spirit abides with the surrendered soul as "the Spirit of light," leading him on to the fuller knowledge of God "whereby His fulness is entered and His perfect love enjoyed." As "the Spirit of wisdom and revelation," He ever guides the believer into all truth essential to the saving of his soul. Smith thought that without the Spirit's illumination both of the Word and the believer's heart the spiritual truths of the Bible are out of reach.[645]

The Birth of the Spirit. The necessity of the new birth is twofold: it rests in "the spiritual nature of Christ's kingdom on the one hand and the fleshly or carnal nature of the human heart on the other."[646] Christ's kingdom which He brought to men, when He came preaching, is not of this world. It is a kingdom of the spirit into which can enter only that which is spiritual, that born from above. Man's inner nature is biased self-ward, sin-ward, and world-ward. It must be changed, as Christ insisted with Nicodemus, if it is to *see* and to enter His kingdom. Nicodemus, one of the finest products of "orthodox" religious education and ethical culture in his day, was under necessity of experiencing a rebirth if he were to become eligible for the heavenly kingdom Christ was bringing to men. "The natural man must be made a spiritual man."[647]

For Smith the new birth was *a radical alteration* of the moral nature of man by which the whole trend of life was changed. It is a "stupendous" miracle by which the moral nature of man is transmuted.

Man has no more power to change his own nature than he has to change the nature of dogs or horses which he might educate to a high degree in the art of imitation; they are dogs and horses still in nature. Likewise man may educate himself so as to modify and mould his conduct; nevertheless his inner nature remains fallen and fierce in possibilities for evil.[648]

> Nothing in the nature of the individual, and nothing in the nature of the aggregation of individuals, nor of any force that man possesses or controls in Nature can work that change whereby he may reach his chief end and glorify God and enjoy Him forever. His every effort in this direction will vanish in the echo: "Can the Ethiopian change his skin or the leopard his spots?" [649]

For Smith the new birth was a mystery, a moral miracle—psychologically unanalyzable, and philosophically undefinable. It was a movement of the divine Spirit by which man became a partaker of the divine nature and a citizen of the kingdom of God. Although not irrational or antirational in nature, the change was supra-rational and made knowable to man only by the Spirit.

> As some things of even our being and life are only known by consciousness, so the things of the Spirit are known by *experience* . . . inwrought by the Spirit Himself in divine revelation, accepted and appropriated by a "faith that laughs at impossibilities and cries, 'It shall be done.' " [650]

This "first thing" of the Spirit's transforming work, designated as the new birth, is also called a "translation from darkness to light and from the kingdom of satan to that of God's dear Son"; it is a passing from spiritual death unto spiritual life, a being quickened from death in trespasses and sin unto life in Christ; it is being "born of God," and becoming "a new creature" in Christ with old things passing away and all things becoming new.[651]

Smith set forth three fundamental scriptural tests of this new life in Christ in any individual experience: First, the test of love. "The love of God, the love of the brethren, and the love of all men's souls inheres in the life which is from above." Second, the test of truth. The new life in Christ "has a perception of truth, an affection for truth, and adjustment to truth, and it steadily seeks an advance of and aggression in truth." Third, the test of heavenly mindedness. This is expressed in "an aversion for the carnal, a subordination of the physical and temporal, an aspiration for the heavenly, and especially by a longing next for 'the more abundant life.' " [652]

The Witness of the Spirit. Smith taught that it was *possible* for Christians in this life to know with certitude spiritual truth, spiritual relationships and spiritual blessings.[653] To him three things had produced great ignorance in the modern church concerning the Spirit's office work of witnesssing: first, the substitution of psychological explanations for the Spirit's workings, amounting to a denial of His person and mission; second, the location of the Spirit's witness in the emotions, feeling, or sensations; and third, the church's excessive stress upon objective Christianity—upon service and the world-wide needs of men—with a subsequent neglect of subjective Christianity or "the spiritual life in the inner man." [654]

The crowning prophecy concerning Christians is this: the Spirit's dispensation, thought Smith, was the promise that "they shall be all taught of God." [655] The Scriptures hold out for them the promise of "the full assurance of faith," of "the full assurance of hope," and of "the full assurance of understanding" during their earthly pilgrimage.[656]

Believing that no one had ever been able either to define or describe adequately the Spirit's witnessing voice, Smith nevertheless attempted to set forth some phases of the *nature* of the witness which the divine Spirit bears *with* (not *to*) the believer's spirit. Since the Spirit himself and the human spirit enter the one into the other, it was not easy for him to distinguish between the two. Even though the two are not identical, "they are so collateral and conjunctive and complemental" as to leave it hard for the common mind to tell where one begins and the other ends.[657]

From Galatians 4:6, Smith deduced the conclusion that "the Holy Spirit enters into our affections and somehow we have the assurance that we are not only new creatures, but sons of God, and we rest our hearts in Him as Father." [658] From I John 5:20, Smith discovered that "Christ is come and has given us superunderstanding—has illuminated our understanding and given us something bordering on inspiration." [659] When given this understanding by the Spirit, the believer knows God in Christ in such a way as to be beyond dispute or debate.

> Now then, in a degree Jesus predicted this knowledge, knowledge of adoption, with regard to the disciples when He was on earth (John 3:11) ... you and I with illuminated understanding and the Spirit's witnessing with our spirit, may be held in a place where we are as sure of God as we are of our own lives and, through positive knowledge, intuitive knowledge, we know the Spirit witnessing to our understanding. Somehow while it is past understanding, it does not ignore the understanding nor despise the understanding, and we do not have to guess, nor fear, nor hope, but we *know* ... God is our Saviour and Father, and Friend.[660]

Besides bearing witness to the believer's affections and understanding, the Spirit also witnesses "with the conscience," confirming and attesting it that it is right in its relationship to God and to others—"right as to honesty, right as to chastity, right as to purity, right as to loyalty." [661] If these things are wrong in the believer's life, the Spirit's witness is withheld.

But underneath and beyond the Spirit's witness to the affections, the understanding and the conscience, there is His witness *with* the faith of the believer's spirit. Not until the individual exercises faith for forgiveness or for cleansing does the Spirit witness with his spirit of the divine work which faith brings. Thus, the order or steps in experience are these: first, faith in the divine promise to accomplish the change now; second, the Spirit's work in the believer, in response to his faith; and third, the Spirit's witness to the work which He has just accomplished. Faith brings that inner "whisper" that the work is done. That whisper is the Holy Spirit's witnesssing voice to believers.[662]

Since only God can know both His own mind and the

depths of each human heart, only He can bear witness *with* man's spirit as to how the divine-human relation stands. Since forgiveness and cleansing are divine acts, only God has the *right* to say that one is born of God or filled with His Spirit. Smith held that the "unconsciousness of sin is not proof of the absence of sin; but the Spirit answers to the blood and tells me I am born of God." [663] Therefore, of necessity, a greater than human knowledge must be communicated to the believer if he is to know God's mind. The Spirit does that work.[664]

The range of the witnessing work of the Spirit extends over all stages of Christian experience "co-extensive with the benefits of the atonement." [665] Taking the things of Christ, the Spirit shows them unto the disciples and reproduces them in believers, attesting the results as genuine. He certifies spiritual truth and blessing; He assures both of adoption and divine union; He witnesses to "individuals and sometimes to Churches, concerning the call of men to preach and to special work"; He witnesses to the acceptability of the believer's life and service unto God, to the believer's sanctification (as clearly and distinctly as to his justification); and He witnesses concerning pending events and persecutions, instanced by Paul's experience enroute to Jerusalem.[666]

As a result of the Spirit's witness believers can live confidently that *sin has gone,* that the fruit of the Spirit is present, and in a "sweet assurance that it is all right" between them and God. However, believers are to train themselves not to rely only upon the direct witness of the Spirit since it is "diversified under different conditions and in different natures." [667] While not always *conscious* of the Spirit's immediate witness, the believer can always be *confident* of his relation to God.[668]

Since the privilege of the Spirit's witness is not for a special class or privileged few, Smith thought no believer ought to rest satisfied without the "direct assurance of the voice Divine" on matters of salvation and service.[669]

The Sanctification of the Spirit. Holding that "too many minimize the Spirit and his work," Smith further believed that even when honored in a general way the Spirit's specific office work as sanctifier is too frequently disregarded. Both Paul and Peter treated the sanctification of the Spirit as the work of the Spirit within believers subsequent to the new birth but prerequisite to eternal salvation.[670]

The Spirit's sanctification of those who are born of the Spirit is integral to the epochal change called in Scripture "the baptism with the Holy Ghost," "crucified with Christ," "filled with the Spirit," "sealed with the Spirit," "the earnest of our inheritance," "the fulness of Christ," and "perfection."[671]

The Spirit's sanctification differs from any "relative sanctifications" of inanimate objects such as altars, temples, *et cetera*, from "official sanctifications" of prophets, priests, and other ministers to sacred offices, from any relative sanctification of infant children of a Christian home, and from the primary or initial sanctification of believers at the time of their conversion. The sanctification of the Spirit is that *entire* sanctification for which Paul prayed in I Thessalonians 5:23, or a being sanctified *wholly*—"that is, 'through and through.' "[672]

There are four principal operations of the Spirit in the entire sanctification of Christians. *Illumination* concerning entire sanctification is His first operation. "No sooner has the Spirit ushered the soul into newness of life [the new birth] than He begins to incite it to something beyond.... The young convert then begins to yearn and to pray ... to 'have nothing in the heart displeasing to Jesus.' "[673] The Spirit illuminates the soul through various means, such as the Scriptures, the preached Word, and the testimonies of other believers; and sometimes "shines directly ... upon the heart itself and convicts *deeply of inbred sin.*"[674]

> But he reserves his brightest light to cast it upon the face of Jesus, that we may see Him, the true standard of Holiness, and upon his precious Blood,

that we may see it has power to cleanse from all sin.[675]

The Spirit then separates the yielding soul from all but Christ. While consecration or the yielding of all is the human approach to entire sanctification, it cannot be fully accomplished without the Spirit's assistance. The soul goes through a process, climaxing in a crisis, which is analogous to Christ's death by crucifixion.

> As Christ through the eternal Spirit offered up himself, so the soul by the Spirit's guidance and help now offers itself up a sacrifice unto God. The laceration of affection, the thorn-pricking of desires, the crushing of ambitions, the forsaking of friends, etc., that is involved is deeply painful, and it is this that makes it analagous [sic] to crucifixion... having simply gained our consent for the separation, He himself supplies us strength to go through with it.... It is not a lifelong separating. It is a present, perfect separation for life. He lets us know when we have come to the *last* tie. He bears witness when the great *transaction is done*. He seals with a betrothal signet. And we now know we are wholly and truly given to Christ.[676]

The objective in the separating work of the Spirit is to bring the believer to the place of faith for the purification of his heart from inbred sin. It is not merely dedication to the Lord's service; it is seeking deliverance from all that hinders perfect devotion to *the Lord himself*.[677]

Having *illuminated* and *separated* the soul from all its inward and outward earthly attachments, the Spirit then brings the soul to "faith ground" in response to which Christ baptizes with the Holy Spirit, *purifying* the heart from its inherited sin.[678] Into the heart made "white and pure and holy within," the Spirit enters to *"inhabit the Soul* he has thus made once more fit for the dwelling place of God." This *inhabitation* by the Spirit is the realization of Christ's promise of the abiding Comforter. It is identical with being filled with the Spirit as found in the Acts of the Apostles and in Ephesians 5:18. With Christ thus indwelling the believer through the Spirit, the believer has found Christian perfection, and his personality, along with others thus conditioned, is the true temple of God in this dispensation.[679]

> And this is what is meant by Perfection: A *perfect separation* from one's self and presentation to Christ. A *perfect purification* of the heart from the blight and being of indwelling sin. A *perfect union* with God through the inhabitation of the Holy Spirit.[680]

Having received by faith the instantaneous cleansing from inherent sin, the soul is conditioned to pursue that "holiness without which no man shall see the Lord." This entire sanctification brings the soul to a holiness "alike in heaven and on earth, and alike in God and in ourselves," save that it is still derived and dependent—whereas God's holiness is absolute; it is still admissible, subject to the contingencies of probation—whereas angelic holiness is inadmissible; and it is a restored holiness, "momentarily supplied by the Holy Spirit from the heart of God and the stream of Calvary's cleansing fountain"—and not innate like Adam's created holiness in Eden.[681] The Spirit then leads the soul forward in the ever-expanding growth of its being and in the ever-extending environment of enlarged opportunities and service for God, revealing *"endless measures of pure love"* to be increasingly appropriated by faith.[682]

Since this is the sanctification of the Spirit, Smith taught that neither time, nor age, nor learning, nor sufferings, nor sorrows, nor service, nor effort, nor death, nor purgatory, are "either efficient or essential to bring us into the grace of sanctification."[683] With the love of the Father as the originating cause, with Christ's shed blood as the procuring (meritorious) cause, with the Spirit as the efficient (effecting) cause, with the Word of truth as the instrumental cause, and the believer's faith as the conditional cause, the grace of entire sanctification may become an immediate experimental fact in the hearts of all who will meet the conditions.[684]

The Guidance of the Spirit. For Smith the doctrine of divine guidance was "one of the most important, the most interesting, and the most intricate in the whole realm of Spiritual Learning."[685] Having personally claimed faith for divine guidance for his life so as always to be in the right place at the right time, he insisted that "no one could fulfil God's pleasure or his own mission on earth without habitual Divine guidance."[686] To further stress its importance, he wrote:

> We are travellers upon an unknown sea. Chart and compass and log book will not suffice. We need a pilot. We are to make the journey but once, a mishap would be final; to come to a wrong destination would be disastrous. We have but limited time to make the trip and reach the landing; if morning and noon are past in meandering, night will overtake us and leave us lost amidst the breakers.[687]

Since "subjective Christianity" had waned in Smith's day, he was convinced that Christians needed anew to "recognize and respect the divine Person of the Holy Ghost above all His ways, and words and works" as the real agent in guiding their lives.[688] Even though the scriptural promises of God's guidance are almost as numerous as the assurances of His care for His own; nevertheless, Smith felt *"few men's lives are guided by God."*[689]

The guidance ministry of the Spirit has been promised only to a certain class and upon certain conditions. The primal requirement, Smith taught, is the "childhood relationship to God. 'As many as are led by the Spirit of God, they are the sons of God.'" None can claim divine guidance who have not repented of sin or are in a rebellious attitude toward the divine will. Secondly, the child of God must earnestly and dependently pray for guidance. Thirdly, the praying one must trust or have faith for the guidance sought. "Commit thy way unto the Lord; trust also in him; and he shall bring it to pass."[690] Pride, prejudices, conceit or self-sufficiency disqualify the soul for divine leadings.[691]

The divine plan or method in guidance is such as to develop the personality of the ones guided. At no time, Smith affirmed, is God's guidance absolute control through the abrogation of the human will. He does not despise the mental and moral faculties in those He has created, and therefore supplements rather than supplants, transcends rather than transgresses, them.[692]

The Holy Spirit's leadings are not confined to any one *channel* of operation. He adapts His guidance to the temperaments and capacities, the moods and individualities, of those whom He guides so that it is out of the reach of none who will seek it.[693] Aiming at guiding the believer, the Spirit teaches (1) by the Scriptures, or (2) by His people, or (3) by His providences, or (4) by the faculties of the mind which He has created.[694]

The Spirit's *modes* may vary between guidance (1) by prevention and restraint, (2) by instruction, (3) by illumination, (4) in judgment (reasoning), and (5) with His eye. Hierarchially arranged, the first mode is the lowest, while the last named is the highest.[695]

Because of limitations of understanding and for the development of a man's character, the Spirit may guide by withdrawing His approving presence or by restraining the human spirit from moving or choosing in certain directions. The Spirit's most preferred mode, thought Smith, is guidance by instruction. This may come through the Scriptures, life experiences, or the counsel of wise and discerning teachers.[696]

An *illumination,* like a flash of light, may be the Spirit's way of settling a problem in a minute. Occasionally "an unmistakable impression" with almost a voice-like reality may settle a matter in a Christian's mind. A dream or a vision, as promised in Acts, chapter two, may be given if "self's desires and affection be nailed to the cross; if one's pride and self-will and eagerness for the spectacular or phenomenal be all subdued." [697]

Basing his belief upon such scriptural promises as "the

meek will he guide in judgment," Smith held that the Spirit may guide in the process of reasoning, enabling a believer to reach a conclusion which would fulfill the divine will for that individual's life. "All our mind therefore, intuitive, reflective and deliberative, is to be employed and enhanced by the Holy Spirit, rather than set aside always by Him in mere mandate in a sort of imperious guidance." [698]

> This then is not suspension of our own faculties to make way for God to substitute His omniscience for our intelligence. No. This is rather promise of light, facts, evidence, advice, suggestion and enablement in the processes of our judgment to bring us to right and proper conclusions. [699]

"Guidance by God's eye" is for those who live in the "realms of purest love and in the atmosphere of simplest faith." This level is reached when all life's interests have been committed to Him and with "utter and absolute confidence both in His skill and in His will," the Christian rests or runs in the way of the divine commandments, knowing that that which is most dear in life is safely and surely devoted to His purposes for his life. This kind of guidance brings the Christian to "the climax of comfort, of rest and of confidence." [700]

In seeking guidance, Smith warned believers against the serious pitfalls into which they might stumble. Christ, Paul, Peter, and John had warned of "false teachers" and their influence upon the minds of disciples. But the believer must also "try the spirits" as to their source and character.

> And first it is necessary for us to recognize that we have three spirits to deal with: There is the Spirit of God which is holy and infallible. There is our own spirit which (after sanctification) is holy but still fallible, and there is the spirit of Satan which is unholy and erratic. [701]

With Satan, the arch-deceiver, often posing as "an angel of light," he seeks to suggest or solicit the believer to take liberties, to demand rights, or to follow personal interests which violate the spirit if not the letter of the plainly written Word. With the human spiritual subject to its own impulses, imaginations, thoughts, and feelings which may be pure but may be neither "preferable, practicable, nor possible," the believer must guard lest he mistake his own affections or desires or judgments for the impressions of God's Spirit.[702] "While there are no mistakes in Divine Guidance, there are mistakes in our interpretation of Divine Guidance."[703]

Smith submitted three major tests with which to detect Satan's seductions and to discriminate between the human impressions and the divine leadings: First, the Spirit's leadings always harmonize with the written Word, maintaining the soul's loyalty to Christ; second, His guidance harmonizes with providence; and third, His guidance is in the direction of holiness and love—He never leads to selfishness or sensuality. "Thus, by his love, by his Providence and by his Scriptures we may know the Holy Spirit of Christ within ourselves."[704]

The province or range within which to expect divine guidance, Smith taught, extends over the whole of life. Nothing too minor or too major, too secular or too sacred, is beyond the scope of the leadings of the Spirit—"for all things secular are made spiritual and sacred by entire devotement to God." "So that matters of business, of marriage, of location of a home, of education and all things else which concern us are proper subjects to submit to the Holy Spirit for guidance."[705] But the more marked and manifest guidance is to be expected in "the direct work of saving souls and building up Christ's kingdom." Since, according to Smith, neither health, prosperity, knowledge, social or climatic conditions are an end in themselves to the Christian, he may seek guidance in those realms so as to augment his spiritual development and effective service.[706]

The Gifts of the Spirit. With the ascension of Christ and the descent of the Holy Spirit, inaugurating the church age or dispensation of the Holy Spirit, spiritual gifts were distributed among the members of the church. In Smith's thought, the Scriptures made a clear distinction between the Holy Spirit as the dispensational gift of the Father and Son to the believer and the Spirit's distribution of spiritual *gifts* to the believers. The former was given to effect salvation from inbred sin and to perfect love within the believer's heart. The latter was to equip for successful Christian service.[707]

Three things, in Smith's thought, were of utmost importance in understanding the Spirit's gifts. First, they are necessary for the successful "advancement of Christ's kingdom on earth." Since His kingdom is one of "righteousness, peace and joy in the Holy Ghost," and since "no man can call Jesus Lord *but by the Holy Ghost,*" it requires the supernatural gifts of the Spirit to properly enforce upon men's minds "the lordship, personality, and the kingly claims of Jesus Christ."[708] "Their end is objective rather than subjective, public rather than personal."[709]

Second, "the Spirit's gifts in themselves do not indicate nor assure spiritual or moral character in their subjects." In the Old Testament Samson and Balaam illustrate this fact, while in the New, Paul affirmed that men might possess the highest gifts and be without that divine love which is the essence of Christianity.[710] "No one of the Spirit's gifts is the Spirit's witness. No one of them is necessary to prove any state of grace."[711]

Third, *"there are different and distinct grades of the Spirit's gifts."* Some gifts served as "signs for unbelievers," while others served to produce the "highest graces" in believers. In the Corinthian and Ephesian epistles, in Smith's view, two grades were set forth. The first grade, listed by themselves in Ephesians, chapter 4, were bestowed for the *"perfecting of the saints . . . for the edifying of the body of Christ."* These gifts—of apostle, prophet, evangelist, and pastor and teacher—are to be earnestly sought, since they are the "best" gifts.[712]

Smith found "carnal Christians" apt to place the lesser gifts of the Spirit above the Spirit himself and the graces

He deigns to bring men in the sanctifying baptism. To him "no enduements nor gifts nor services of the believer can equal or substitute holiness in his own heart."[713]

Frequently among those stressing the gifts of the Spirit, Smith found "healing" and "tongues" unscripturally taught. In the matter of healing, Paul, who possessed the "gift of healing," did not have power for its universal exercise, not even always upon himself. Paul's own physical affliction "seemed to withstand even his own best prayers," God having promised him grace to endure successfully what He did not take away.[714] Paul also stressed the superiority of prophesying over tongues in the church when he said he would rather speak "five words that can be understood to profit than ten thousand words in an unknown tongue."[715] Smith disclaimed any relation between the Holiness Movement as he represented it and the modern Tongues Movement with its earliest emphasis upon "speaking with tongues" as evidence of the baptism with the Holy Spirit. At this point Smith viewed their doctrine and practice as "neither Scriptural, Sensible, nor Spiritual."[716]

The two gifts of the Spirit, which Smith emphasized as of greatest value in promoting the gospel enterprise in the world, are the gifts of prophecy and of discerning of spirits. The former is the telling forth of the gospel, while the latter enables the believer to "discern the signs of the times," and the deceptions and counterfeits preying upon the Christian church.[717]

Predicted by Joel and cited again by Peter, the gift of prophecy for "handmaidens as well as servants, daughters as well as sons, is shown as pre-eminent and as perpetual as an evangelistic factor throughout the gospel age."[718] The gift involves first a *"superior illumination"* on the deep things of God and, secondly, an "unctious utterance" of these things to the edification and comfort of those who will hear and heed.[719]

The Unity of the Spirit. Smith called the unity of the Spirit a "miracle of grace," when he recalled the diversities within which unity was to be achieved. From the Scriptures Smith concluded that Jesus spoke of a "unity of *all ages,* and of *all races,* and of *all types,* and *temperaments,* and *trainings* of true believers." [720] Basing much of his teaching at this point upon Christ's prayer in the fourth Gospel, chapter 17, Smith held that Christian unity rests upon union with the divine—analogically, experientially, and organically. In the first place, Jesus had likened the unity of believers both between themselves and between him and the Father, to that "supernatural, mystical, incomprehensible" unity of the Trinity. Second, Jesus had said, "I in them and thou in me, that they may be made perfect in one." Paul experienced and witnessed to this when he said, "For me to live is Christ," and "Christ liveth in me." Third, Jesus anticipated the whole church through the centuries when He prayed, "Not these alone; but them also which shall believe on me—that they all may be one" [721]

From Jesus' teaching Smith deduced four things essential to the unity of the Spirit:

>(1) Christianity's lawful due to the world is *Salvation.*
>(2) The world's salvation is contingent upon true Christian unity.
>(3) Christian Unity is only possible as a result of Divine union in the believing soul.
>(4) Divine union results from the answers to the Savior's prayer and sacrifice of Himself that the Father would *sanctify them* through the truth.[722]

Distinguishing between sectarianism (a child of carnality) and denominationalism (sometimes a child of providence), he recognized the havoc wrought by the former and the benefits contributed by the latter. Sectarianism, leading to competition and contention, he deplored. But he likewise was not optimistic about the federations and amalgamations, which silenced sectarianism "at a sacrifice of principle for policy under a flag of truce." [723]

While acknowledging many commendable facts and features of possibility in church mergers, Smith nevertheless urged that denominational amalgamations are not to be confounded or identified with Christian unity. In his thought

> "The unity of the Spirit" allows for much diversity, not of "gifts" only, but of "administrations" and "operations" (See I Cor. 12:4, 5, 6). Real spiritual unity may co-exist with much variety in different and distinctive church societies, even as the pure and perfect love of the Spirit may, and does, obtain in different individuals of any and all of these societies.[724]

Denominations, he thought, were children of the Spirit's providences to meet the "localities, languages, governmental restrictions, ancestral heritages, etc.," incident to the worldwide propagation of Christianity. "As there were twelve tribes, but *one Israel,* so the body has various members, but one life within it all; and different 'branches' of the church may all yet be as of *one Vine.*" [725]

However, under the present economy, Smith believed some divisions are inevitable. With compromise on vital Biblical truths and testimonies, the catering to the non-revivalistic drift of thought and method, the condoning of worldly policies within the church, he believed that loyalty to Christ and obedience to the Holy Spirit would precipitate separations within some branches of the organized church, just as divisions developed under the preaching of the apostles as recorded in the book of Acts.[726]

According to Smith, the cure of sectarianism and the checking of excessive denominationalism was to be found in the mighty baptism with the Holy Spirit upon all believers in any one church and in all the denominations. "Let pentecost come to any church and factions will die out. The world's evangelization, the church's true orthodoxy, the church's true unity, all are assured by the pentecostal baptism and the coming of the Comforter." [727]

With evangelism pitched to the key of both conversion for the sinner and the baptism wtih the Holy Spirit for all believers, the decimated ranks of Christendom can be closed and the church can gird on her strength for a successful world-wide evangelism. Smith repeatedly urged,

> Interdenominational evangelism is the need of the hour. Neither no-churchism, all-one churchism, community churchism, no detached and independent tabernaclism can solve the problems of a nation-wide revival.... And no denomination need merge its identity, nor default upon its own providential trust in order to maintain, not an undenominational, but an interdenominational unity.[728]

But the unity of the Spirit does not necessitate *uniformity* in several matters, including the time, place, or order of Christian service. Liberty as to the day of worship; the mode, number, and necessity of the sacraments; and certain doctrinal emphases (as in Calvinism and Arminianism) are still compatible with unity in the Holy Spirit. Diversity of cultural views on matters not absolutely essential to salvation may be held by those united in heart through saving faith.[729]

The unity of the Spirit is not achieved without human cooperation under the domination of the Spirit's graces. The Pauline injunction to endeavor to keep the unity of the Spirit in the bonds of peace, requires at least three passive virtues: "These are lowliness, meekness, and longsuffering. None of these encompass power to do any big things, but they make for patience with readiness to put up with many little things which may be done unto us."[730] By these unity in the Spirit can be a reality.

The Intercession of the Spirit. Smith was convinced that the greatest power God has released for man in this world is neither the power of the human mind nor physical force but the *"power of prayer."*[731] Since prayer is *"a universal instinct and institution,"* Christianity did not initiate it, but rather directs it.[732]

Under the Spirit's dispensation, Christians are made both the temple of the Holy Spirit and priests unto God. Having become the dwelling place of the Spirit, Christians are not only "the habitation of His person," but "the holy place of His intercession."[733]

> As Christ is representing the affairs of men in heaven, so the Spirit is in the holy temple of our hearts representing the affairs of God on earth. And we are the vehicles and agencies of his prayers. The Holy Ghost prays through us.[734]

However, the Spirit's intercessions are always in cooperation with the intercessory praying of the believer. The latter needs this divine factor in his prayer life for at least four reasons: First, without it, he is ignorant of the will of God on many matters; second, his spiritual inertia and indolence are best overcome by the Spirit's help; third, without the Spirit's help he cannot overcome Satan's resistance to his approach to God; and fourth, prayer tends to be self-bounded without the Holy Spirit's world-embracing love possessing the Christian.[735]

In fulfilling his priestly function in intercessory prayer the Christian experientially enters "an acquaintance and kinship with the intercession of Christ at the right hand of the Father in heaven."[736] That fellowship in intercession enables the believer to become a participant with Christ in effecting the work of salvation.

In Romans 8:27, Paul informed his readers of an experience in prayer which would transcend their human ability to express or understand it.

> This is the crowning "thing of the Spirit" when by utter abandonment to Him in the attitude of prayer, in response to our faith, the Spirit will make intercession through us, beyond not only our own power of expression, but beyond also our own perception of what we ask.[737]

Since Jesus' supreme objective in redemption was not to get souls *to heaven* but rather *to get them to God,* that objective can be largely realized in this life by the Spirit's ministry in the realm of intercession *in* and *with* and *through* the believer.[738] For the Spirit can give the believer "direct access to God Himself" as an immediate result of the mediation of Christ. Therefore, in the Spirit's dispensation, the Christian is given *"a place and privilege in prayer beyond any that even God's people had ever enjoyed before."* [739] "And by the daily and hourly intercession of the Holy Ghost our circumstances are all efficiently related to God's great, sovereign plan for ourselves and for the universe."[740]

The Grieving of the Spirit. Following New Testament terminology, Smith warned against "quenching," "grieving," "resisting," "lying to," or "blaspheming" the Holy Spirit.[741] He found "two great lies in circulation concerning the possible sinning of Christians," both of which relate to the doctrine of the Spirit.

> The first is that such sinning is inevitable so long as we are in the body, and does not affect the Christian's *standing* with God....
>
> The other great lie with which the devil has dismayed and depressed many sensitive souls is *that they are guilty of having committed the sin against the Holy Ghost, for which there is no forgiveness neither here nor hereafter.*[742]

While any and all sinning, according to Smith, is really against the Holy Spirit, yet there are degrees of sinning against Him, until wilfulness becomes apostasy, as in the case of Judas.[743]

Recognizing the possibility but denying the necessity of Christians grieving the Spirit through sins of commission and quenching Him through sins of omission, he maintained "ample provision is made to keep the Christian from sinning at all." [744] However, when the Christian through weakness and unwatchfulness, as in the case of Peter, falls into sin, by meeting afresh the conditions of repentance and faith, he can be forgiven and restored to his rightful relation with the Spirit.[745]

The Scriptures warn Christians not to "grieve the Holy Spirit of God whereby we are sealed unto the day of redemption." That "sealing" Smith held to be one and the same with the sanctifying baptism with the Spirit which purifies the nature and stamps the image of Christ upon it. To guard against offending the Spirit, breaking the seal, and destroying the likeness to Jesus, the Christian must allow nothing in his soul contrary to the pure love of Christ.[746]

If all sin is really against the Holy Spirit and since sin tends to deceive, "it is best and wise to be very vigilant against *habits* of 'grieving' or 'quenching,' as the distance may not be great between backsliding [as instanced by Peter] and *apostasy* [as instanced by Judas]." [747] However, of the many hundreds of distressed souls who contacted Smith concerning the possibility of their having committed the unpardonable or apostate's sin, the sin unto death, only two he believed had really committed it.[748]

The Supply of the Spirit. For Smith the baptism with the Holy Spirit was "the crowning benefit of Christ's Redemption" from sin, and the Comforter's abiding presence in the believer's heart was "at once both the source of holiness" in his life, and the surety of his hope at Christ's second coming.[749]

Christ had promised "another Comforter" to abide with His disciples forever. Since He had been the "other," what Christ did for the disciples the Spirit would continue to do for them. The latters' fellowship with Jesus had led "to His solving their perplexities, sharing their burdens, allaying their fears, and assuring their hopes." [750] To those who receive and retain the fulness of the Spirit, thought Smith, the Spirit comes to abide in constant readiness for their relief "against the sorrows, and sufferings and struggles of life in this world of conflict." [751]

Smith chose the scriptural expression of "the supply of the Spirit" to cover "those multiplied *measures* of light and love and power which special occasions of opportunity and obligation may call for." [752]

Turning to the book of Acts, Smith found there what the supply of the Spirit meant both to individuals and the collective body of the Church. While the early Christians, including Paul, were *"born* of the Spirit and *baptized* with the Spirit and *endowed* by the Spirit," yet they were continually realizing their need of *"the supply of the Spirit* to meet the exigencies of each passing hour." [753] Accurately speaking, there is one baptism with the Spirit, but many subsequent refreshings, quickenings, anointings, and enduements by the Spirit for life's service.[754]

It was at this point that Smith disclaimed that either he or other Christians could rely only upon blessed experiences and certain states of grace. Rather, he insisted upon momentary dependence upon "the personal Holy Spirit Himself to supply the readiness, the aptitude, the wisdom, and the words" with which to meet each succeeding test or trust. This supply of the Spirit, claimed Smith, is "the very love and life of Jesus Christ coursing through one to make him fit for whatever may come or go." [755]

In the case of Stephen, the first Christian martyr, a man already full of the Holy Spirit, Smith found that the added supply of the Spirit meant for him (1) *adaptation* to new conditions; (2) *power* in advanced service; (3) *illumination* upon Scripture; (4) comforting *vision;* (5) dauntless *courage;* (6) *placid expression* of countenance; and (7) *Christ-like prayer* for his murderers.[756]

For the "collective body of believers and leaders, at a most strategic juncture in the advancing history of the church," the supply of the Spirit meant great boldness and power, unusual sacrifices and great grace with which to face successfully "their greater opposition, their enlarged opportunity, and their added obligations" and be prepared for even greater, more aggressive exploits for Christ.[757]

For Smith the supply of the Spirit today meant the immediate administration of any and all spiritual blessings and assistance required by individuals and the church to meet victoriously the material, physical, social, intellectual, moral and spiritual demands of a Christ-centered, Spirit-led, church-reviving, soul-winning, world-evangelizing Christianity.[758]

CHAPTER SEVEN

The Gospel of Grace and Glory—*Cont.*

The grace of God realized in the recovery of man individually and collectively, and his full restoration to the glory originally planned for him by the God of glory are the phases of Smith's thought treated in this chapter. The stages of man's recovery from sin have been shown to be justification, sanctification and glorification. As soon as a man is justified he becomes a member of Christ's body, called the church, which is a fact of history, founded upon Christ in fellowship with believers, formed with manifold features, functioning as a living organism with a view of furthering its faith among men. Confronted by various foes and often failing itself in its visible form individually and corporately, the church invisible has been promised a triumphant future.

The future of the church involves the restored glory of man when God's glory is manifested anew through Christ's personal return to earth to be glorified in His saints, to judge the ungodly, and to make manifest His own glorious kingdom of righteousness which shall know no end.

The Grace of God Realized: The Recovery of Man

The gospel of grace and glory manifest *in* and *through* redeemed lives was for Smith "the most wonderful of all truth," "the most stupendous of all problems," and "the most glorious of all results." While creation and providence declare much of God's glory, the redemption of men is "His unspeakable glory." [759]

Grace for Individuals

As stated earlier, Smith found the gist of the whole gospel story, about which the "Blessed Book was written," in two great doctrinal hemispheres which were bound into one sphere by a third doctrine.[760] The "Fall of Man" was to him "the underlying and outstanding fact of human history, the fundamental doctrine of the Bible; and the controlling fact of both God's policy or dealings with man in Providence and occasions of God's communication with man in Revelation."[761] But the "Recovery of Man" is the crowning doctrine of the Bible, thought Smith.

> What one of the hemispheres of the earth is to the other, what day is to night, so is the Book of Revelation to the Book of Genesis. The Holy City is Redemption's counterpart to the blighted and blasted garden. To the sentence, "Dust thou art and unto dust shalt thou return," comes the answer, "The leaves of the trees were for the healing of the nations, and there shall be no more curse." These two—Man's Fall and Man's Recovery are the Alpha and Omega of Doctrine.[762]

With these two doctrines bound together by a third, the doctrine of Christ, the Scriptures indicate that but for the fall of man the revelation of Christ would have been unnecessary and that the recovery of man would have been impossible without His revelation.[763]

Smith found that the threefold aspect of man's fall was more than met by the threefold aspect of salvation through Christ. For him the doctrine of the fall meant: first, the *universality* of the fall and its entailing effects upon the race; secondly, the *twofoldness* of the fall—bringing man "under God's condemnation without ability to regain His favor" and marring or shattering in man the original divine image, that likeness to God in righteousness and true holiness; and thirdly, the *eternal consequences* of sin, begun in time and enduring for the impenitent to all eternity.[764]

The doctrine of man's restoration involved three major steps: first, *justification* through Jesus' blood by which fallen man recovers his lost place and favor with God ("the only possible stepping stone to further grace and future glory");[765] second, *entire sanctification* by the Holy Spirit, recovering fallen man's lost likeness to God in righteousness and true holiness (the qualifying fitness for "man's final glorification");[766] and third, *glorification* by resurrection and restoration, which recovers redeemed man from all the consequences of sin—"both his own and the sins of the fallen race"—giving him for his eternal home a resurrected body and a "new heaven and a new earth wherein dwelleth righteousness." [767]

As the fall of man, from the rebellion in Eden to the eternal punishment on the other side of the last judgment, has been working itself out by degrees, so the recovery of man, from the beginning of the Spirit's strivings with the souls of sinful men to the eternal kingdom on the other side of the final judgment, has been by degrees. Within the redemptive scheme, with its crises and processes, the three major crises in their successive order are: justification, sanctification, and glorification. While the approach to these crises is usually gradual, the entrance *upon* each state (beyond each crisis) is instantaneous, and the progress *within* each state is indefinite in degree. The progress is from faith to faith, from grace to grace, and from glory to glory.[768]

The individual and individualizing factor in Christianity was repeatedly stressed by Smith. The gospel was to be taken to every creature; everyone shall stand at the judgment seat of Christ and give an account of himself to God. No matter how many are justified, sanctified or resurrected at a time, thought Smith, it is with each one as an individual work.[769]

Thus, his understanding of the gospel led him to hold that "everything in the gospel, everywhere and all the time tends to *the man*. Not to the solidarity of humanity, but to each and every one of us. The incalculable and incomparable worth of *one soul* is ever before the mind of Jesus." [770]

The divine "callings" of the gospel which are successively sounded out to individual men, Smith affirmed, are five in number. The first call is to all unsaved men; it is the call to repentance. The second call is to all Christians; it is the call to holiness. The third call extended in this life is likewise to all Christians; it is the call to serve or minister ("all are called to the ministry"). The fourth call comes after death to all humans; it is a call to judgment, to give an accounting of one's stewardship. The fifth call (which only true believers will hear) is to "inherit the kingdom prepared from the foundation of the world." [771]

The call to repentance may be turned down; the call to holiness may be despised; the call to the ministry may be neglected; and the call to inherit the kingdom will never be heard unless the first three calls are heeded. But the call to accounting for one's stewardship cannot be evaded; it is irresistible. The first three and the last of these calls are determined by each individual's choice, but *all must respond* to the call to judgment or accounting. Smith saw one of these calls imperative (to holiness), one as possible (to minister), one as probable (to inherit the kingdom), and two of them as universal (to repentance and to judgment). "Many are called, but few are chosen." [772]

Justification. The necessity of the grace of justification in Smith's thought grew out of the fact that man is a sinner, standing under the wrath or righteous condemnation of God and without power in himself to regain favor with Him. As a sinner, man is condemned to die eternally for his sin, having forfeited his right to live in God's moral universe. Smith viewed justification by faith as "the base" of all human hopes of the hereafter and the ground of all human possibilities of grace here and now.[773]

The *nature* of "justification unto life" is found in its forgiveness or pardon of sins, in its "removal of the sentence of death," in its turning away of the divine wrath, and "the renewal to the soul that trusts in Jesus of the right to live." Having been pardoned, the liberated soul is now protected "against further trouble from the law on account of those his past offenses." It entitles him, too, to the "privileges and powers of citizenship" in the kingdom of God.[774] This reinstatement in divine favor is so perfect that the once guilty souls are now given *a standing* before the divine tribunal as though they had never sinned, and henceforth treated as godly or righteous.[775]

Smith did not feel that he or his colleagues in the Holiness Movement had made too much of sanctification, but he did wonder if they had made too little of justification. Of justification he wrote,

> It is the birthday of our life. It is the foundation of God's temple within us. It is the daybreak of heaven to our souls. It is our credential to glory. Without it, we are debarred from the gift of the Holy Spirit and the fulness of God's love in our hearts.[776]

He held that justification or forgiveness of sins was the greatest provision with which God ever blessed sinners. He saw it related to the soul's eternal life as the day of one's birth is related to his earthly life. It met man's basic need for a readjustment to and a right relation with the moral government of God.

The *ground* for the divine act of the justification of sinners is God's love and the blood of Christ. Since "God's justice could not revoke his sentences, nor suspend his law, nor overlook our offenses, his love provided a way of escape." [777] That way of escape was the atoning death of Christ which, "being infinite in merit, and being suffered for us, has furnished a full expiation of our guilt, and the appeasement of the righteous demands of the Lord." [778]

The *effects* immediately derived from justification are: (1) absolution of sin's guilt; (2) reconciliation and peace with God; (3) access into the grace of entire sanctification; and (4) hope of eternal life, being delivered from the wrath to come through Christ.[779]

The *conditions* which men must meet in order to be justified are these: a turning from and a turning to—from self to the Lord. The former, Smith called repentance, the latter faith, and the whole process when completed *conversion*.[780]

The negative step of *turning from self*, in Smith's thought, "embraces a repudiation of sin as the practice of life, a rejection of worldly wisdom as the standard of light, and a renunciation of the law as the hope of salvation."[781] Since self is prone to cleave to sin, to look to reason and to trust works of righteousness for its salvation, in turning from self, the soul finds that "Christ condemns sin, puts a premium on simplicity, and fulfills the law."[782] That self from which man must turn may be reprobate, refined, or even religious; nevertheless, as in the case of Paul, it must turn resolutely and absolutely from all forms of sin, inwardly and outwardly, crude or highly polished, if it is "to come into the light of the knowledge of the glory of God."[783]

Within the Scriptures Smith found "three chief studies of the nature of Repentance." Jesus' portrayal of a penitent in the parable of the prodigal son, John the Baptist's definition of repentance in his response to the inquirers who came to him, and King David's example of penitence, gave him his Biblical basis for holding to a threefoldness in all cases of true repentance: (1) It is a recognition of God's moral government, and of a day of judgment. (2) It is acknowledgement of guiltiness and helplessness, with a plea for mercy. (3) It is a solemn vow to renounce all sin, and to follow Christ as the Lord of one's life.[784] Without such repentance, with its deep sorrow and contrition over sin and its turning in abhorrence from sin, there is no other way for man to rise to faith in Christ as Saviour.

Smith held that "godly sorrow which worketh repentance unto salvation" was both a grace from God and an act by man. Basing his view in part upon II Timothy, chapter 2, he believed that repentance first "must be inwrought by the Holy Spirit" if men are to pass the levels of mere sentiment and remorse and find that repentance which is not to be repented of, mentioned by Paul in II Corinthians, chapter 7. [785]

The positive step of *turning to the Lord*, according to Smith, involved: a turning to the Lord's people; to the Lord's Word of truth; to the Lord's Spirit as teacher, helper, and guide in the way of light; "to the Cross of the Lord—as the propitiation for guilt and the fountain for cleansing"; and to the Lord himself—as "the worthy object of our confidence, the sufficient Source of our salvation, the lawful Sovereign of our wills." [786] For Smith, the turning was not complete until the soul had reached an entire consecration of all to Christ. For those in the justified state but not fully sanctified the turning was not as yet complete.

This whole process he called *faith*, although the crisis aspect in entering the justified state was very marked in Smith's thought. For him, saving faith was "a turning to the Lord" which was more than human "avidity" for things new or strange or preposterous. It was more than a human "credence for one another's word in matters of business and earthly interest." Rather, it was a faith, grounded on the divine promises and holding Christ as its chief object, which was as "adapted to revelations as sight is to light, or intellect is to reason." [787]

The love of God manifested toward sinful man as revealed in the gospel was so transcendant to man's powers of reason, thought Smith, that it could only be revealed to faith.[788] But for him that was integral to man's glory.

> For the most glorious of all man's faculties, powers and possibilities is his capability of believing. It is here he becomes almost Divine, "for all things are possible to him that believeth." Man's shame has all come through unbelief, and likewise all his sorrow, and all man's honor and his joy come through faith. In the natural state faith is dethroned, reason perverted and sense exalted, but under grace faith sways the sceptre of being, reason is prince over a realm rightfully his own, and holds sense as his servant.[789]

According to Smith, man's volitions alone cannot exercise

saving faith for any degree of salvation. He held to a synergism in which the human agency is active, but which is complemented by "a generation of the Holy Spirit conditioned upon a yielded will on our part and an assent to the truth of God as it is in Jesus Christ.[790] Possessing both active and passive factors, faith contained for Smith four aspects: it was an assent to, and an acceptance, appropriation, and application of the truth of salvation as it is in Jesus Christ.[791]

Smith further made clear that faith itself does not have "merit" although it does have "quality." Men are not saved because of faith, nor by faith itself, nor without it. But rather faith is that medium through which God transmits His saving grace to the believing soul; it is the receiver of the power of God unto salvation.[792]

The *concomitants* of "justification unto life" by faith in Jesus Christ, according to Smith, are regeneration, adoption, and assurance. Regeneration, although logically subsequent to the divine act of justification, occurs simultaneously in experience in the lives of those "truly converted." While justification is God's act for men, regeneration is His act within them.

> And all truly converted persons realize that when by justifying grace they are accorded *a standing* with God as though they had never sinned, they also at the same time received a state of heart which gave them both disposition and power to avoid all forms of actual sinning—no matter what the temptation may be.[793]

Regeneration, in Smith's doctrine, was one and the same with the new birth, offered by Christ to Nicodemus and enjoyed by the disciples during Christ's earthly ministry. Its inner nature was set forth for him in John 1:12, 13, where he discovered it to be "a positive generation of the life of God in the soul of him that believes on Jesus."[794] This "injection of a holy principle of life" into the believer is a reviving within the soul of its capacity, capability, and craving for the divine nature. Regeneration adds a new life to the believer's human nature but it does not destroy "the seed of sin" that was there from birth.[795]

Having been a *"partaker of the very nature of Satan,"* man becomes through the regenerating act of God a partaker of the divine nature. In this degree of salvation he is well on the way to the recovery and restoration of the divine image within him and is conditioned to partake increasingly of the fulness of God through time and eternity. However, it is when the soul has "put off the old man" in the experience of entire sanctification that he is "filled and flooded with the divine nature." [796]

Since Smith believed that regeneration brought man "into the glory of life, even a life Divine in righteousness and in love," which motivates and empowers the soul to live righteously, it is not surprising to find him making much of the difference between imputed and imparted righteousness.[797]

Basing some of his expositions at this point upon Romans, chapter 3, he held that the merits of Christ's atoning death were imputed to a believer for a propitiation or covering of his past sins; whereas, "the law of the Spirit of life in Christ Jesus" is imparted to believers, making it possible now "that the righteousness of the law might be fulfilled in us, who walk not after the flesh, but after the spirit." [798] Christ fulfilled the law of ordinances *for* men which is imputed to them, but He fulfills the moral law of righteousness *in* them that believe by imparting to them a new nature and "the Spirit of life" which becomes manifest in holiness of character and righteousness of conduct.[799] By the act of imputation God gives the penitent believer a new *standing* before His law, but His act of impartation gives man a new *state* of character or nature. "Both are provided for in the blood of Christ and must ever be held in inseparable union. The forfeit of the one is the forfeit of the other." [800] Both were necessary to cover man's full need. While imputation is logically prior to impartation, giving man a new judicial standing within

God's government, nevertheless God never imputes without imparting righteousness which gives man a new ethical or moral state and power with which to fulfill the law's demand of love.[801]

Having lost the "natural right" to sonship in the fall, mankind forfeited the son-Father relation with God and consequently was disinherited by God. Only as men are redeemed and become the children of God by faith in Jesus Christ, as stated in Galatians 3:26 and Ephesians 1:5–7, can the Father-son relation be re-established and man become again an heir of God and of eternal life.[802]

When God forgives the penitent believer, He accepts him "in the beloved" (Christ) and at the same moment *adopts* him back into His family, reinstating him to all the rights and privileges of a son. The blessing of adoption, concomitant with justification and regeneration, is not a "creative" but a redemptive relation, predestinated for those "in Christ." It is the induction of believers "into holy relations with the people of God and with God himself." [803]

As the natural sonship of Adam was forfeitable in Eden, so the redemptive sonship of believers by adoption while on probation is forfeitable.

> The very same gracious work that is styled the Birth of the Spirit, is also termed "Adoption," and is referred to as having the name written in heaven, and in the "Book of Life." Among the admonitions given us by Christ is that ... danger of having our names blotted out of the Book of Life.[804]

Smith declared that in the realm of grace *"no one need be in uncertainty as to his standing or as to his state,"* inasmuch as the witness of the Spirit is integral to the epoch called conversion.[805]

While the divine Spirit alone can witness *with* the believer's spirit as to the latter's *standing* before God, it is the believer's spirit that is made especially conscious of a new *state* or nature within itself.[806]

While the two were distinguishable in his thinking,

Smith could not separate between the divine witness and the witness of the human spirit. His analysis, however, led him to hold to a *direct* assurance, almost a voice to the inner or hidden self, but originating outside the self, bearing witness as to the self's inner state and heavenly standing.[808]

The human witness he believed had both a negative and a positive aspect. Negatively, the consciousness of sins being "washed away" is real; and positively, there is the awareness of the fruit of the Spirit—"love, joy, peace, longsuffering gentleness, goodness, faith, meekness, temperance"—in the heart and manifest in the life. The witness of faith is a second factor in the positive aspects of the human witness. When one believes the written record which God has given of His Son, then a witness of faith rises within the believer's soul which has an evidencing value to him. When faith is rightly based and rightly centered, it is "the evidence of things not seen." [809]

> Yet since this is not a mere intellectual acceptance of the letter of the record; but a believing from the heart with a personal appropriation of the touch of one's own self; and since such a faith is enabled and assisted by the Holy Spirit ... we repeat that it is quite probable that some measure of the Spirit's witness is involved in even their witness of their own spirit which the believer has in himself....
>
> Nevertheless, when upon simple faith in the record that God has given of His Son—that "He taketh away the sin of the world" ... one faithfully confesses to having received Christ as a perfect Saviour, there soon follows a sealing blessing which none can ever doubt as the witness of the Holy Spirit.[810]

Analyzing his own and others' experiences of salvation, Smith concluded that "the divine assurance in its fullness is rolled in upon the soul" only when one has witnessed to or confessed openly his acceptance by faith of divine grace.[811]

Reminding himself and others of human fallibility in this as in other realms, Smith nevertheless asserted that

> ... despite our inability to comprehend it, and our liability to err here as elsewhere, there is nevertheless granted to humble, trustful souls, a deep, sweet assurance, which comes neither from our own reasonings nor from our fancies or self-congratulations (but often in spite of all our fears and in the face of our self-distrust), telling us " 'Tis done," or " 'Tis true." [812]

Smith maintained that three chief marks were necessary to mark one as a Christian at all: first, he must have the Spirit of Christ, which is "the Spirit of love to God and man"; second, he must have outward victory over sin. "These two tests apply to our Christian experience—the love test within and the power over sin test without." Third, he must have "the aspiration for Holiness." [813]

Since repentance includes "a solemn vow to renounce all sin, and to follow Christ as the Lord of one's life," and regeneration is the impartation of the life of God in the soul, manifesting itself in righteousness, the believer authenticates his conversion and maintains his justified state by a life in righteousness or good works.[814]

The life of good works fulfills the Pauline command, in Philippians 2:12, to work out one's own salvation with fear and trembling. For Smith that did not mean that "good works" have any meritorious value to atone for anyone's sins—past, present or future—but meant rather that they were "evidence and fruit" of one's salvation. Good works have value for the Christian in that they are "a proof of the merit of Christ's Blood applied in our behalf, and of the effectiveness of his grace through us." [815]

Christ came not to destroy the moral law but to fulfill it. He carried the whole moral law into "the Gospel Dispensation" by fulfilling it not *for* men but *in* them by His Spirit.[816] That, therefore, implies that "the first outworking of our salvation is obedience to the Word of God, as in the Decalogue and the Sermon on the Mount. 'Faith without such work is dead.' " [817]

To work out one's own salvation meant for Smith the

working out of "three remaining problems" of the Christian's salvation, namely: sanctification, preservation and fructification.

> For each of these three are conditions to be met, and exercises to be wrought (as there was of Repentance for our Justification.) And it is the working out of our salvation thus, that will (not entitle but) qualify us to ... receive the final and fixed and forever state of salvation.[818]

Smith viewed the doctrine of non-forfeitable grace or the unconditional eternal security for believers in this life as one of the major heresies of the times.[819] "The idea of being able to retain a relation of sonship, and a standing of justification, without a life of unbroken righteousness, is an atrocious hallucination and heresy."[820] As he interpreted the Scriptures, the individual who is born of the Spirit was begotten to love both God and his fellow men, which is really the fulfilling of the law according to Galatians 5:14. Instead of the Spirit's dispensation, with its promised liberty, being an era of exemption from the law, it is rather a freedom from sin so as to keep the moral law of God, the quintessence of which is divine love.[821]

Smith found that Paul in I Corinthians, chapter 10, Peter in his second epistle, chapter 2, James in chapter 5, and John in his first epistle were unitedly protesting against the idea that professing Christians are exempt from the penalty and consequences of sins committed after the experience of justification by faith. In I John 2:1, 2, Smith found that the *hope* of the "sinning" Christian is *"on the very same ground as that of the sinful world."*

> This is most significant and conclusive that the Christian is *no exception* as to man's dependence upon Christ's death for mercy: and further that the Christian has no *preferred stock* in this atoning Mercy. All the good works he may have done before have no propitiatory merit for any forgiveness for evil works now. He is on the very ground that other sinners are.[822]

Turning to Jesus' teaching, Smith claimed that Jesus faithfully showed the necessity of "one's conduct and character" conforming to the Sermon on the Mount now, if he is to have "any hope of an heavenly abode hereafter."[823]

Smith believed that following one's justification (and subsequent sanctification) he is on probation to be tested, "proven and developed," in all the moral likeness of Christ, and to be of service to God through others.

> Moreover, I am not only detained here, but I am *retained* on some mission for my Savior in the service of the Kingdom. Somehow my salvation is yet wrapped up in my participation in the saving of others. ... And besides my problem of self preservation against all the assaults and all the wiles of the foe, I have the further problem of the fruitfulness of my life's service for God and for souls.[824]

For him probation involved for the Christian his testing to prove his graces, his chastening to correct his errors, his "schooling in discipline to deepen and train" his motives, his suffering of consequences to arouse him to his deficiencies, and sometimes his punishment to rebuke his presumptions.[825]

Smith divided the testings, chastenings, schoolings, sufferings and temptations through which the Christian passes into two broad classes: trials and temptations. "*Trials* are in the *permissive will of God;* and have proof and development of our graces in view. *Temptations* are from the *designing will of Satan,* and are meant to shake our faith and shatter our love for and likeness to Jesus."[826] In the category called "trials," Smith placed the losses of health, of prestige, of property, of loved ones in death, and of other values which human unfaithfulness or neglect and natural causes might destroy. All these are the agencies of trial, but God makes them "work together for good to them that love God" (Rom. 8:28).

> And the following verse there shows that the good He has in mind is "that we should be *conformed to the*

image of his Son." So while the wise men of heathendom are still puzzling over the problem of human suffering, *"We know"* that God has a way of making it work for our good.[827]

The temptations from Satan are also part of the "all things" which God can overrule for man's good. These enticements or solicitations from the evil one are camouflaged as "goods" for the Christian.

> Now these three, *appetency* for knowledge, *appetite* for food pleasant or necessary, and *ambition* for place and power, were all inherent in our constitution as seen here in Eve: and they are not expelled by holiness as shown here in Satan's approachment to Jesus.... Restraint of appetite, restriction of curiosity or love of learning to proper channels; and contentment with a servant's place, must barricade Satan's approach to our souls through the normal avenues of human life.[828]

Satan's temptations may be so intertwined with the trials through human and natural causes that they are scarcely distinguishable; nevertheless both are more or less faced by the Christian until he has finished his earthly probation. Smith believed that just as men engage in athletics and study to develop their persons, so God permits temptations and trials to develop the Christian's faith which builds character, expands the soul, and brings one into a deeper love of the unseen God. He also held that God is achieving good with the angelic order through the Christian's testings.[829]

Smith taught that only as Christians faithfully participate in the *means of grace* can they be kept from falling from grace. While temptations and trials may become the *occasions* for the forfeiture of grace, they need not necessitate it.[830]

According to Smith, clear teaching on the "relation of the means of grace to grace itself" was the need of the times for two reasons: first, "the prevailing disuse of the most important means of grace"; and second, "the dependence by some upon means of grace for what they were never designed to substitute or accomplish." [831]

He found the relation to be most intimate between the means of grace and "the revelation, reproduction and reflection" of God's glory and grace in believers. Five facts were evident to him in this regard, based upon his own observation of Christians' worship, his study of the history of spirituality in the church, and "the precepts and precedents of the Saviour and the Apostles":

> (1) That all of those who find salvation (in any of its degrees) find it in the use of some one or more of those exercises which we call "means of grace."
> (2) That the great majority of them find it in connection (directly or indirectly) with some public means of grace.
> (3) That the neglect of the means of grace is always both a certain cause and a sure evidence of decline in grace itself.
> (4) That souls on the stretch for an advancing glory in the Divine life invariably find themselves drawn into a more ardent and diligent use of all possible "means of grace."
> (5) That a genuine revival of religion always revives the "means of grace" in attendance, interest and power.[832]

Having learned that the means of grace are not *grace* itself or not to be identified "with the faith that obtains grace, but are only helps to that faith," and that an undue exaltation of the means defeats grace, the Christian is ready to make those acts of worship "means" to an end, instead of the end in themselves. When the "means" is mistaken for the end, ritualism is mistaken for redemption, as occurred in the history of Pharisaical Judaism.[833]

Recognizing that there are differences between the acknowledged means of grace—some designed "to serve the objective end of a monument of religion before the world" and others "to minister the deep things of God to the believing soul"—Smith believed that the majority of professing Christians adopt the public and objective means of grace and almost lose sight of the private and subjective means. Neither is to be left undone.[834]

He further affirmed that the *true test* of a means of grace is not "its conformity with accepted usage of public church service nor its adherence to any orthodox formula or traditional requirement, but rather to its effectiveness in propagating and promoting spiritual life." [835]

Holding that "Providence" had so ordered things that public abuse or disuse by the majority in Christendom of the means of grace need not rob the individual of access to his supply of divine grace, Smith listed as the most important "means" the following: " 'praying in the Holy Ghost,' private assimilation of God's Word, judicious exercises of fasting, personal ministration to the sick and afflicted, both of material and spiritual substance." [836] With him the private took precedence over the public means of grace, and of the latter none were to be so highly regarded as "the preaching of the Gospel by men anointed with the Holy Ghost sent down from heaven." [837]

These "means," both private and public, were with a view of keeping the believer in vital relation to Jesus, the living Saviour. According to Smith, good works, correct creed, means of grace, devout desires, or diligent discipline in themselves could no more *keep* the Christian than they could remove his guilt, recover the lost image of God, successfully resist evil, or represent him before God. The former are only *conditions* to be met, in order to keep personally related to "a Living Person beyond any personality or life of our own." "We rest our faith on no mere plan of Redemption but upon a *Living Redeemer*. We draw our love from no mere reservoir nor ocean of sentiment, but from the heart beats of the living, loving Son of God." [838]

Sanctification. Since God chose to redeem man by degrees, partly because of His wisdom and man's fallen condition, Smith saw entire sanctification as the second major part in the redemptive scheme by which man is to be recovered to a greater than his original glory. As God created the world on successive days and as He made mankind in parts ("first Adam and then Eve"), and as He made the Bible in parts (first the Old and then the New Testament), and even gave the gospel in parts ("first, 'the beginning of the gospel' in the ministry and baptism of John" and the second "in the ministry and redemption of Jesus Christ"), so He has administered salvation in parts and to be realized in a definite and consecutive order: first, justification or free salvation; second, sanctification or full salvation; and third, glorification or final salvation. To Smith these were perfect parts of a perfect whole, each part a necessary preparation for entrance into the next part.[839]

While these three parts were definite and distinct in Smith's thought, yet they were not totally separable, because of an overlapping *relation* between them. Especially was this true in the relation between justification and sanctification. In free salvation (or justification), believers are sanctified in part. This partial sanctification is relative, outward, and inward. All justified persons are *relatively* sanctified unto God by their separation from the world and sinners; they are outwardly sanctified by their freedom from sinful living made possible through "the washing of regeneration"; and they are further *inwardly* sanctified to the extent that in the new birth (a concomitant of justification) they receive love, which is the seed of God's holiness, into their hearts. Thus, Paul in addressing the Corinthian Christians addressed them as "sanctified in Christ Jesus" and then designated them as "yet carnal" and as but "babes in Christ."[840]

The *necessity* of an entire sanctification, which Paul held before the Corinthians in II Corinthians 7:1, and before the Thessalonian converts in I Thessalonians 5:23, lies in that aspect of the sin problem which each individual inherits from Adam, the first natural and federal head of the human race. While justification has perfectly cared for the past sins which the individual has personally committed, it remains for entire sanctification to remove the sin bias which he has inherited.[841]

Smith found several reasons for putting great stress upon the necessity of the grace of entire sanctification in the believer's life. Among those reasons were these: first, the newly justified souls have deep longing "for a full and free deliverance somewhere, sometime, somehow, from the innate proclivities to unrighteousness which hinder and oppose the principle of righteousness which grace placed within them." [842] Salvation would not be full and complete if it did not meet the need and answer the cry "for a perfect solace and satisfaction" to the inner sin problem.

Smith further held that entire sanctification was requisite to continued holy living and service here and to admission to the presence of God and the "environment, associations, and occupation of heaven." Without holiness the soul would find heavenly associations and the person of God an embarrassment to and incompatible with his own nature. Further, "Christ's redemption would have failed of its purpose here on earth or would have been thwarted by the absence of faith in man had the least stain of sin been found to remain ... or any lack of the Spirit's fulness been unmet in his being." [843]

Smith was convinced that the "provisions of Christ's death, the promises of God's word, and the power of the Holy Spirit furnish a complete solution of the believer's sin problem." [844] He further believed that this solution was fully adapted to the probationary character and the remaining imperfections of both person and environment in this life.

He labored to make clear his understanding of what was, and what was not, the *nature* of Christian holiness or Christian perfection promised in Scripture. In the first place, "*there is a distinct limit* as to what it is that is perfect." [845] It is not a perfection of what the hand can do or of what the head can think, but it is a perfection of the heart's love and devotion to its God and to the well-being of others.[846] It is not a "perfection of physical or mental state, nor of temporal circumstances or conditions, but rather a *perfect acceptance of and adaptation to the probation that is involved in the imperfections of our lot.*" [847] It is, therefore, not perfection of social or economic conditions, or deliverance from those experiences that bring sorrow and loss and pain to men. But it is "strengthening *with might by his spirit* [sic] *in the inner man*" so that one may spiritually triumph over all earthly or bodily handicaps. It is a perfection limited to "*that which Christianity contemplates for man while on earth and in the body.*" [848]

When discussing the *nature* of entire sanctification which perfectly cleanses the moral nature of inherent depravity and perfects the soul in love to God and man—all through the merit of Christ's blood and accomplished through the ministry of the Spirit—Smith used various terms with which to relate the facts integral to this crisis in salvation. Whatever the terms, he always stressed, not a paradoxical, but at least a dual aspect in this epochal change. It was both an emptying and a filling, a death and a resurrection, a cleansing and an impartation, a purification and an inhabitation, a laying aside and a putting on, a destruction and a creation, a separation and a union, a freedom from sin and a fulfilling of righteousness.[849]

Smith claimed that entire sanctification is "the glory of righteousness brought to the soul by the Lord our righteousness; it is divestment, investment and empowerment of the soul unto righteousness." [850] Turning to Luke 1:74, 75, he found a "monumental text" which set forth for him both the *extent* and *duration* of this grace:

> "That He would grant unto us, that we being delivered out of the hand of our enemies might serve Him without fear, in holiness and righteousness before Him all the days of our lives." The deliverance is total (see also v. 71), the spirit of the service is perfect ("without fear"), the service itself is complete, being both inward and outward ("in holiness and righteousness"); the judgment thereof is infallible ("before Him"), and

the continuance of it is perpetual ("all the days of our life"). Truly, this is glorious![851]

While the righteousness of nature was begun within the believer in regeneration, it is in entire sanctification that fullness of righteousness is imparted and the believer has that righteousness which "exceeds the righteousness of the scribes and Pharisees." While this is called the "righteousness of Christ" and "righteousness by faith," it was also called by Christ "your righteousness," inasmuch as the believer receives it and makes it his own by a decisive faith.[852]

The effects of inwrought holiness in the believer, thought Smith, could be epitomized as follows: In relation to one's self, holiness is *soul health* because the "soul's disease of sin has been cured." In relation to others, holiness is helpfulness; "Sordid selfishness has been extinguished and love's service and sacrifice for our neighbor has become the rule of life." In relation to God, holiness is *harmony*: "There is an *amen* to whatever He does or allows: a *'Yea, Lord'* to whatever He asks or commands. And *contentment with thanksgiving* for one's lot, and PRAISE FOR HIMSELF." [853] This harmony between the soul and God brings the soul in this life into a present fulfillment of the promise, "Blessed are the pure in heart; for they shall see God." That for Smith was the realization of the Pauline Scripture in II Corinthians 3:18: "But we all, with open face beholding as in a glass the glory of the Lord, are changed into the same image from glory to glory even as by the Spirit of the Lord." [854]

Since Christianity has not altered in any way the essential nature and final consequences of sin itself, it is extremely imperative, thought Smith, that the new believer hasten his progress toward entire sanctification lest he lapse back into sinning through the promptings of the sinful bias of his unsanctified nature.[855] To remain outside of entire sanctification not only brings peril to each individual soul, but also produces evils within the church, as instanced in the Corinthian congregation founded by Paul. To them it meant babyhood instead of manhood in Christian character and conduct; it meant schism due to carnal envy, jealousy and rivalry; it meant defectiveness in "the character and quality of the good works of the Church;" and fourthly, it issued in the undue elevation of "worldly wisdom in the Church of Christ." In such a state the church loses her power and influence to be "the mighty force it should be for the extension of the Kingdom of Christ." [856]

The *conditions,* which Smith taught as requisite for the believer to enter this second major part of salvation, were three: repentance in believers, entire consecration, and perfect faith. Smith was insistent that all Christians seeking this "deeper work of grace," be ever mindful that they are *"dealing with sin."* Since many have looked upon holiness as a delightful state of joy, and others have thought of it primarily in terms of enduement with power, Smith stressed that *the fundamental thing* is *"purification"* and that joy and power are resultants of *"cleansing from all sin."* [857] Not only is it a dealing with sin, but a specific *form* of sin. Smith differentiated here between the "motions" of sin within the personality such as pride, man-fear, unbelief, resentment, hatred, anger, *et cetera,* and the *unitary* principle or spring of evil from which these motions of sin take their rise. While conversion (justification and its concomitants) has a threefold effect upon this inbred sin it does not extirpate it from the nature. Converting grace "subjugates it," "makes the child of God a legitimate candidate under grace for its removal," and "opens the way for the revelation of its presence" in the convert's heart.[858]

Conviction for holiness does not first grow out of the sense of guilt for having the carnal mind, but out of the "uncleanness" of it and "the privilege and necessity of having it removed." Sometimes the conviction is a condemnation growing out of reflections upon past failures in the Christian walk and warfare. Often it is *"the conscious* inability to do the good" which the regenerated heart and

Spirit of God prompt one to do. This *"chronic impotence"* is usually quickly followed by a sense of "inward conflict with one's self," and the consciousness of dispositions and tempers which the believer knows are unholy. But "the purest and most normal type of all is the conviction which results from simple faith ... in God's word ... in the testimony of God's witnesses." When the soul humbly believes what has been revealed in the Scriptures about his unsanctified heart and in simplicity of faith seeks deliverance from it, even before feeling its stirrings, or being defeated and deceived by it, he can reach "the Canaan of Perfect Love, without the discomforts of the wilderness route." [859]

Smith turned to the experience of Paul, "the pattern Christian," for an example of entire consecration, required to obtain entire sanctification. Paul's "complete world-renunciation and self-abnegation" was not exceptional to him, thought Smith, but exemplary of what all Christians must do in spirit if they are to obtain a clean heart, filled with Christ's love, and indwelt by the Holy Spirit—which is the essence of entire sanctification.[860]

For the believer, rejoicing in the mercies extended to him in forgiveness of sins and restored favor with God, *entire consecration* is really a sacrifice of love to his Lord. Smith stressed that the Scriptures consistently esteemed the giving of one's self to the Lord as surpassing "benevolence, humanitarianism and any or all forms of material sacrifices." [861] He saw love as "the motive," and the *"hope of Christian perfection* as the incentive in entire consecration," as presented by Paul in Romans 12: 1, 2.[862]

Paul's own experience is a further illustration of the fact, thought Smith, that one's self-giving can become a completed transaction in a moment and then maintained as a continuous fact throughout life. Having finished his perfect consecration to Christ, and having sustained the attitude of being the property of another, Paul called himself a bond-servant, that is, a *love* slave of Jesus Christ, and declared that he put a low estimate upon his sacrifice compared to his victory—he counted it as "refuse" and therefore did not pity himself for his self-yielding or attach any merit or sin-atoning worth to his sacrifice. He did it all that he might *win* Christ from whom he received the righteousness of God by faith.[863]

Smith further distinguished between the character of consecration on the part of the believer and repentance on the part of a sinner. Thought he, the former differs from the latter much the same as "a loyal citizen's enlistment and devotion of himself to the service of his country differs from the surrender of a rebel." The sinner surrenders himself in repentance to find peace with God, whereas the believer yields himself to God's eternal ownership that he might know the God of peace in His fulness and be perfected in love toward Him.[864]

Consecration is to be distinguished from entire sanctification, urged Smith, in the sense that the former is an act of the believer in letting go of all, while the latter is God taking complete possession of it for himself. In consecration the self is yielded up for crucifixion, whereas in entire sanctification "the body of sin is destroyed, and Christ in the person of the Holy Spirit immediately takes up His abode in the heart." [865]

Smith held that not until one had perfectly yielded himself by the Spirit's help to be the Lord's forever, without any reservation whatsoever, could that believer exercise *faith* for the cleansing of his heart from inbred sin. He claimed, however, that like Wesley, he preached entire sanctification by faith and, therefore, since it is by faith, then it is obtainable immediately.[866]

He held that the faith by which one is sanctified is "different from every other kind of faith" in three particulars: first, it is *"the faith of God's own child.* Regeneration has made all things new within us. Even our faith is different. It possesses the vital quality of the life-giving Spirit of God. It is now a confidence based upon the relation of sonship." Second, it is "faith for cleansing."

> This is not the same as covering; neither is it the same as control. It goes to the very root of the matter of sin. It strikes at the very germ of this innate leprosy. It cannot be content even with victory over sin. It can no longer endure *its presence*. It insists upon not a cleaner but a *clean* heart. It must be "whiter than snow." [867]

Third, it is "*a faith that abandons* the whole being to the will of God, and results in the fulness of God's love in all parts of the soul, and in all departments of life." [868]

When the regenerate soul is fully yielded, the Holy Spirit is present to generate in his heart this faith which brings the sanctifying baptism. Usually the soul passes through three stages in reaching this level of faith. With Christ the High Priest as the particular object of sanctifying faith, the soul reaching up must believe that He is *able* to sanctify wholly, that He is *willing* to do it for the believer, and that He *does* it immediately. By a present-tense faith in Christ as sanctifier, the believer enters instantaneously into the relation of divine union, that state of Christian holiness in which the abiding Spirit perfectly cleanses the heart and perfects it in divine love Godward and manward.[869]

Paul called this the "perfecting of faith." According to Smith, it is not perfect faith in *scope* or *strength,* but in condition and quality, whereby it can trust in Christ for a present, perfect salvation from sin and that "without a doubt." Such a faith has yielded "every affection and ambition and desire and pleasure and possession to be nailed to the cross," and Christ has become its all.[870]

When asked to set forth the essential points of his doctrine of entire sanctification which he claimed to have derived from the Scriptures and to have tested in experience, Smith gave the following summary:

> The depravity or carnality of man's nature.
> The imperative necessity of regeneration in every case to begin... the Christian life.
> That carnality, though subdued and subjugated, remains after regeneration.

> That the Blood of Christ provided for its complete removal in this present life.
> That this removal connects with the promised baptism with the Spirit.
> That the baptism with the Spirit is not the same as, but is subsequent to, the birth of the Spirit.
> That it is instantaneous.
> That it is to be earnestly sought.
> That it is conditioned on entire consecration.
> That it is received by faith.
> That it results in the abiding presence of God.[871]

Smith recognized great intellectual and spiritual hindrances in bringing some believers to the point of believing on Christ for an immediate and entire sanctification of the heart and life. Among the intellectual difficulties which some must overcome is the idea that sin is located in the physical nature of man and is consequently ineradicable until the body dies. Such a view, claimed Smith, is nowhere countenanced in Scripture.[872]

Smith centered the spiritual difficulties to becoming sanctified wholly in the will of the believer.

> One of the greatest hindrances to becoming sanctified is wanting our own way instead of God's way. When did the devil make man an idolator? When the serpent came to Eve he proposed to her to make herself her God instead of the GOD.... No matter what holds you back it is the idolatry of self, your own will, your own plans, or your own ambitions, instead of God's plan for you.[873]

Its Constituents. Integral to the grace of entire sanctification are the two facts of purity and perfect love. Purity designates the exclusion of all contrary to love, whereas perfect love describes that positive aspect of the soul in its conformity to the divine nature.[874]

Purity of intention, claimed Smith, can exist only where evil desires have been purged away and the inner self united and simplified. Whereas the regenerate believer is plagued by a double-mindedness which produces an inner wavering between loyalties—self or Christ—amounting to an inner instability, the fully sanctified soul is freed from all that keeps him from *willing one thing*.[875] With singleness of purpose, he wills to act always out of pure love to God and man. He lives to glorify God and do good unto others. "This man may now truthfully and exaltingly cry, 'He restoreth my soul.' "[876] "Now then, a pure heart is that which lends the quality of pureness to all the conversation, transactions and influences of a human soul."[877]

A pure heart filled with perfect love was portrayed, thought Smith, by Paul in his hymn of love in I Corinthians, chapter 13. Love's expulsion of the sevenfold forms of evil—envy, boasting, pride, self-seeking, unseemliness, irritability, and evil thoughts—indicates "the certainty and completeness of *cleansing* in this state of Perfect Love." Its sevenfold inclusion of longsuffering, kindness, truth-loving, hope, faith, forbearance and endurance, impels and enables the Christian to " 'walk in the ways of God's commandments.' And all the Law is fulfilled in this one word: Thou shalt love!"[878]

John's first epistle led Smith to hold that perfect love is both a practice, a state, and a relation.

> Yes, it is all three of these—a life of loving service and sacrifice in Jesus' name—a state of pure love flowing through all the avenues of the nature; and a relation of divine union binding us in love's wedlock with our Lord.[879]

For Smith this was the antithesis of the state of total depravity in the moral nature; it was the state of total love.

But perfect love is *"compatible with many deficiencies if not defects."* For instance, a young bride may have perfect wifely devotion to her husband in that all other suitors or admirers are excluded and all her abilities and affections are devoted to him. "Yet her inexperience and lack of knowledge and skill in housekeeping may cost *him* many discomforts and delays and possibly some damages and expense."[880] While still struggling to overcome her deficiencies as a housekeeper, she may have as perfect a love toward her husband as ever she could have even after her imperfections have been overcome.

Perfect love out of a purified heart is not therefore to be identified with, or to tarry for, a well-skilled hand, or a well-trained mind, or a well-balanced temperament, or a finished character. It is rather a quality of nature and spirit with which to work at the task of building character, improving one's temperament, mind, and skill.[881] It is not "the measures or the might of love" that constitute perfection with a Christian, but rather "the banishment of all but love from the heart and practice, and the abiding in loving companionship with Christ." [882]

For an "authorized pattern" of a pure heart filled with perfect love in pursuit of the unattained, Smith turned to Paul's testimony in Philippians, chapter 3, where the apostle disclaimed having attained three things while at the same time claiming two other important facts in his life. Paul disclaimed "physical perfection," a *"finished probation,"* and a *"Final Degree of Christian Progress."* But he did claim a kind of spiritual perfection and successful progress toward a perfection yet to be attained.[883]

From the general movement of thought in the New Testament, Smith was convinced that progression in divine things is as necessary to salvation as justification and sanctification. But sanctification, thought he, was the *cause* rather than the *consequence* of constant spiritual progression.[884] "We are perfected in love in order that unhindered we may pursue the path of ascent. Cessation or stagnation is defeat and death and damnation." [885]

Believing that much error prevailed concerning the *nature* of growth in grace, Smith maintained that while spiritual growth is begun the moment a soul is regenerated, it nevertheless needs the divine work of entire sanctification to remove the sinful barrier to that soul's growth. Entire sanctification is the translating of the soul into Christ in such a fulness that "all subsequent promotion is 'from glory to glory'—that is, promotion in the positive and glorious realm of spiritual being rather than a never ending translating from sin and shame to righteousness and glory." [886]

> Too much attention cannot be given, nor too much importance attached to this point.... It is right here that a subtle pessimism concerning the possibilities or probabilities of grace prevents both the glory of God and the glory of man. The idea that growth in grace is to consist in a life-long and never-ending getting rid of sins has no place in Scripture, and is fatal to the true idea of a life-long walk and a life-long advancement in that holiness and righteousness of Christ, which has no negative element. The key to the sure and steady and swift ascent in the scale of glory is in a perfect translation into the kingdom of glory. Thus Paul (in Ephesians iv: 13–15) prefaces our growing up into Him in all things with our having come to the measure of the stature of the fullness of Christ. And the failure to grow steadily and symmetrically, which is so general, is due to a lack of the fulness of Christ, which is the perfect qualification for growth.[887]

Smith further stressed that as in nature and in providence, so in grace God has employed both the law of progression and "the law of Divine Interposition." Neither cancels out the other, but both are necessary to carrying forward the divine work in the soul. Just as in nature there are "the crises of germination in vegetation" and "of generation in the animal," and as there are "great revolutions in Providential history," so in Christian grace once a degree of life or change has started, the law of progression takes over. These crises furnish the law of gradual progress with its "starting points" and "objective points." [888]

> And the great reason why progress in holiness has been so unsteady and unsatisfactory with many is because a lack of faith to lay hold upon God for a supernatural beginning, and consummation has robbed their minds of the necessary start and stimulus for the onward move.[889]

Since some had developed the idea that all growth is imperceptible, Smith further objected by stating that the epochal experiences of conviction, regeneration and sanctification both "establish the precedent and illustrate the law" by which continuous spiritual progress is to be realized. As the transitions from a sinning life to Christianhood, and from the mixed state of the regenerate heart to the state of heart purity, were "sharply-defined transformations from glory to glory," so the transitions from "faith to faith," from "grace to grace," and from "glory to glory," in the fully sanctified life are "steady, distinct and definite" ascents.

> For, instead of growth being that insensible, undefined, or often undiscoverable thing... these steps of advance are often made by a revelation so vivid, a faith so conscious, and a result so marked, that it is scarcely to be wondered that some have been misled into attaching to these subsequent developments a prominence equal to that of their justification and their sanctification. Yet, while they are quite analogous, and are under the same general law of spiritual change, yet they are different in that the great epochal saving blessings have a negative or destructive side in translating us from darkness to sunlight, while these are all the more strictly on the positive side, not changing us from sin and shame to righteousness and glory, but promoting us from one degree, which is already glorious and righteous, to another, which is greater in measure of both righteousness and light.[890]

While Smith believed that "God's Law of Progress is nowhere more insistent than in the spiritual life," he nevertheless did not believe that progress is a necessary "reflex action of Christian work," nor that it is automatic or inevitable. Instead he reiterated in his writings and preachments the necessity of following Paul's pattern of pursuit in Philippians, chapter 3, where all else, even past Christian blessings and successes, are secondary to his present progression in the knowledge of Christ. While time can move the Christian *toward* eternity, it cannot of itself bear him *to* eternal life.[891]

> This we must seek, yea, we must strive to enter in. There are distinct and definite stages in the inner life,

even as in the outer life. These are illustrated by childhood, young manhood and fatherhood by the Apostle John. (See I John 2:12–15) And with this likeness of the spiritual to the physical (which is recognized also in other Scriptures) there is also one difference; in the physical we may simply *grow* to these stages successively, but in the spiritual we must go! [892]

Recalling that he himself had had difficulty seeing the compatibility of perfect love with probation and with progression, especially the latter, Smith illustrated his mature view on progression (after heart purity) in perfect love thus: "A friend taking me through his great orchard once showed me how *'an apple could be perfect, though it was still little and green and hard.'*" [893] Progression in the maturing of the disease-free apple, its enlargements, its ripening and its flavoring, illustrated for Smith the difference between purity and maturity, between perfection as a quality of nature and an unfolding development of that nature. [894]

The lines along which Christian progression must move, thought Smith, are these:

> In the realm of spiritual life there are unnumbered and indescribable degrees of advancement to be made in knowledge, in courage, in prayer, in persuasiveness, in meekness, in patience and in the every-day, every-way reflection about us of the life that is within us.
>
> In holiness there are establishments, intensifications, both of the earnestness of our consecration and the ardor of our love, and increased wisdom, too in our testimony and in our ways and means of spreading the truth, and an ever-growing force in impressing holiness upon others, together with a constant replenishing of our being with fresh supplies of the Spirit of Christ.
>
> Then, in the way of the cross, there are ever-widening and deepening conceptions of humanity's needs, an inflamed passion for man's salvation, improvement, development and increase of gifts... but withal a growing facility in the greatest of all arts—the art of self-denial... for the glory of God. [895]

The laws of progression in grace, according to Smith's

study and experience, he condensed to two words: exertion and expectation. A full-fledged synergism obtained in Smith's view of progression as it did in repentance, faith, conversion, and sanctification. By human disciplines or "daily dozens" for the soul and expectations of "fresh blessings of a supernatural order," the perfect-hearted Christian can move forward "to boundless advancement." [896] The disciplines which Smith recommended were:

> Bible reading, meditation, petition, supplication, and intercession; kind words and deeds for others, as well as thanksgiving and praise to God, and withal habits of quick retirement within ourselves and acts of abandonment to the indwelling Spirit, who... will be ever ready to make intercession for us according to the will of God.[897]

When a believer becomes entirely sanctified, there is no change in the probationary character of his earthly life except that he has become conditioned to meet more successfully (by continued faith and obedience) the tests and trials incident to the rest of his temporal existence. No state of grace or ascent into holiness in this life can render the believer impeccable. As John Fletcher, Wesley's colleague, lost the grace of entire sanctification four or five times, so others have lost all grace and after having preached to others have become moral derelicts and spiritual castaways.[898]

Three things, claimed Smith, yet remain to be worked out by the believer "to make his calling and election sure" for final salvation. These are: first, a progressive development in Christlikeness as evidenced in His earthly life; second, the fulfillment of the life work entrusted to him by Christ for the advancement of His kingdom; and third, continuous victory over satanic forces and the spirit of Antichrist seeking to overthrow the faith of his soul.[899]

Quoting Wesley, Smith believed, "It is a small matter to get a soul saved or to get a soul sanctified, compared with keeping a soul saved and keeping a soul sanctified." [900]

He therefore made much of the doctrine of preservation, looking upon preservation from the human side as the greatest thing in redemption in this life.[901]

From his study of the New Testament, he concluded that Jude was the leading exponent of preservation, who related the believer's keeping himself in the love of God to God's preservation, as much as Paul had related the believer's consecration to God's sanctifying work and as John the Baptist had related the sinner's repentance to God's remission of sins.

> Thus it is made clear, that as Christ's ability to save to the uttermost did not suspend the necessity of our meeting the conditions to secure our full salvation, so neither does God's ability to keep us from falling suspend the necessity of our meeting the conditions of perseverance in order to our enjoying the blessing of His ability of our preservation. In brief, it is made clear that in order to our being kept, by God, we must keep ourselves where and at what God would have us....[902]

In Smith's thought, perseverance and preservation were inseparable for the believer to the very end of his earthly life. He claimed that Jude showed that "no environment has been found able" to keep moral beings from falling, as instanced by the angels in heaven; "no superior gifts and *ministries* are able to insure our eternal safety"; and "Jude has shown plainly that *no great epochal experience* though as truly divine as was the crossing of the Red Sea, is able to 'keep us from falling.'"[903]

While ever confronted with the possibility of falling—even as holy angels and as Adam and Eve had done—the fully sanctified, however, have the presence of a divine Guardian and the power of His resurrection to keep them in the midst of all the permissive providences and temptations incident to this life.[904]

Glorification

The third major part of "the great salvation" as Paul

taught it, thought Smith, is glorification or final salvation which begins for the believer at the moment of death and continues to all eternity.[905] Standing within time as a Christian, Smith related the three great epochs of salvation thus:

> Our justification has disposed of our past. Our sanctification provides for the present, and our hope of glorification assures for the future.
>
> . . . .
>
> One's previous justification is requisite for his sanctification; and one's present sanctification is prior to, and pre-requisite for his glorification.[906]

Approaching the same epochs with different Biblical language, Smith spoke of these three stages in terms of life. Regeneration (concomitant with justification) is life begun and is "the earnest" of the second stage and "partakes of all the essential qualities of life eternal." It is, thought he, "the gift of God to encourage and enable the soul" to seek and sacrifice for "The Life More Abundant." Entire sanctification, which brings the fullness of the Spirit of life into the soul, makes actual the more abundant life in the believer. But, claimed Smith, neither the life nor life more abundant is the crown of life or glorification.

> This is conditioned upon our being "faithful unto death" (See Rev. 2:10). Paul, though possessed of Life and of the Life More Abundant, was still pursuing "the prize of the Crown of Life" when he wrote Phil. 3: 13-14.[907]

Smith seemed confident that the Scriptures hold out no hope of any future probations for men beyond the privileges and bounds of time. Death, being man's last enemy, is not a saviour or transformer of character. Death does not change; it only seals the character which has been determined by choices made in this life. Death ends the possibility of a moral change of character by putting men beyond or past it.[908]

While men's characters have been in a process of change

and formation in this life, at the stage of glorification Christians will share in the "unalterability of God's own character."[909]

Having declared that sanctification is prerequisite to one's glorification, Smith made it clear that those having been justified and dying before having received the light upon and grace of entire sanctification, like the dying thief on the cross, find mercy with God inasmuch as their sanctification and "full fitting for heaven is doubtless unconditionally provided by the atoning Blood of Christ." The dying justified believer stands in the same relation to the atoning merits of Christ for the entire sanctification of his soul as the infant does (who needs sanctification) before reaching the age of accountability.[910]

Smith held that Paul's "masterful treatise on the Resurrection"—Christ's and the Christians'—was written "to offset the materialism and rationalism" of the Corinthian Church which was finding philosophical difficulty with the doctrine of the resurrection and therefore objecting to it.[911]

Smith believed himself thoroughly scriptural in holding to a bodily resurrection for the saints even as the Saviour had. Inasmuch as man's perfect body was a part of his original glory in creation, Smith felt that redemption would not be complete if it did not restore his body to an estate free from sins' consequential effects upon the physical. He based his view upon direct statements of the Bible plus the high estimate which Christianity has generally put upon the body.

> Christianity puts a great premium on the body. This we will see from three viewpoints:
> *First,* it is the supreme sacrifice that a Christian is enjoined to present to GOD. (Rom. 12:1)
> *Second,* it alone can furnish all the instruments and implements for the soul's service for God on earth. (Rom. 6:13)
> *Third,* it was HIS BODY THAT CHRIST gave unto death for our salvation. And it was the *resurrection of His body* that attested the *acceptance* of His sacrifice

in our behalf. And the assurance this gives of the resurrection of our own bodies establishes the fact of the everlasting distinction of man from mere spirit, by the immortalizing of his body, and the making eternal the conjunction of soul and body which God had effected in the creation of man.[912]

While entire sanctification brings a moral and spiritual likeness to Christ in the believer's heart now, yet the Scriptures held before him the hope of the resurrection of the physical body to an incorruptible spiritual state which will "seal and crown the moral likeness" to Christ with a body like unto His own glorious body.[913]

Smith found scriptural ground for believing that each degree of salvation contains an "earnest" of the greater glory that shall come in the Christian's full recovery to glorify God and enjoy Him forever. The gracious help granted by God to the physical here and now, especially as instanced by bodily healing through direct divine touches, is but "an earnest of the physical glory" which awaits believers in their resurrection bodies.[914] The supernatural and instantaneous factors involved in the resurrection of the Christians' bodies were also prefigured in the supernatural intervention for the new birth and entire sanctification of their souls.[915]

In the resurrection, marriage, having been instituted for "the propagating of the race," ends, and its temporal relationships are sublimated to the point that "the possibility of the family relationship for effecting and perpetuating a higher and more sacred and everlasting relationship is beyond that of any other institution or organization of which we have any knowledge whatever." [916]

This resurrection body will be of such a nature as to fully equip immortalized man for "an arena of life" in which all its surroundings, as well as itself, have been "divested of all that pertains to death and decay." [917] This arena will be that realm or hemisphere of glory of the eternal Christ in His pre-creational and post-redemptional majesty and felicity.

By the aid of faith, Smith had no difficulty in his mind harmonizing finished probation, fixedness of character, and perpetual progression for Christians. He believed that the perfection which man is to know in redemption is not the perfection of finished progression, but a perfect harmonizing of man's whole being with God until he will ever ascend into deity but also ever increase in his capacity of assimilating the divine likeness. Man is "doubtlessly, infinitely and eternally called" to progress in God and is so constitutionally made that he craves to do it.[918]

> .... Christ's kingdom is both eternal and infinite; and ... our being while creaturely and finite is nevertheless unceasing in its expansion, and ever increasing in its capability of achievements. And fear of having to halt before having half accomplished what we have purposed will never again recur to us.[919]

The Glorious Church

The Fact of the Church. Smith was one who refused to entirely separate or to completely merge the church of Christ and the kingdom of God. He viewed the latter as a sphere of reality in which there are the heavenly and the earthly, the present and the future, aspects. The true church is a spiritual organism or "fellowship" within which the life of the kingdom of God is presently realized: "For the kingdom of God is not meat and drink, but righteousness, peace and joy in the Holy Ghost."[920] While the church in any one of its ecclesiastical formations or in entirety is not *the* kingdom of God, it is nevertheless "the earthly vehicle or medium of the Spiritual Kingdom of the Lord Jesus. It is meant to propagate the kingdom and conserve its interest in this dispensation."[921]

Smith saw in the Old Testament era a preparation for and a type of the New Testament church. To him Abraham's seed after the flesh were a type of the New Testament church. John the Baptist, who came preaching the gospel of repentance, was preparing the soul for the immediate plant-

The Church

A Glorious Church

Respectfully dedicated to Rev. Joseph H. Smith
Copyright, 1892, by R. E. Hudson. By per.

R. E. Hudson

1. Do you hear them com-ing, broth-er,— Throng-ing up the steeps of light, Clad in glo-rious shin-ing gar-ments,— Blood-washed gar-ments pure and white?
2. Do you hear the stir-ring an-thems Fill-ing all the earth and sky? 'Tis a grand, vic-to-rious ar-my, Lift its ban-ner up on high!
3. Nev-er fear the clouds of sor-row, Nev-er fear the storms of sin,— We shall tri-umph on the mor-row, E-ven now our joys be-gin.
4. Wave the ban-ner, shout His prais-es, For our vic-to-ry is nigh! We shall join our con-q'ring Sav-ior, We shall reign with Him on high!

CHORUS

'Tis a glo-rious church with-out spot or wrin-kle, Washed in the blood of the Lamb; 'Tis a glo-rious church, with-out spot or wrin-kle, Washed in the blood of the Lamb.

ing of the church by Jesus when he began his public ministry. With the church's full inauguration on the day of Pentecost, the church age or dispensation ushered in the best days that had ever come to man since the fall in Eden.[922]

As the church visible is not to be identified with the kingdom of God, neither is it to be always identified with Christianity. Since society generally can degenerate, so the church can fall away from its true nature and calling, and thereby fail truly to embody and represent vital Christianity before the world of men.[923] For Smith, true Christianity and its medium of expression, the church of Christ, were as divine in origin as creation and as the Scriptures. "But as there is an apocrypha that bears some resemblance to Holy Scriptures yet lacks inspiration of the Holy Spirit," so there are counterfeits of the church which must be distinguished from the true church.[924] He believed the church to be the most glorious of all institutions among men when true to its divine origin and goal, but the most despicable if it failed in its mission as some churches he felt were failing in his generation.[925]

The Foundation of the Church. Smith's Biblical studies inclined him to set forth the church under the analogies and figures employed in the Scriptures: The church was presented by Paul as a husbandry, a repository of truth, a building, a body, a bride, a family, a flock, and an army. Peter presented it as a holy nation a royal priesthood, a chosen generation, a peculiar people, and a band of pilgrims; whereas John presented it as a family and its resultant fellowship.[926]

Basing his conclusion upon the content of the fourth Gospel, chapter 1, Smith dated the beginning of the Christian Church at the very opening of Christ's public ministry. Of that historic beginning, he wrote:

> It did not begin in the temple, nor in a synagogue, nor a meeting house. It began in Jesus' lodging house.

> "Where dwellest thou?"... "Come and see."... "And they abode with him that day." (vs. 39) That was the beginning of the Church. *Its Foundation was Fellowship with Christ.*[927]

While Jesus founded the church at the very opening of His public ministry, it was not until the occasion of Peter's great confession of Christ's divine sonship that the real foundation of the church was disclosed.[928] According to Smith, the church is a divinely human institution, founded not upon a man or wholly upon Christ, but upon an *experimental knowledge* of Christ through a divine revelation of Him to human hearts as the Son of God and Saviour of men.[929] It was this experiential knowledge of and fellowship with Jesus Christ through the Spirit and its accompanying fellowship with the apostles and saints of all ages through the Scriptures and the Spirit which constituted for Smith the very genius of the church.

> Not for historical data and record and reference only is the narrative of the gospel written; but that believers now and in all generations may experience the very same super-relationships which the apostles had among themselves; and not only so, but the very same sublime relationship which they had *with Christ and God Himself.*[930]

Just as fellowship had a primary place in Christ's relation to His disciples while He was on earth, so now it is primary in the church's relation to Him and will *"continue throughout the everlasting ages.... Fellowship is never final; it is forever."* [931] It is to be "a fellowship and kinship like to that of a family relationship" and analogous to and "somewhat in harmony with that of the unity of the trinity: 'as thou Father art in me, and I in thee, that they also may be one in us.' (See John 17:21)" [932]

Smith rejected the sacraments, church membership, and orthodox theology as the ground of this fellowship but affirmed that according to First John, chapter 1, it is righteousness of life and purity of heart, supernaturally begotten in the believer, which constitute the ground and proof of such a fellowship.[933]

No local congregation or ecclesiasticism, thought Smith, could rest its claim to be a church on its orthodoxy, or its authority, or its antiquity, or its birthright privileges and obligations. That which constitutes a true church is spiritual adaptability, that is, faithfulness to feeding the spiritual life of its members with divine truth in its regenerating, sanctifying and edifying stages, thereby creating and sustaining a divine-human fellowship.[934]

Smith was convinced that God had set in the book of Acts "the model for a New Testament Church" for all time, which He meant for men to follow as much as He had intended for them to copy the pattern of the tabernacle given to Moses on the mount. Just as that pattern was retained and not varied in either the tabernacle or the temple in Israel's history, so the church was to "continue steadfast" in the skeletal features essential to New Testament Christianity and its world-wide propagation as outlined in Acts.[935]

As spiritual as was Smith's emphasis upon the church, he did not go to the one extreme of denying the necessity of an external organization of the church, nor did he go to the other extreme of affirming that the Scriptures gave a formal plan of organization which must be adhered to regardless of time or place or extenuating circumstances under which it was to take its rise. He rather held to the view that the New Testament laid down general principles for organization but no specific church polity. He believed the church must have some kind of polity in order to survive, and since no divinely ordered polity had been revealed, it therefore was left up to the church, and to each church, to determine its own polity.[936]

The principles which he believed "a true-to-type pentecostal church" was to retain and by which she was to chart her course across the centuries were these: (1) a ministry of power through concentrating upon prayer and the Word of God; (2) a laity adhering to the apostles' doctrine—

later formulated as the apostles' creed; (3) a spiritual fellowship in love feasts and the sacramental commemorations of Christ's death; (4) a self-supporting program through sacrifice, and care for their own poor instead of dependence upon the world's charity; (5) a maintained spiritual gladness; and (6) a continuously evangelistic outreach toward the world.[937]

> Many incidental and secondary matters, as of polity, economics, and adjustments to varied and versatile circumstances, are left for successive legislation. But these are constitutional and charter principles.[938]

The Features of the Church. For Smith the Scriptures spoke clearly of the church of Christ in its manifold characteristics. He distinguished between its local and universal, its redemptive and providential, its visible and invisible, its diversified and united, its militant and triumphant, its imperfect and holy, its individual and corporate, its necessary and voluntary, its apostolic and confessional, its ministerial and lay, its real and ideal features.

Smith thought that Christ had the universal aspect of the church in mind, "the church in magnitude," when He said, "I will build my church." This was doubtless also in Paul's mind when he employed these expressions: "The church which he has purchased with his own blood," and "Christ also loved the church." The "church in miniature" or its local aspect was in the apostle's mind when he wrote these lines: "the church that is in their house," and "the church in thy house." [939]

Smith's study of Scripture led him to see that the Lord not only addressed the church as a whole, but also each of the seven churches which were severally located at Ephesus, Smyrna, Pergamos, Thyatira, Sardis, Philadelphia, and Laodicea. The latter were but the "providential settings" or place of the church of Christ, while the church as a whole in its dispensation-long and world-wide, its earthly and heavenly, modes of existence were its "redemptional setting" in the divine scheme of things. "While the Church of Christ is as colossal as the starry heavens, each and every church may have its fixed place in the firmament and be a center and a reflector of the same pure light as illumines the whole sky by night."[940]

Distinguishing between the visible or the external manifestation of the church and its invisible or its inner nature, Smith repeatedly declared that not all men associated with the visibly organized ecclesiasticisms were really in nature members of the true church of Christ. He regarded the latter as "the mystical body of Christ" which is invisible and is scattered among the various local, denominational units of Christendom. Only those individuals make up the invisible body of Christ who have had their names written down in the Lamb's book of life in heaven as an accompaniment of the salvation experience into which individuals enter by faith in Jesus Christ.[941]

For Smith the church must also be recognized as having both a militant and a triumphant aspect. The former designates the church as it engages in its redemptive conflict with sin in this world, whereas the latter has reference to the redeemed in heaven who have successfully passed their earthly probation with its struggles, sufferings, and sorrows.[942]

The church's unity and diversity engaged Smith's thought and received attention in his public ministries. He held that diversity of denominations need not, and in some instances did not, destroy the essential unity of the church.

> God's people may enjoy the state of heart-purity and even the life of Pentecostal power, whose sectarian distinction may be as varied as were the dialects of those who spoke and those who received the present gracious and great blessings of the Gospel on that Day of Pentecost.[943]

Smith urged that men were not to look everyone on his own works for Christ, "'but each also upon the work of others,' and that not with a critical but rather an appreciative eye." He saw the redemptive unities of the churches as far greater than their providential diversities.

> Despite those things which differentiate us as: locality, language, nativity, various views on matters not vital, there are things which identify us, such as reverence for the Holy Scriptures, dependence upon the Cross of Calvary; Righteousness and Good Works; and the Hope of Heaven.[944]

Smith's view of the gospel led him to stress especially the individual and the individualizing factor in the church. "Not simply 'mankind' but 'every man' had the great apostle's attention and consideration. And this with respect to his present personal and his future and eternal salvation... (Col. 1:28)." "Great as is the Church of our Lord Jesus Christ... The Good Shepherd leaves the ninety and nine to seek and to save the one that was lost...."[945] Smith was persuaded that the true objective and end of Christianity was not in the 'solidarity of humanity,' but in the *soul* of each man, that is, in *individualism,* inasmuch as the whole of Christian doctrine "resolves itself and converges into the Personality of Christ."

> Society is but the aftermath of Creation. When God made a man of the dust of the ground and breathed into his nostrils the breath of His own life in moral and spiritual likeness to Himself, *He completed His work of human creation.* And the soul of a man reaches its maximum worth then and there. *What mankind is in the world is what fallen man has made of himself.* And Redemption is God's provision and administration by mediation of His Son and ministration of His Spirit for the *recovery of a man's lost likeness to God.*[946]

The individual aspect of the church gave Smith ground for stressing the voluntary and independent nature of the choice involved in the "whosoever will" call of the gospel. It allowed for the possibility and often the necessity of choosing contrary to the environmental trends in becoming and remaining a Christian. On the other hand, Smith held that *"open identification with the visible Church of Christ is an obligation that rests upon every Christian,"* which in turn necessitates cooperation with other members of the corporate body for the maintenance and progress of the visible church. Therefore, a twofold necessity rests upon Christians in that it is necessary for them to accept and propagate the nature of the spiritual body and fellowship into which they are ingrafted by the Spirit.[947]

Smith did not anticipate a holy visible church in its world-wide extension and expression. Inasmuch as the writer of the Acts had to record corruptions, and the messages of Revelation to the seven churches of Asia carried rebukes for backslidings and apostasy within the first-century church, and inasmuch as both Christ and the apostles predicted evils creeping into the church from outside as well as rising up from within, Smith was not optimistic about *all* members of the visible church meeting the standard of apostolic faith and holiness of heart and life.[948] He taught that some church degenerations and corruptions are inevitable in *some* degree if not in the *same* degree in all periods or in all places of the church's existence. He viewed these degeneracies as "a part of the probation of souls" and, therefore, not wholly escapable in this dispensation.[949] Since the "Lord contemplated no ideally perfect and absolutely true and clean civilization in the world during this dispensation," Smith believed that the encroachment of the world upon the church was a constant threat to her purity, against which both ministers and laymen must give the closest of vigilance.[950] Jesus promised that both the tares, sown by the enemies of Christianity, and the wheat of the church would grow together until the harvest, that is, until the end of the church age. As there is no impeccability for the individual in this life so there is no absolute immunity against corrupters for the church corporately.[951]

Smith also insisted that the church must be apostolic and confessional to meet the requirement of the divine pattern for the entire church age. That is, those who constitute the church must continue in "the apostles' doctrine" and confess their faith publicly as one with that which was formulated in the apostles' creed. Since Paul had inextricably united the apostles with Christ in the foundation of the church, according to Ephesians 2:20, it necessarily followed for Smith that New Testament Christians must retain and profess "the faith once for all delivered unto the saints" by the apostles.[952]

In the light of Ephesians 4:11-16, Smith felt compelled to view the distinction between a specially called ministry and the laity in the church as divine in origin. According to his interpretation, God sovereignly chooses each man and woman whom He would set apart for the work of full-time Christian service. The New Testament minister, thought Smith, is in line with the Old Testament prophet in that he does not enter the sacred service by virtue of family or ecclesiastical or humanitarian connections and ambitions. He is personally called by God for a special task for his day within the church and to the world.[953]

From the same Ephesian passage, Smith was convinced that all the members of the body of Christ are to "minister" just as far as their natural and spiritual gifts and providential opportunities permit them to do good to the souls and bodies of men. While God distinguishes between the offices of the clergy and the laity, He has put no difference between their privileges in divine grace, of divine fellowship, and of intercessory prayer.[954]

The supreme mission of the specially called ministers is to the church, for the perfecting of the saints preparatory to their spiritual ministry to the world of Christless men, as well as to each other as believers.[955]

Smith further stressed the place of women as well as men in the God-called, full-time Christian ministry, citing Philip's four daughters in the early church as an argument for the divine call upon some women to preach the gospel.[956]

Believing Paul to be the pattern New Testament preacher, Smith concluded that the whole church is the "lawful heritage of all ministers of Perfection," and that preaching perfection to the church and regeneration to the world were equally binding upon a truly Pauline ministry.[957]

According to Smith's ecclesiology, no one church as it is found in this world could justly claim *everything* in doctrine, polity, and ethics as superior to and unpossessed by any other branch of the church. He held that since the visible church is humanly organized and staffed it has defaulted in some way or another, sooner or later, in its doctrine, or polity, or ethics and that the ideal church without flaws and failings is yet to be. In fact, it will not be a reality until the divine head of the church, Jesus Christ, gathers the church unto himself in eternity and removes from the minds and bodies of men the handicaps and scars of the racial fall.[958]

To Smith the crowning attractiveness and loveliness of the church lay not in her prestige or members but in her spirituality. By that he meant not intellectuality or aesthetics or cultural refinement but the life of the Holy Spirit barring sin from and permeating the being of believers. It is this spirituality of the church that makes her more loved by the spiritually minded than any other object in this world.[959] As the individual's rights in the church cease with the loss of his spirituality, so the church's claim to the love and loyalty of her members, thought Smith, can be only in proportion to her spirituality.[960]

The Function of the Church. Smith viewed the church's primary function as fourfold. In the first place, the church is "the repository of inspired truth." According to Paul's first letter to Timothy, chapter 3, the church is "the house of God," "the pillar and ground of truth," which "stands to lighten the world concerning Time and Eternity; Men and God; and Christ the Mediator." [961] As the house of God, the church becomes God's dwelling place on earth in which He is fitting believers for His heavenly kingdom, and through which He is demonstrating to the world that He has sent Christ to be the Saviour of men.[962]

This "truth" of which the church is the repository, guardian, and steward is a mystery to the world until it is opened to them by the Spirit through the church. When this mystery is opened by the Spirit, it is plainly seen to center in the person of Christ. Thus the church exists to make Christ known to men and to bring them into a saving relation to Him.[963]

> How necessary it is for the church to hold close to its own business!... Salvation from hell hereafter, and from sin here, is the high calling and divine purpose of the Church of the Lord Jesus Christ. The radiance... this pillar of Truth may shine upon these other matters is but a side light of reflection. Man may get enough from learning and experience to help him in things that are merely worldly for himself; but to glorify God in his life here and reach the true end of his being, he needs the Truth as it is in Jesus—and the stewardship hereof is committed to the Spirit-indwelt Church of Christ.[964]

The church is also an "institute of worship." It exists to lead men into that "highest function of the human soul" which is the worship of the thrice-holy God.[965] To Smith worship was a larger than *time* or *place* or *form* consideration which men might attach to it. The spirit of worship was of supreme importance with him. According to his understanding of Scripture and experience, true worship is far removed from "the doleful, the sad, the depressing and the melancholic!" Rather it means gladness, singing, thanksgiving, and praise as one meditates upon God himself—His natural and moral attributes—and upon what He has done for men and given to them.[966]

Smith made much of the "means of grace" in worship, both in their private and public form, emphasizing the need of distinguishing between the means of grace and "the faith which obtains grace." [967] Basing his view upon Jesus' teaching in Matthew 12:1–8, Smith believed that "deeds of *mercy and necessity have precedence over ordinances of religion* in the will of God." [968] For him the spiritual relation to

God and the ethical relation to men are primary, and any ritual or ceremonial observances in worship were secondary in Christianity.

Smith believed that sacramental worship was intended to have both a subjective and an objective value for the Christian. As to the ordinance of the Lord's Supper, it was to symbolize both the death of Christ and the soul's feeding upon Christ as the source and sustenance of its spiritual life. It was also a symbol prophetic of Christ's second coming. "Humanity is so constructed, and still so much like children, that we need pictures and symbols to show us truths and memorials *lest we forget*." [969]

Pointing out in Acts, chapter 8, Philip's *"conservatism about water baptism,"* Smith strongly emphasized the "prior importance of faith in Christ for salvation," if the rite itself was to be significant and a means of grace. Whether following the mode of sprinkling or pouring or immersion, he held that baptism in itself was neither meritorious nor absolutely essential to salvation, as evidenced by the death of the dying thief to whom Christ promised a place in Paradise without any sacrament. [970]

The theologian herein studied looked upon the church not only as a repository of inspired truth by which God reached downward to man and as an institute of worship through which man reaches upward to God, but also as an "institute of evangelism" through which God and redeemed lives reach outward to the world of men.

Having accepted Dr. S. A. Keen's definition of evangelism—"Evangelism is the precipitation of salvation"—Smith viewed the church as God's means of bringing together the saving Christ and the lost world, thereby making immediate salvation available to the world. [971] Nor is this ministry of the church merely a formal function; rather, it is the life passion and desire of the new life in Christ to want to save others. Evangelism is the natural functioning of the spiritual life received from Christ. [972]

Individual Christians or the church have not yet reached

their "chief end, nor fulfilled the glory of God," when they themselves are "saved by the vicarious sacrifice of Jesus." The "final object of Christ's grace" in believers is to get others saved through them who have found righteousness and true holiness in Christ.[973]

Smith held that the *"two greatest arts of which men are capable"* are intercession and evangelism. To excel in these two is the calling and obligation of the church.[974] "In *Evangelism* one by the help of the Spirit is able to bring men to God. In *intercession* one may prevail and bring God to men. And one need not be a theologian or a prophet to do this."[975]

Smith sought to correct what he believed to be two basic errors in current views of evangelism. The first error is that evangelism is to be confined to those who have been especially separated for the work of special evangelism. Smith cited Paul's exhortation to Timothy to do the work of an evangelist (even though Timothy was to administer the affairs of the church) as his spiritual evidence that whatever place one has in the church, it is to be employed as a means to further the work of evangelism. The second error is the view that evangelism is to be limited to the winning of converts, or at best to winning converts and Christian believers to entire sanctification.[976]

> The function of an evangelist applies to every truth of the Gospel, just as the experiential knowledge applies to every truth. The work of an evangelist applies to every grace as well as to the great epochs. Now to put it this way, if I am preaching on the word *grace*, or patience or benevolence, I am not...to be content, beloved, unless they have received patience and benevolence, etc. I am not to be content unless...I have precipitated the truth into their hearts. That gives you some idea how the work of an evangelist extends through the whole line of Christian work and to everyone.[977]

Evangelism aims at immediacy or the bringing of souls to act then and there upon the gospel truth they have received. Unless immediate acceptance of and obedience to the truth is pressed, the enemies of gospel truth snatch it away and little is assimilated to have a gradual and ultimate effect upon individuals. Evangelism presses for immediate decision. "It believes in crisis." [978]

Smith further believed that Christ also instituted the church to exert a savory salt-like influence upon the world that it might stay its degeneracy. But the church's savoring function and its leavening power to raise civilization to higher levels are the by-products of the church's direct evangelistic outreach. For the church, however, to become directly absorbed in the "world's interests, activities and concerns" and make them the church's program is to default on what the Lord *sent* the church to do and also to fail in that which she is *attempting* to do.[979] The modern church's absorption in current civic issues, he claimed, has demonstrated two things:

> (1) That the turning of the churches from the souls of men to the problems of society has not solved these problems.
> (2) That this leaving of the Word of God to serve tables has famished the flock of God and has left not only the outside world without the light of life, but many that are "masters in Israel" and experts in religious politics "know not these things" that are essential for entrance into the kingdom of God.[980]

But when the church majors upon her mission of ministering personal holiness, urged Smith, "good citizenship, right social conditions and proper stand on the right side of public moral questions are assured." [981] In proportion as the church lowers the gospel standard of righteousness, the world becomes more confused and wicked.[982] When the church substitutes reform in society for redemption unto righteousness in human nature, it is seeking an end without sufficient means. Asked Smith, "How can an unsanctified church effect a *millennial like* civilization?" [983] On the basis of Luke 6: 39–49, he affirmed:

> Now the Saviour makes it plain and very emphatic here that *all such zeal for the moral betterment of society that is in excess of zeal* for the purification of one's own heart is *hypocrisy*....
>
> Self-purification must have priority over civil or social reformation.... It is not in the nature of the case that the civil reform shall partake of the righteousness of the Kingdom if its agent is not himself righteous in life and holy in heart.... Our human nature if "yet carnal" will taint and blight all our efforts at the betterment of others.[984]

While the church may serve as leaven in the dough of society to raise its ideals and morals, its standards of living and its control of evil, yet that is not the kingdom of Christ. "His kingdom, of which the best possible Christian civilization here can be but an earnest and a taste," is yet to be manifested at His second coming.[985] Therefore, the highest ambition of the church "in Christian culture and in Christian work should be to acquire and distribute means" whereby the Holy Spirit may be aided in all of His ministries of striving, illuminating, regenerating, witnessing, sanctifying, energizing, guiding, and fortifying human souls until Christ returns.[986]

The Faith of the Church. Believing his generation had placed too much emphasis upon doubt, Smith labored to minister faith to his hearers both in its creedal and character aspects. In regard to its doctrinal content, Smith held that the faith of the church must be *evangelical*. According to him, the Apostles' Creed was basic, if not inclusive of all essential, to the Christian faith.[987]

> Nothing short of the truth of Christ can move men's hearts from sin or hold them to righteousness. Hence the Evangelist... must have the mind of God upon Sin, upon Judgment, upon Present Probation and Future Destiny, upon the Deity of Christ, the Atonement of His Death, upon the Holy Spirit, and Holiness, and upon the Church and her Mission and God's great purpose in the World.
>
> And his perception of these things should be di-

rected, sustained and corroborated by a knowledge of the didactic, historic and prophetic Scriptures.[988]

If scripturally derived and spiritually discerned, the faith of the church, thought Smith, would set forth the concept of holiness as "the central point into which all the rays of the gospel converge."[989] As the central idea of Christianity,

> Holiness is the hub of the wheel. Many other good things, as Prohibition, war on white slavery, proper education, Near East Relief, etc., are like spokes to the wheel; but, holiness is the hub.... And the fact is, too [sic] that no one of the spokes is of any account, at least as part of the wheel—unless it be fitted in properly and joined tightly to the hub. Hence... sofar as salvation and heaven and eternal reward are concerned, and the real glory of Christ, all such other matters as we have mentioned are useless, save as they are properly related to holiness.[990]

But the faith of the church must be experiential inasmuch as the cornerstone of the church is the "spiritual knowledge of Christ as the Son of God."[991] Herein lies the character aspect of faith. "Creed will control the course of life, fix the character of the man, and determine his destiny."[992] Therefore, thought Smith, it is a matter of eternal import what one believes about God, about man, about sin, about Christ, and about redemption.

Rejecting the idea that Christian faith is something to be gradually and personally evolved in the experience of each individual, Smith urged that the ministry give special attention to its responsibility to "minister" faith to men since faith, both for forgiveness of sins and perfection of love, comes by hearing God's Word on these matters. The Pauline commission in Acts, chapter 26, suggested to Smith "the basal place of a *full Gospel* in the Christian system" of faith.[993]

Without experiential faith in Christ, issuing in the new birth, thought Smith, no one is a member of the true body of Christ and should not be admitted to the membership of the visible church. This transforming faith, to be a reality, is a work of the Spirit, a work of the minister of divine truth, and a work of the believer in Christ.[994]

Convinced that an evangelical and experiential Christian faith will also be ethically expressed, Smith warned against zeal for "the *work* of Holiness" which would divert one from "the *life* of Holiness."[995]

> This does not require simply adherence to righteousness, as to honesty, truthfulness, and cleanness in our conversation. Common citizenship requires this: and surely repentance, regeneration and justification will assure such consistency. But the experience of Holiness stands for more—much more than this. Our testimony to this state lays claim to PATIENCE under trial, MEEKNESS under oppression, QUIETNESS midst contention, and to PEACEFULNESS as well as PEACEABLENESS at all times. And not only so, but KINDNESS, ungrudging FORGIVENESS, continuous CONTENTMENT, and ceaseless THANKSGIVING and PRAISE.[996]

To realize its mission, the church's faith must ever be evangelistic. Its objective is the souls of men everywhere. When the church possesses experientially the evangelical faith, the following, claimed Smith, results: "Missions and mission field evangelism are the normal outflow of the rivers of living water from Spirit-filled hearts, whether of ministers, churches or humble individual Christians!"[997]

The church achieves unity of spirit, if not in organization, when she becomes holy in nature through the transforming power of an experiential evangelicalism at its deepest level. "Holiness with its Perfect Love and...its one Spirit in Christ erases all divisive boundary lines from between true Christians."[998] When the church loses herself in the supreme task of soul-saving, sectarianism and proselytism fade away, and denominationalism is regarded as so many "different rooms opening into the one great court of the Lord," or as the several regiments in the one great Christian army.[999]

The church's faith is inescapably *eschatological*. "And the Book of Revelation fore-announces the greatest of all social events of the universe as the *Marriage of the Lamb, for whom his wife has made herself ready* (Revelation 19)." With Christ's love for His church likened unto the nature and quality of marital love, the church's faith in a glorious consummation to her probation is as natural, thought Smith, as for human courtship to anticipate and be climaxed in marriage.[1000]

The Failure of the Church. Smith held the church's failure moved along a definitely discernible line of decline. The church's first departure from her essential genius is at the point of Christian experience of spirituality. With the loss of spirituality the evangelistic passion or soul-winning concern soon wanes. Following the forfeit of spirituality and soul-winning, the church is then in danger of departing from "sound doctrine." "The decline of the church, together with that of the world *in morals*, keeps pace (at rapid step) with *the absence of doctrinal preaching* from the pulpit, the displacement of the Apostles' Creed from many of the rituals."[1001] With the departure from scriptural teaching, the ethical standards of Christianity are weakened, and the social influence of the church fades.[1002] According to Smith's interpretation, if the church fails at the spiritual level; if she loses the fervor for the immortal souls of men, the truth (doctrine) by which they are saved seems less significant and is more easily exchanged for heretical or non-Christian views. "Yet... these manifold failures of men under the gospel... do not argue nor involve *the failure of the gospel itself*."[1003]

The Future of the Church. The hope of the church within history and beyond it received considerable attention in Smith's ministry. Within his day Smith still looked for another great revival of Christianity. Basing his expectation upon the dispensational interpretation of the Holy Spirit's ministry and upon the power of prayer, Smith taught that revivalism within the church and aggressive evangelism among the unchurched would effectively appear again in Christendom.[1004]

But Smith held out no hope of the church successfully converting all individuals to Christianity. He stressed an every-creature evangelism but did not believe the Scriptures prophesied a universal Christianizing of society before the second coming of Christ.[1005]

The *patient* waiting for the coming of Christ keeps the church's gaze upon the future. "There can be no perfect Christianity that omits or overlooks or slights the future things of Christ's Gospel." [1006] The future includes resurrection and reward for the righteous, with regal powers imparted for ruling and judging with Christ in God's moral universe.[1007]

The Glory of God Manifested Anew: The Restored Glory of Man

The Two Hemispheres of Glory

Smith's view of Christian thought under the caption of "the Gospel of grace and glory" included "both a heavenly and an earthly hemisphere of glory." Without the celestial fulfillment of God's purposes, the terrestrial glory of God in creation, providence, and redemption would be incomplete.[1008]

In the earthly life of believers the glory of redeeming grace has begun, but in the heavenly hemisphere God will share His glory with the redeemed in such a way as to cause "the glory of God and the true glory of man to converge into one." Only in realms celestial, where the third major stage of salvation is effected, will the chief end of man be realized. Smith called that state final salvation or *glorification*.[1009]

He believed that the glory of grace, realizable in this life by faith through the birth of the Spirit and the baptism with the Spirit, is but "the profile of the glory" which awaits the church at the coming again of the Lord Jesus Christ. The glory that is now available is analogous in three ways to the glory which shall be revealed at the second advent of Christ: (1) both center in beholding the glory of the Lord—one by faith, the other by sight; (2) both result in the believer's transformation—one moral and the other a physical one; and (3) both require a supernatural deliverance and, therefore, both are called redemption—one redemption from the penalty and pollution of sin, the other from the presence and the scars of sin.[1010]

The Glorious Appearing of Christ

Smith interpreted the Scriptures as revealing Deity not only in His pre-creational existence and in His creative, providential, and redemptive activities within history, but also in His termination of history and inauguration of a post-temporal, eternal future. He urged that Biblical prophecies pointed not only to an end of time, but also to the end of the present order of earth and the heavens.[1011]

> ...there has never been any uncertainty as to the revelation of *the fact* of the Second Coming of Christ. And while Scripture is silent as to the day and the hour of his appearing it is nevertheless explicit and emphatic...that *"He will come again."* "He will come *as the disciples saw Him go."* His coming will consummate the dispensation of man's probation and *usher in the great and notable day of the Lord....* His appearing will be *sudden* as the *lightening* [sic].
> His coming will be as *unexpected and unprepared for by the world* as was *Noah's flood.* While its immediateness is nowhere declared its *imminence* is so everywhere impressed that we are neither fanatical or irrational in assuming and asserting that *it may be soon.*[1012]

To Smith the signs of the approaching end of time, consummated by the coming of Christ, seemed to have multiplied during his lifetime. Earthquakes, continued war between nations, human perplexities, delusions, false christs, and atheism moved him to declare in 1927 that the end would be soon. While impressed by the progress of science, Smith nevertheless taught that Christ will no more respect Gentile constructions than He respected the Jewish temple when He declared: "Not one stone shall be left upon another." [1013]

Unlike some of Smith's closest colleagues, he did not set forth a milliennial view in connection with his doctrine on the second advent of Christ. To this investigator, Smith seems to have come closer to the a-millennial than to either the pre-millennial or post-millennial position. For him the millennial issue was insignificant compared to the fact and certain accompaniments of Christ's personal visible sudden return in the clouds of heaven with power and great glory.[1014]

Glorified in His Saints. To the believer "the glorious appearing" of Christ is the *blessed hope* of the Christian life. It will be an hour of a fuller revelation of God in Christ, of divine glory in which redeemed man is to share, and of the believers themselves. During the church age the believer's true life has been hidden, his motives often misjudged and his person mistreated; but in that day he shall be revealed with his Lord to the world of unbelievers.[1015] Everyone who has died in the faith will be bodily resurrected and, in a "glorified body," will live with Christ forevermore. To the living believer at Christ's coming, there shall be an Enoch-like and Elijah-like translation from the terrestrial to the celestial body which will occur at the moment Christ appears.[1016] That bodily redemption will give the believer a body fashioned like unto Christ's own glorious body, which is now immortalized and incorruptible. In that state "not only 'sickness and sorrow, but pain and death are felt and feared no more.'"[1017]

The state of glorification will further mean to the believer, according to Smith, (1) "deliverance from the presence and power of the wicked one and his allies"; (2) the crowning of life and righteousness by fixing, establishing, and empowering the believer "beyond all contingency forevermore"; (3) the manifestation and completion of the believer's union with his Lord in holiness; (4) union with believers of all generations and especially loved ones who have died in the faith; (5) the reward for faithful service during time by an "increased trust and power in the glorious kingdom," involving "a peculiar and glorious relationship" with those whom one has been instrumental in redeeming; and (6) the seeing of Christ as He really is, which is "the crown of glory." [1018] Of that climactic event, Smith wrote, "Every vestige of our fallen estate, and our former unfittedness for Him or lack of harmony, or need of adjustment has vanished.... We not only are His, but we are made one with Him for-ever." [1019] Full-fledged believers will have boldness at Christ's coming again (in judgment) because their hearts, having been perfected in love, are made free from fear of God's righteous judgment.[1020]

Judgment Against Sinners. As the deceased believer will be resurrected to everlasting life at Christ's return, so the unbelieving dead will be resurrected to "condemnation and oblivion," to contempt and eternal separation from the life-giving Christ. To both the resurrected sinner and the living unbeliever Christ's appearing will be "a revelation of the righteousness and of the wrath of God ... a vindication of the Divine government and character before all the nations." [1021]

> It will convince all the ungodly of all their ungodly deeds and will clear the Divine government in judging the unrighteous. This shining forth from His righteous throne will reveal the heart and the lives of men... and the punishment of evilworkers will commend itself to all by this revelation of everlasting righteousness; ....[1022]

Relating the idea of judgment to that of holiness which Smith held as central to all theology, he affirmed:

> Judgment truth is close akin to Holiness Truth. It is the burning thought of a future judgment that impels one to a holy life in the present. All human history will be reviewed at that day, and every man's case passed upon in the light of *where* he has lived and *when* and *how* ... men shall be judged according to their nations, times, light and opportunities, and according to their generation.[1023]

Smith's emphasis upon the judgment-to-come did not include as definite a distinction between the *time* and the *order* of the judging of Christians to determine their eternal reward and the judging of the living nations at Christ's return, and the judging of angels who fell from their original state of holiness, and the judgment of ungodly men of all centuries of human history, as some millenarian "fundamentalists" have made.[1024]

Smith made much of "the wrath of the Lamb" in portraying the last judgment and Christ as the final arbiter in the destiny of human souls.

> ...THE WRATH OF THE LAMB, it is founded upon faith both in the nature of Christ and in the government of God, and stands supported by the trenchant truth of revelation and the words of Christ himself.
> Surely as was the Curse of the Creator pronounced upon the ground which He himself had made but man had defiled, and surely as the curse of the Law-giver was pronounced upon him that continued not in all the commandments of the Law to do them, so, indeed, is the Curse of the Savior yet to be pronounced upon them that reject and neglect this great Salvation He has bought.[1025]

Smith held that "the curse of Christ" was identical with what Paul called "everlasting destruction from the presence of God and from the glory of his power." He taught that such "punishment" was not simply the consequence of wrong-doing working itself out in human personality, but the direct punishment of sin through penalties determined and "administered by sovereign edict." "It is assignment to the domain of a different and new demoniacal order of beings, 'hell prepared for the devil and his angels.' And it is forever. 'These shall go away into EVERLASTING punishment.' "[1026]

The Glorious Kingdom of Christ

For Smith the Christian hope of Christ's appearing would mean not *the setting up* of His kingdom but the glorious manifestation of His kingdom long since set up. Recognizing that this view was not easily made clear to many students of Scripture, Smith nevertheless affirmed that three things concerning Christ were increasingly clear to him:

> (1) That already "all power is given unto Him in heaven and in earth." "That He is now highly exalted at the right hand of the Father, far above all principality and power." "God ... hath put all things under His feet." (2) "But now we see not yet all things put under Him." This universal reign of Christ upon His mediatorial throne is a matter of faith rather than of sight even to His own devout followers, and the world does not recognize it at all. (3) Christ's coming shall not only bring to light the hidden things of darkness with respect to men's motives and conduct, but it will reveal or manifest His own kingdom, so that the recognition of it will be as universal as its power. A revelation this which ... will be the joy and glory of His own.[1027]

At that future day the believers will be as dependent upon the royal, kingly office of Christ as they have been dependent upon His past prophetic ministry and sacrificial work, and as they are *now* upon His priestly office carried on on His mediatorial throne at the Father's right hand.[1028] But Christ will share His throne of glory with the redeemed who have suffered in this world for righteousness' sake.

> As He is set down with the Father upon His throne, we shall sit with Him on His throne.
>
> Angels and archangels and all the host of heaven ... as they worship God and the Lamb, will rejoice to serve us who have washed our robes and made them white in the blood of the Lamb.

> We shall have stations and areas, and honors together with riches of treasure...in reward pro rata to the faithfulness and fruitfulness of our kingdom service here.[1029]

When Christ shall have banished *death*, the last enemy of mankind, "by a resurrection as universal as death has been," and after a dissolution of the earth and heavens that now are in order to usher in "the new heavens and the new earth wherein dwelleth righteousness," Christ the Son will "return the Kingdom of the cleansed world to the Father" that the Father may be "all in all" in the ages to come.[1030]

Smith held that God had foreordained "the things of the Spirit" for believers in this dispensation—making His acquaintance, fellowship, and indwelling a reality here and now—in order "to qualify and fit" them "for the environment of the skies, the company of angels and occupation with God and all the heavenly hosts in His ceaseless exploits of love throughout the infinite domain of His universe."[1031]

Forever united with Christ by creational and redemptive ties, glorified men enter upon their eternal destiny to find their chief end realized in glorifying God and enjoying Him forever. At that level and under that mode of celestial existence God's glory and man's have converged and become identical.[1032]

CHAPTER EIGHT

Summary

THE DISTINCTIVENESS OF THIS STUDY

To the present time no official history of the National Holiness Association has been written; consequently, neither the reading public nor serious students have had full access to the historical antecedents of a "movement" which has sustained a uniquely American institution—the camp meeting—during an era in American Protestantism which it was almost entirely abandoned by the older denominations. This movement has unceasingly emphasized year-around evangelism, given birth to numerous educational institutions, occasioned the publishing of several religious periodicals and a large body of devotional and doctrinal literature which have helped to influence pietistically and ecumenically (in spirit) a segment of America's religious life. It has championed some reforms, and zealously promoted home and foreign missionary endeavor.

Just as the historical literature of the movement has been meager so the biographical and autobiographical productions of its members have been inadequate for a representative presentation of its accredited leaders to those unacquainted with these modern "sons" of John Wesley. Standing midway between the original members of the National Camp-meeting Association for the Promotion of Holiness (formed in 1867) and the contemporary leaders of the National Holiness Association, Joseph H. Smith was chronologically related to the movement as no other man has been. Having been regarded by his most popular colleagues as the foremost expositor-evangelist of the movement, Smith's theology may be looked upon as representative of the religious thinking of sizable groups in American Protestantism holding membership in scores of different denominations.

Summary

Claiming that doctrinal Christianity issued from the person Christ and that in this life Christ can be experienced in the heart by faith, no part of Smith's theology was without its experiential aspect and reference. Whatever came in for theological consideration between the divine purposes before creation and the ultimate will of deity beyond the last judgment, Smith related all to an inseparable union of the "Christ for us" and of the "Christ in us" verities which turned doctrine into discipline, belief into performance, and an objective, future salvation into a subjective, present one, manifesting itself in daily, practical morality.

Central to the whole of his system was the thought of holiness—holiness in God, in angels, in original man, in redeemed man and in the society of the eternal future. Like Wesley he presented Christianity as essentially a religion of salvation from sin, experientially available to *all* men *by faith* in Jesus Christ but to be successively appropriated as justification, entire sanctification, and glorification. Denying that entire sanctification is received at regeneration, and declaring that it may be experienced before death, Smith's strong emphasis was upon the instantaneousness of entire sanctification by an act of faith and the patient persistence in that grace by a fixed attitude of faith. Holding that each work of divine grace is in some degree a foretaste of and analogous to the next degree of salvation to be obtained, Smith incessantly held out the inescapable necessity for progress and advancement from faith to faith, from grace to grace, from victory to victory, and from glory to glory in the Christian life.

Relying upon the Scriptures as historically trustworthy, as prophetically reliable, and as the only infallible guide for faith and practice, Smith did not anticipate an easy or universal victory for Christianity in the world. He rather portrayed an extensive rejection of Christianity—in spirit not in form—as a climactic feature of this gospel dispensation. He did not anticipate the Christianizing of society or an earthly Utopia through the teaching of the gospel, but rather the intensifying of the spirit of antichrist until the second advent of Christ who would forcibly put down all forms of spiritual, moral, and social evil, and usher in His everlasting reign in righteousness over the new heaven and the new earth. With the manifestation of the latter, the glory of man's recovered likeness to God in character (which was originally forfeited in Eden) is crowned with the glory of eternal fellowship with the Godhead, holy angels, and redeemed men in the grandeurs of a redeemed universe.

Appendix A

CONFERENCE MEMOIR[1034]

"Joseph H. Smith was born June 4, 1855. He married Sallie A. Markle in his early twenties. In his twenty-seventh year he was admitted by Bishop E. G. Andrews into the Philadelphia Conference, with sessions being held in Frankford, Philadelphia, March 15–21, 1882. His first appointment was Raubsville, then Cherry Valley, Lahaska, and Marshallton. The brethren early discovered his ability as an evangelist, and, in 1887, he was granted the supernumerary relation in order to engage exclusively in evangelistic labors. In 1901 he was given the title of Conference Evangelist, which he held until his retirement in 1923.

"Not long after his entry into the office of conference evangelist his wife died, and as his labors carried him across the nation, he changed his address from Pennsylvania, to Indiana and even later to California, where he followed his boyhood hero, William Taylor of Virginia. So Redlands, California, was his 'home' for many years.

"He was remarried December 6, 1908, to Jean Kincaid who survives him, as do his children: a preacher son, J. Hunter Smith; a doctor son, John J. Smith; a missionary daughter, Grace Smith; and a married daughter, Mrs. B. A. Flynn.

"Brother Smith always preached a constructive and upbuilding Gospel, never indulging in censorious criticism of the Church or its ministry. He was a living example of the Wesleyan doctrine of Christian Perfection which he stressed. As men of our Annual Conference have attested, no one ever gave a clearer message on this doctrine. His messages were never queer. They were scriptural and plain, and he excelled in the expository type of preaching. At other times, his speech was always seasoned with grace and wisdom. He was ever upon the quest for souls, yet, as duly eager for the believer's growth in grace. The Lord of the Harvest richly rewarded his abundant labors with a great multitude of souls 'washed in the Blood of the Lamb,' receiving pardon and purity.

"Across the nation, the term, 'School of the Prophets' is associated with his name. To multiplied scores it meant a time of imbibing rare and rich spiritual morsels of truth from God's Word which developed and matured their spiritual lives. A great host will rise up 'in the land that is fairer than day' to call him blessed. His name is also associated with the Friday Holiness Meeting of Philadelphia which was always well attended and added to the spiritual tone of the churches, and is remembered by the names of Drs. E. I. D. Pepper, John Thompson, Alfred Cookman, and George M. Brodhead.

"Joseph H. Smith died, April 8, 1946. Funeral services were held in the First Methodist Church of Redlands, California, with the Revs. Charles H. Babcock, Fred H. Ross, and local pastors of the Methodist, Nazarene, and Presbyterian churches participating. Internment was in the Hillside Cemetery in Redlands."

Appendix B

SCHOOLS, COLLEGES AND SEMINARIES CURRENTLY AUXILIARY TO THE CHRISTIAN HOLINESS ASSOCIATION

Name	Location
Aldersgate College	Moose Jaw, Saskatchewan, Canada
Asbury College	Wilmore, Kentucky
Asbury Theological Seminary	Wilmore, Kentucky
Azusa Pacific College	Azusa, California
Bartlesville Wesleyan College	Bartlesville, Oklahoma
Bethany Bible College	Sussex, New Brunswick, Canada
Bethany Nazarene College	Bethany, Oklahoma
Bethel College	Mishawaka, Indiana
Brainerd Indian School	Hot Springs, South Dakota
Canadian Nazarene College	Winnipeg, Manitoba, Canada
Central College	Central, South Carolina
Circleville Bible College	Circleville, Ohio
Eastern Nazarene College	Wollaston, Massachusetts
Emmanuel Bible College	Kitchener, Ontario, Canada
George Fox College	Newberg, Oregon
God's Bible School	Cincinnati, Ohio
Greenville College	Greenville, Illinois
Houghton Academy	Houghton, New York
Houghton College	Houghton, New York
John Wesley College	Greensboro, North Carolina
Kentucky Mountain Bible Institute	Vancleve, Kentucky
Malone College	Canton, Ohio
Marion College	Marion, Indiana
Messiah College	Grantham, Pennsylvania
Mid-America Nazarene College	Olathe, Kansas
Mountain View Bible College	Didsbury, Alberta, Canada
Mount Carmel High School	Vancleve, Kentucky
Mount Vernon Nazarene College	Mount Vernon, Ohio

Nazarene Bible College	Colorado Springs, Colorado
Nazarene Theological Seminary	Kansas City, Missouri
Niagara Christian College	Port Erie, Ontario, Canada
Northwest Nazarene College	Nampa, Idaho
Olivet Nazarene College	Kankakee, Illinois
Point Loma College (formerly Pasadena College)	San Diego, California
Roberts Wesleyan College	North Chili, New York
Salvation Army	
Officers' Training School (Central)	Chicago, Illinois
Officers' Training School (Eastern)	Suffern, New York
Officers' Training School (Southern)	Atlanta, Georgia
Officers' Training School (Western)	San Francisco, California
Seattle Pacific College	Seattle, Washington
Spring Arbor College	Spring Arbor, Michigan
Taylor University	Upland, Indiana
Trevecca Nazarene College	Nashville, Tennessee
United Wesleyan College	Allentown, Pennsylvania
Vennard College	University Park, Iowa
Western Evangelical Seminary	Portland, Oregon

Appendix C

HOLINESS PERIODICALS

The Advocate of Christian Holiness	Consolidated with *The Christian Witness*
The American Holiness Journal	Still published
Banner of Holiness	Discontinued
Banner of Zion	Discontinued
Beulah Christian	Consolidated with *Herald of Holiness*
Beulah Items	Discontinued
The Beauty of Holiness	Consolidated with *Guide to Holiness*
The Best Life	Discontinued
The Bible Christian	Discontinued
The Christian Apologist	Discontinued
Christian Harvester	Discontinued
The Christian Standard and Home Journal	Consolidated with *The Christian Witness*
The Christian Voice	Discontinued
The Christian Witness	Still published
Christian Worker	Discontinued
The Contribution	Discontinued
Das Evangelische Magazin	Discontinued
Divine Life and International Expositor of Scriptural Holiness	Discontinued
The Evangelist	Discontinued
Fire and Hammer	Discontinued
Friends' Expositor	Discontinued
German Guide to Holiness	Discontinued
God's Revivalist	Still published
The Good Way	Discontinued
Guide to Holiness	Consolidated with *The Christian Witness*
Heart and Life Magazine	Still published

The Harvester	Discontinued
The Herald	Until recently, *The Pentecostal Herald*
The Herald of Full Salvation	Discontinued
Herald of Holiness	Still published
The Highway and Banner	Discontinued
Highway and Hedges	Discontinued
Highway of Holiness	Discontinued
Holiness Evangel	Discontinued
The Holiness Movement	Discontinued
The Kingdom	Discontinued
The King's Messenger	Discontinued
Lamp of Life	Discontinued
Line and Plummet	Discontinued
The Living Epistle	Discontinued
The Meridian Messenger	Discontinued
The Methodist Monthly	Discontinued
Nazarene Messenger	Consolidated with *Herald of Holiness*
The Ocean Grove Record	Discontinued
The Pacific Pentecost	Discontinued
The Pentecost Century	Discontinued
The Pentecostal Era	Discontinued
The Pentecostal Evangel	Discontinued
Penuel, An Advocate of Scriptural Holiness	Discontinued
Purity Journal	Discontinued
Ram's Horn	Discontinued
Salvation News	Discontinued
The Soul Winner	Discontinued
The Southern Methodist Home Altar	Discontinued
Standard of Holiness	Still published
Tennessee Methodist	Discontinued
Texas Holiness Advocate	Discontinued
Texas Holiness Banner	Discontinued
The Times of Refreshing	Discontinued
Triumphs of Faith	Discontinued
The Way of Faith	Consolidated with *The Pentecostal Herald*
The Way of Life	Discontinued
Zion's Outlook	Discontinued

Appendix D

CONSTITUTION OF THE CHRISTIAN HOLINESS ASSOCIATION

MOTTO

"I am, O Lord, wholly and forever Thine."—John S. Inskip

ARTICLE I

Name

The name of this organization shall be CHRISTIAN HOLINESS ASSOCIATION

ARTICLE II

Jurisdiction

The jurisdiction of the Association shall extend to any country, state or territory where qualified persons or organizations may desire to affiliate with the Association.

ARTICLE III

Purpose

Section 1: The purpose of this Association shall be to effect the closest possible fellowship and cooperation among all denominations, religious organizations, and associations, educational institutions, individual churches, and persons who are in accord with the Statement of Faith of this Association and the Wesleyan position on Scriptural Holiness; and further, to secure the conversion of sinners, the entire sanctification of believers as a second definite work of grace, to promote a spiritual awakening, and to seek generally to edify the body of Christ.

Section 2: This Association shall not organize churches, work in opposition to any church, or support the interest of any one church, denomination or organization above another.

ARTICLE IV
Statement of Faith

The Christian Holiness Association is a body of churches, organizations, and individuals who accept the inspiration and infallibility of sacred Scripture and the evangelical doctrine that pertains to divine revelation, the incarnation, the resurrection, the second coming of Christ, the Holy Spirit, and the Church as affirmed in the historic Christian creeds. The particular concern of this fellowship is the biblical doctrine of sanctification identified historically in what is known as the Wesleyan position.

The Association believes that personal salvation includes both the new birth and entire sanctification wrought by God in the heart by faith. Entire sanctification is a crisis experience subsequent to conversion which results in a heart cleansed from all sin and filled with the Holy Spirit. This grace is witnessed to by the Holy Spirit. It is maintained by that faith which expresses itself in constant obedience to God's revealed will and results in a moment-by-moment cleansing.

ARTICLE V
Associate Relationships

The constituents of this Association shall be organizational and individual associates.

Section 1: Organizational Associates. Denominations, conferences/districts, individual churches, educational institutions, interdenominational associations, camp meetings or non-denominational organizations, who agree with the objectives and Statement of Faith of the Association may, upon application and subsequent approval of the Board of Administration, affiliate with the Association.

An organizational associate shall be represented in the Annual Convention and on the Board of Administration by the highest level judicatory in associate relationship from that affiliate body.

Section 2: Individual Associates. Any individual who is in accord with the objectives and Statement of Faith of this Association may become a member upon application with the subsequent approval of the Board of Administration and payment of annual dues.

Section 3: This Association reserves the right to take action upon the acceptance or rejection of any individual, or organization at any time for due cause.

ARTICLE VI

Organization

Section 1: Annual Convention. The Annual Convention is the highest authority of the Christian Holiness Association. The delegate members from constituent groups of the Association, the Association officers, and members of the Board of Administration shall constitute the voting body of the Annual Convention. It shall organize itself to transact the business of the Association, and elect those officers necessary for the operation of the Association.

Section 2: Board of Administration. There shall be a Board of Administration which shall have authority to transact all business in the interim between the Annual Conventions.

Section 3: Executive Committee. There shall be an Executive Committee which shall act in the interim between the meetings of the Board of Administration.

Section 4: Board of Directors. There shall be a Board of Directors which shall manage the corporate affairs of the Association in accordance with the charter of the said corporation, a California corporation on file with the Secretary of State, and the County Clerk of Los Angeles County, and the Bylaws of the same which are on file in the national office of the Association.

Section 5: Debts. The private property of members is exempt from corporate debts.

ARTICLE VII

Amendments

These articles may be amended upon the majority vote of the membership present and voting at any Annual Convention, except Article IV, Statement of Faith, and Article V, Membership, which shall require a two-thirds vote of the membership present and voting, provided that any proposed change shall have been submitted in writing to the membership at the previous convention.

Member Denominations of CHA

Brethren in Christ
Church of the Nazarene
Churches of Christ in Christian Union
Evangelical Church of North America
Evangelical Friends Alliance
Evangelical Methodist Church
Free Methodist Church of North America
Holiness Christian Church of USA
The Salvation Army of Canada
The Salvation Army in the United States
The Wesleyan Church

Cooperating Denominations

The Church of God (Anderson)
Congregational Methodist Church
The Holiness Methodist Church
Methodist Protestant Church
Primitive Methodist Church

Inter-Denominational Missionary Agencies

OMS International, Inc.
World Gospel Mission

Footnotes

CHAPTER ONE

1. R. N. Flew, *The Idea of Perfection*, p. xiii; W. E. Sangster, *The Path to Perfection*, p. 7.
2. William R. Cannon, *The Theology of John Wesley*, p. 13.
3. Elmer T. Clark, *The Small Sects in America*, rev. ed., pp. 72–74; William W. Sweet, *The Story of Religion in America;* William W. Sweet, *Revivalism in America.*
4. J. B. Chapman, *Bud Robinson, A Brother Beloved*, p. 51.
5. C. W. Butler, Interview between author and, Detroit, Michigan, June 26, 1952.
6. Edwin A. Burtt, *Types of Religious Philosophy*, pp. 139–166, 455–458; Henry Nelson Wieman and Bernard Eugene Meland, *American Philosophies of Religion*, pp. 61–76.
7. Harald Lindstrom, *Wesley and Sanctification*, 1946; Adolph Koeberle, *The Quest for Holiness*, 1938; *et cetera.*
8. W. E. Sangster, *The Path to Perfection*, 1943; William R. Cannon, *The Theology of John Wesley*, 1946; *et cetera.*
9. The writings of a'Kempis, Fenelon, and Law have recently been reprinted.
10. George Allen Turner, *The More Excellent Way*, p. 17.
11. Flew, *op. cit.*, p. ix.
12. Walter M. Horton, *Toward a Reborn Church*, *passim.*
13. John Wesley, *Plain Account of Christian Perfection*, pp. 4–5.
14. Luke Tyerman, *Life and Times of the Reverend John Wesley, M.A.*, p. v.
15. Flew, *op. cit.*, p. xi.
16. All Biblical quotations in this study have been taken from the Authorized Version, 1611.
17. Joseph H. Smith, *Pauline Perfection*, pp. 27–32.
18. C. W. Butler, Interview between author and, Detroit, Michigan, June 26, 1952.
19. Smith, "A Letter About the Tongues' Movement," *Heart and Life*, April, 1927, pp. 12–14.
20. John Paul, "Memory Column," *Pentecostal Herald*, January 11, 1950, p. 5.
21. C. W. Butler, Interview between author and, Detroit, Michigan, June 26, 1952.
22. Smith, *From Glory to Glory*, *passim.*
23. *Ibid.*
24. *Ibid.*
25. *Ibid.*

CHAPTER TWO

26. J. L. Neve, *Churches and Sects of Christendom*, pp. 379–380.
27. William W. Sweet, *The Story of Religion in America*, p. 190.
28. William W. Sweet, *Methodism in America*, p. 35; George Allen Turner, *The Most Excellent Way*, p. 163, dates May 28, and Neve, *op. cit.*, dates it May 29.
29. Turner, *op. cit.*, p. 151f.; Wesley, *Plain Account of Christian Perfection*, pp. 3–4.
30. Turner, *op. cit.*, p. 152.
31. Sweet, *Methodism in America*, pp. 35–41.
32. Wesley, *op. cit.*, pp. 5–7.
33. *Ibid.*
34. *Ibid., passim.*
35. John Paul, "The Story of Scriptural Holiness," *The Christian Witness*, May 6, 1937, p. 8.
36. Halford E. Luccock and Paul Hutchinson, *The Story of Methodism*, 1926, *passim.*
37. Merrill E. Gaddis, "Christian Perfectionism in America," unpublished Ph.D. dissertation at the University of Chicago, June, 1929, pp. 217–218.
38. Wesley, *op. cit.*, p. 105.
39. Luccock and Hutchinson, *op. cit.*, p. 204.
40. Sweet, *Methodism in American History*, pp. 119–120.
41. Gaddis, *op. cit.*, p. 213.
42. *Ibid.*, pp. 207ff., 233.
43. Abel Stevens, *History of Methodist Episcopal Church*, vol. IV, p. 247.
44. Gaddis, *op. cit.*, pp. 241ff.
45. Luccock and Hutchinson, *op. cit.*, pp. 59–60.
46. O. P. Fitzgerald, *The Class-Meeting*, p. 33.
47. Wesley, *op. cit.*, p. 84.
48. Wesley, in J. A. Wood, *Christian Perfection as Taught by John Wesley*, p. 93; in Turner, *op. cit.*, p. 170.
49. Wood, *op. cit., passim.*
50. Sweet, *The Story of Religion in America*, p. 8.
51. *Ibid.*, pp. 329–331. The date of the first camp meeting is variously given. F. G. Beardsley, *A History of American Revivals*, p. 192, gives the year 1799; Paul H. Douglass, *The Story of German Methodism*, p. 90, has set 1796 as the date of the first camp meeting.
52. Paul H. Douglass, *The Story of German Methodism*, p. 90.
53. In 1849 one Methodist camp meeting preacher estimated "that four-fifths of all cases of entire sanctification among us are traceable, directly or indirectly, to this powerful instrument." *An Essay on Camp-Meetings*, p. 32.
54. Gaddis, *op. cit.*, pp. 375ff.
55. *Ibid.*
56. *Ibid.*
57. W. McDonald and John E. Searles, *The Life of Rev. John S. Inskip*, pp. 186ff.

FOOTNOTES

58. Luccock and Hutchinson, *op. cit.*, pp. 302, 403.
59. Gaddis, *op. cit.*, p. 437; Frank G. Beardsley, *A History of American Revivals*, pp. 202–203.
60. J. Edwin Orr, *The Second Evangelical Awakening in Britain*, pp. 126–127.
61. Luccock and Hutchinson, *op. cit.*, pp. 364–365.
62. Sweet, *Methodism in American History*, pp. 366–367.
63. George Hughes, *Fragrant Memories of the Tuesday Meeting and Guide to Holiness*, p. 164.
64. Henry B. Ridgaway, *The Life of Edmund S. Janes, D.D., L.L.D.*, pp. 292–299.
65. Richard Wheatley, *The Life and Letters of Mrs. Phoebe Palmer, passim*; A. M. Hills, *Holiness and Power, passim*.
66. Wheatley, *op. cit.*, pp. 13–14.
67. John A. Roche, *The Life of Mrs. Sarah A. Lankford Palmer*, pp. 17ff.
68. Sarah Worrall was born in New York City on April 23, 1806.
69. Roche, *op. cit.*, pp. 37–39, 109–111; Hughes, *op. cit.*, pp. 10–12.
70. *Supra*, p. 22.
71. Hughes, *op. cit.*, p. 12.
72. Phoebe was born in New York City, December 18, 1807; Walter C. Palmer was born February 9, 1804.
73. George Hughes, *The Beloved Physician*, pp. 18, 31.
74. *Ibid., passim.*
75. Wheatley, *op. cit.*, pp. 43–44.
76. *Ibid., passim.*
77. Hughes, *The Beloved Physician, passim.*
78. Wheatley, *op. cit., passim.*
79. *Ibid.*, pp. 237–239.
80. Hughes, *The Beloved Physician*, p. 28.
81. B. B. Warfield, *Studies in Perfectionism*, vol. II, p. 359.
82. Wheatley, *op. cit.*, pp. 518–523.
83. Warfield, *op. cit.*, p. 355.
84. Wheatley, *op. cit.*, pp. 247–248.
85. Quoted in Hughes, *Fragrant Memories*, pp. 38–42.
86. Roche, in Wheatley, *op. cit.*, pp. 248–249.
87. *Ibid.*, pp. 250–254.
88. *Ibid., passim*; Hughes, *Fragrant Memories, passim.*
89. Wheatley, *op. cit,, passim.*
90. *Ibid.*, p. 243.
91. Hughes, *Fragrant Memories*, p. 219.
92. "Rev. Timothy Merritt," *Advocate of Bible Holiness*, July 1882, pp. 193–195.
93. Merritt, in Hughes, *Fragrant Memories*, p. 166.
94. In *Fragrant Memories*, p. 171, Hughes claimed *The Guide to Christian Perfection* was the first magazine in history concerned chiefly with Christian holiness, whereas *The Oberlin Evangelist*, published as a perfectionist semi-monthly, began in November, 1838; see Warfield, *op. cit.*, pp. 7–8.

A THEOLOGY OF CHRISTIAN EXPERIENCE

95. Hughes, *Fragrant Memories*, pp. 176ff.
96. *Ibid.*
97. Hughes, *Fragrant Memories*, p. 157.
98. Rev. S. A. Keen, *Praise Papers*, p. 22.
99. Warfield, *op. cit.*, p. 351, footnote; Wheatley, *op. cit.*, pp. 479–510:
100. *Ibid.*, p. 507.
101. *Ibid.*, p. 509.
102. *Ibid.*, pp. 258–259.
103. *Ibid.*, pp. 258–478.
104. *Ibid.*
105. *Ibid.*
106. *Ibid.*, p. 283.
107. *Ibid.*, p. 244.
108. *Ibid.*, p. 552.
109. *Ibid.*, p. 562.
110. *Ibid.*
111. *Ibid.*, p. 298.
112. *Ibid.*, p. 502.
113. Orr, *op. cit.*, pp. 14–15.
114. *Ibid.*, p. 14, footnote.
115. Wheatley, *op. cit.*, pp. 299–300.
116. *Ibid.*, p. 301.
117. *Ibid.*, p. 317.
118. *Ibid.*, pp. 322–323.
119. *Ibid.*, p. 328.
120. *Ibid.*, p. 329.
121. *Ibid.*, pp. 331–332.
122. *Ibid.*, p. 333.
123. *Ibid.*, p. 332.
124. Orr, *op. cit.*, p. 5.
125. *Ibid.*, pp. 5, 263; Mrs. Phoebe Palmer, *Four Years in the Old World*, passim.
126. Wheatley, *op. cit.*, p. 400.
127. Orr, *op. cit.*, p. 263.
128. *Ibid.*, pp. 262–267
129. *Ibid.*, passim.
130. T. Dewitt Talmadge, in Wheatley, *op. cit.*, 633–634.
131. Roche, *op. cit.*, pp. 223–224.
132. Hughes, *The Beloved Physician*, p. 246.
133. *Ibid.*, pp. 244–245.
134. Wm. McDonald, "The Advance of Holiness," *Advocate of Christian Holiness*, January, 1875, pp. 140–141.
135. Hughes, *The Beloved Physician*, pp. 164ff.
136. Wheatley, *op. cit.*, p. 636.
137. Hughes, *The Beloved Physician*, p. 188; Wheatley, *op. cit.*, p. 315; Abel Stevens, *Life and Times of Nathan Bangs, D.D.*, p. 368.
138. Wheatley, *op. cit.*, pp. iv–vi.
139. *Ibid.*, passim; Hughes, *The Beloved Physician*, passim; Hughes, *Fragrant Memories of the Tuesday Meeting and Guide to Holiness*, passim.

FOOTNOTES

140. Hughes, *The Beloved Physician*, pp. 239ff.
141. *Supra*, p. 33.
142. Gaddis, *op. cit.*, p. 312.
143. *Ibid.*, p. 340.
144. Roche, *op. cit.*, pp. 238-239.
145. John A. Wood, *Autobiography of Rev. J. A. Wood*, pp. 9-19.
146. *Ibid.*, pp. 19-20.
147. *Ibid.*, p. 46.
148. *Ibid.*
149. *Ibid.*, p. 49.
150. *Ibid.*, pp. 58-59.
151. *Ibid.*, p. 73.
152. W. McDonald and John E. Searles, *The Life of Rev. John S. Inskip*, pp. 186-187.
153. Incorrectly Osborne has been popularly credited by some with having been the first one to even suggest a special holiness camp meeting; see *The National Association for the Promotion of Holiness*, 1932-1936, p. 4.
154. McDonald and Searles, *op. cit.*, p. 178.
155. *Ibid.*, p. 188.
156. *Ibid.*, p. 194.
157. *Ibid.*, p. 190.
158. *Ibid.*, p. 192.
159. *Ibid.*, p. 193f.
160. McDonald and Searles, *op. cit.*, p. 194; Adam Wallace, *A Modern Pentecost*, pp. 168-169.
161. McDonald and Searles, *op. cit.*, pp. 9-17.
162. *Ibid.*, p. 33.
163. *Ibid.*, p. 48.
164. *Ibid.*
165. *Ibid.*, p. 72.
166. *Ibid.*, p. 104.
167. *Ibid.*, p. 125.
168. *Ibid.*, p. 126.
169. *Ibid.*, pp. 129ff.
170. *Ibid.*, p. 133.
171. J. S. Inskip, *Methodism Explained and Defended*, p. 61.
172. *Ibid.*, pp. 59-61.
173. *Ibid.*, p. 61.
174. Roche, *op. cit.*, p. 123.
175. McDonald and Searles, *op. cit.*, p. 151.
176. *Ibid.*
177. *Ibid.*, pp. 151ff.
178. *Ibid.*, p. 153.
179. *Ibid.*, p. 154f.
180. *Ibid.*, p. 162.
181. *Ibid.*, p. 163.
182. *Ibid.*, p. 180.
183. *Ibid.*, p. 181.

184. *Ibid.*, pp. 176, 183.
185. *Ibid.*, p. 186.
186. *Ibid.*
187. Wallace, *op. cit.*, p. 199.
188. *Ibid.*, p. 202.
189. McDonald and Searles, *op. cit.*, pp. 217ff.
190. *Ibid.*, pp. 222–223.
191. *Ibid.*, pp. 226–240.
192. *Ibid.*, pp. 256ff.
193. *Ibid.*, pp. 256ff.
194. *Ibid.*, p. 281.
195. *Ibid.*, p. 197.
196. A. McLean and J. W. Eaton, *Penuel; or Face to Face with God*, pp. 479–483.
197. McDonald and Searles, *op. cit.*, pp. 273ff.
198. *Ibid.*, p. 297.
199. *Ibid.*, p. 313f.
200. *Ibid.*, p. 324.
201. *Ibid.*, p. 329.
202. *Ibid.*, p. 333.
203. *Ibid.*, pp. 334ff.
204. *Ibid.*, p. 346f.
205. *Ibid.*, p. 356.
206. *Ibid.*, pp. 299–302; *Advocate of Christian Holiness*, July, 1874, p. 20.
207. *Advocate of Christian Holiness*, William McDonald, ed., vols. I–V, *passim*.
208. Jesse T. Peck, in Hughes, *The Beloved Physician*, pp. 246–248.
209. *Echoes of the General Holiness Assembly*, S. B. Shaw, ed., pp. 21–27; C. W. Butler, Interview between author and, Detroit, Michigan, June 21, 1952.
210. McDonald authored three significant books: *Scriptural Way of Holiness; Marquis De Renty, or Holiness Exemplified by a Roman Catholic;* and *New Testament Standard of Piety, or Our Love Made Perfect.*
211. George Asbury McLaughlin, *Autobiography of George Asbury McLaughlin*, *passim*.
212. George Hughes, "The Beginning of the National Holiness Movement," *Heart and Life*, pp. 5–7.
213. *Official Minutes of the National Association for the Promotion of Holiness for 1907*, Nashville, Tennessee.
214. McLaughlin, *op. cit.*; *The National Association for the Promotion of Holiness*: 1932–1936, p. 1.
215. Gaddis, *op. cit.*, pp. 449–460.
216. *Ibid.*; Sweet, *Methodism in American History*, pp. 342ff.
217. *Echoes of the General Holiness Assembly*, p. 325f.
218. *Ibid.*
219. *Ibid.*
220. *Ibid.*; Gaddis, *op. cit.*, *passim*.

FOOTNOTES

221. C. W. Butler, Interview between author and, Detroit, Michigan, June 20, 1952.
222. Rev. W. A. Dodge, "The Holiness Movement in the South," *The Pentecostal Herald*, December 14, 1898, p. 6.
223. Rev. G. W. Mathews, "The Holiness Movement in the Southeast," *The Pentecostal Herald*, March 25, 1908, pp. 4–5.
224. Rev. John Paul, "Propagation of Holiness in the Central South," *The Pentecostal Herald*, March 25, 1908, p. 11; J. C. McPheeters, "Joseph H. Smith," *The Pentecostal Herald*, July 3, 1946, p. 8.
225. C. W. Butler, Interview between author and, Detroit, Michigan, June 20, 1952.
226. Rev. John Paul, "Propagation of Holiness in the Central South," *The Pentecostal Herald*, March 25, 1908, p. 11.
227. C. W. Butler, Interview between author and, Detroit, Michigan, June 20, 1952.
228. Rev. E. C. DeJernett, "The Holiness Movement in Texas," *The Pentecostal Herald*, March 25, 1908, pp. 6–7.
229. *Ibid.*
230. *Ibid.*
231. W. B. Godbey, *Bible Theology*, p. 100.
232. Rev. C. B. Jernigan, *Pioneer Days of the Holiness Movement in the Southwest*, pp. 150–157.
233. Rev. T. H. B. Anderson, "Some Views of the Coast's Revival," *The Pentecostal Herald*, March 25, 1908, pp. 7, 10; *ibid.*, April 1, 1908, p. 3; C. W. Butler, Interview between author and, Detroit, Michigan, June 20, 1952.
234. Rev. Isaiah Reid, "Beginning of the Movement in the Central Northwest," *The Pentecostal Herald*, March 25, 1908, p. 6.
235. *Ibid.*; C. W. Butler, Interview between author and, Detroit, Michigan, June 20, 1952.
236. *1906 Year Book and Minutes of the Iowa Holiness Association*, published by the General Secretary, Globe Presses, Oskaloosa, Iowa, 1906, *passim*.
237. *Ibid.*
238. C. J. Fowler, "President's Report..." *The Christian Witness*, June 11, 1908, p. 8.
239. Rev. Isaiah Reid, "The Des Moines, Ia., Double Annual Campmeeting," *The Pentecostal Herald*, June 29, 1904, p. 4.
240. *Ibid.*; *1906 Year Book and Minutes of the Iowa Holiness Association*, *passim*; Fowler, "President's Report..." *The Christian Witness*, June 11, 1908, p. 8.
241. W. W. Cary, *Story of the National Holiness Missionary Society*, pp. 5–10.
242. Paul E. Haines, "'And Their Works Do Follow Them,'" *The Missionary Standard*, March, 1951, p. 3.
243. Appendix B.
244. Appendix C.

245. "A 'Movement' not an 'Ecclesiasticism,'" *The Christian Witness*, September 7, 1899, p. 5; C. W. Butler, Interview between author and, Detroit, Michigan, June 20, 1952.
246. Whitcomb was elected but never served.
247. C. W. Butler, Interview between author and, Detroit, Michigan, June 20, 1952.
248. Smith, "The National Association for the Promotion of Holiness," *The Christian Witness*, May 19, 1927, p. 2.
249. *Ibid.*
250. *Ibid.*
251. C. W. Butler, "A New Interdenominationalism," *Heart and Life*, February, 1932, pp. 31–32; C. W. Butler, Interview between author and, Detroit, Michigan, June 20, 1952.
252. C. W. Butler, Interview between author and, Detroit, Michigan, June 20, 1952.
253. Rev. John Paul, "What Has Most Hindered the Progress of the Holiness Movement," *The Pentecostal Herald*, June 9, 1904, p. 9.
254. *Supra*, p. 20.

CHAPTER THREE

255. Pennsylvania, *A Guide to the Keystone State*, pp. 106–107.
256. Joseph H. Smith, "His Grace...Not in Vain," *God's Revivalist*, December 3, 1925, p. 2f.
257. *Ibid.*
258. *Ibid.*
259. Byron J. Rees, "Mountain Lake Park, Maryland," *The Pentecostal Herald*, July 20, 1898, p. 6.
260. Smith, "His Grace..Not in Vain," *God's Revivalist*, December 10 1925, p. 2f.
261. *Ibid.*
262. *Ibid.*
263. *Ibid.*
264. *Ibid.*
265. *Ibid.*; Joseph H. Smith, "Ohio State Meeting (Mt. Vernon) Last Day (continued)," *The Christian Witness*, November 2, 1899, pp. 2, 9.
266. Joseph H. Smith, "My Sixty-Third Anniversary," *God's Revivalist*, April 15, 1937, p. 5.
267. Smith, "His Grace...Not in Vain," *God's Revivalist*, December 10, 1925, p. 2f.
268. *Ibid.*
269. *Ibid.*
270. *Ibid.*
271. Joseph H. Smith, "My Experience of Entire Sanctification," *Heart and Life*, June, 1932, p. 1f.
272. *Ibid.*
273. *Ibid.*
274. *Ibid.*
275. Joseph H. Smith, "Pentecostal Preaching," *Heart and Life*, June, 1941, pp. 4–7.

FOOTNOTES

276. *Ibid.*
277. *Ibid.*, pp. 7, 14.
278. *Ibid.*
279. Joseph H. Smith, "A Pattern in Holiness," *God's Revivalist*, May 1, 1924, pp. 2, 3.
280. *Ibid.*
281. *Ibid.*
282. Joseph H. Smith, "The Menace to Our Evangelism," *Heart and Life*, August, 1927, pp. 14, 15.
283. E. Merton Coulter, *A Short History of Georgia*, 1933, pp. 328–330.
284. *Minutes of the Annual Conferences of the Methodist Episcopal Church, for the year 1875, passim.*
285. Appendix A.
286. Smith, "A Pattern in Holiness," *God's Revivalist*, May 1, 1924, p. 3f.
287. *Ibid.*
288. Smith, "The Relation of Holiness to the World," *God's Revivalist*, September 9, 1926, p. 4.
289. Appendix A.
290. Smith, "A Pattern in Holiness," *God's Revivalist*, May 1, 1924, pp. 2, 4.
291. Appendix A.
292. Smith, "A Pattern in Holiness," *God's Revivalist*, May 1, 1924, pp. 2, 4.
293. *Ibid.*
294. *Ibid.*
295. Joseph H. Smith, Correspondence between J. Hunter Smith and, dated March 10, 1927.
296. Smith, "A Pattern in Holiness," *God's Revivalist*, May 8, 1924, pp. 2–3.
297. *Ibid.*
298. W. W. Cary, unpublished record of an interview between Joseph H. Smith and, Cincinnati, Ohio, April 25, 1936.
299. Smith, "A Pattern in Holiness," *God's Revivalist*, May 8, 1924, pp. 3–4.
300. *Ibid.*
301. *Ibid.*
302. Joseph H. Smith, "Camp Meeting Nuggets," *Friends' Expositor*, October, 1892, pp. 714–715.
303. David B. Updegraff, "Items," *Friends' Expositor*, October, 1888, p. 215.
304. David B. Updegraff, "Field Notes," *ibid.*, October 1890, p. 458.
305. Gaddis, *op. cit.*, p. 534.
306. George A. McLaughlin, "We Call Attention," *The Christian Witness*, May 25, 1899, p. 8.
307. *The Christian Witness*, February 11, 1897, p. 15.
308. *Ibid.*, pp. 3–4.
309. C. W. Butler, Interview between author and, Detroit, Michigan, June 25, 1950.
310. *Infra.*, pp. 73, 74.

311. Joseph H. Smith, "School of the Prophets," *Heart and Life*, August 1922, p. 8.
312. David B. Updegraff, "Missionary Training Institutes," *Friends' Expositor*, January, 1892, p. 619.
313. Joseph H. Smith, *Training in Pentecostal Evangelism*, p. 10.
314. Smith, *Training in Pentecostal Evangelism*, pp. 10–11.
315. *Ibid.*
316. Mary Ella Bowie, *Alabaster and Spikenard, The Life of Iva Durham Vennard, D.D.*, pp. 68–71, 102–161, 180–183.
317. Smith, *Training in Pentecostal Evangelism, passim.*
318. *Ibid.*, p. 14.
319. *Ibid.*, p. 19.
320. Joseph H. Smith, "The Things of the Spirit," *Heart and Life*, May, 1920, p. 7.
321. Smith, *Training in Pentecostal Evangelism*, p. 24.
322. *Ibid.*
323. *Ibid.*, pp. 44, 45.
324. *Ibid.*, pp. 62–64.
325. *Ibid., passim.*
326. Joseph H. Smith, "That Good and Perfect Will of God," *God's Revivalist*, December 13, 1923, p. 3; Appendix A.
327. Mrs. E. E. Williams, *Pentecostal Services... At Mountain Lake Park*, p. 190f.
328. Smith, *Training in Pentecostal Evangelism*, p. 111.
329. Ezra S. Tipple, *Drew Theological Seminary*, p. 256.
330. Smith, *Training in Pentecostal Evangelism*, p. 67.
331. Williams, *op. cit.*, pp. 70–75.
332. Joseph H. Smith, "The Great Camp Meeting of 1939," *God's Revivalist*, September 7, 1939, p. 1.
333. H. C. Morrison, "Central Holiness Camp Meeting," *The Pentecostal Herald*, June 6, 1928, p. 5.
334. *Ibid.*
335. Joseph H. Smith, "The Revival That is Needed in Your Town," *Heart and Life*, November, 1931, p. 8.
336. E. S. Dunham, "The Propagation of Holiness in the General Church," *The Christian Witness*, December 6, 1914, p. 3.
337. "Preachers and Workers." *Program, Forty-Ninth Annual Camp Meeting For the Three Chicago Districts*, Des Plaines, July 15–27, 1908, Chicago, p. 8.
338. Smith, *Training in Pentecostal Evangelism*, p. 81.
339. A. R. Archibald, "A Pentecostal Conference," *The Christian Witness*, October 7, 1897, p. 17.
340. H. C. Morrison, "Editorial," *The Pentecostal Herald*, June 22, 1904, pp. 1, 8.
341. *Ibid.*
342. Joseph H. Smith, "Evangelistic Meetings at General Conference," *The Pentecostal Herald*, April 22, 1908, p. 4; H. C. Morrison, *Some Chapters of My Life Story*, pp. 191–192.

FOOTNOTES

343. C. W. Butler, Interview between author and, Detroit, Michigan, June 26, 1952.
344. Joseph H. Smith, "Methodism and Holiness," *Heart and Life*, May, 1925, pp. 10–11.
345. Gaddis, *op. cit.*, pp. 443–540.
346. Elmer T. Clark, *The Small Sects in America*, pp. 72–84.
347. Joseph H. Smith, "The Holiness Movement and Methodism," *The Pentecostal Herald*, September 4, 1912, p. 2.
348. *Ibid.*, September 11, 1912, p. 2.
349. *Ibid.*
350. Smith, "Methodism and Holiness," *Heart and Life*, May, 1925, pp. 10–11.
351. *Ibid.*
352. "Joseph H. Smith's Itinerary of Campmeetings For 1933," *The Pentecostal Herald*, October 4, 1933, pp. 6–7.
353. Smith, "Methodism and Holiness," *Heart and Life*, May, 1925, pp. 10–11.
354. "Asburians Assist in Philadelphia Revival," *Asbury Alumnus*, November, 1949, p. 1.
355. J. C. McPheeters, "The General Conference of the Methodist Church," *The Herald*, May 28, 1952, p. 1.
356. T. Otto Nall, "Evangelism in the Nation's Capital," *The Christian Advocate*, April 3, 1952, pp. 5, 26.
357. McPheeters, "The General Conference of the Methodist Church," *The Herald*, May 28, 1952, p. 1.
358. "Asburians Assist in Philadelphia Revival," *Asbury Alumnus*, November, 1949, p. 1.
359. Smith, "A Pattern in Holiness," *God's Revivalist*, May 8, 1924, p. 4.
360. C. W. Butler, Interview between author and, Detroit, Michigan, July 11, 12, 1950.
361. *Ibid.*; *Official Minutes of National Association for the Promotion of Holiness for 1926–1928.*
362. Joseph H. Smith, "A Notable Day in the Holiness Movement," *The Pentecostal Herald*, October 10, 1928, p. 7.
363. Joseph H. Smith, "The Second Rise of the Holiness Movement," *The Pentecostal Herald*, April 1, 1925, p. 3.
364. William R. Cannon, *The Theology of John Wesley*, p. 7.
365. Joseph H. Smith, *From Glory to Glory*, pp. 17–18.
366. Joseph H. Smith, *Pauline Perfection*, pp. 2, 15–17.
367. Smith, *Pauline Perfection*, p. 7.
368. *Infra*, pp. 208–226.
369. Smith, "Wise," *Heart and Life*, August 1915, p. 9f.
370. Bishop Arthur Wesley, Interview between author and, Chicago, Illinois, July 9, 1948.
371. Smith, "Spiritual Life Suggestions," *The Christian Witness*, February 18, 1937, p. 10.
372. *Supra*, pp. 73, 74.

373. J. C. McPheeters, "Joseph H. Smith," *The Pentecostal Herald*, June 19, 1946, p. 8; Frank M. Thomas, "Doctor Gross Alexander," *The Methodist Review*, January, 1916, pp. 3–19.
374. *Flames of Living Fire*, Bernie Smith, ed., p. 44.
375. J. B. Chapman, *Bud Robinson, A Brother Beloved*, p. 51.
376. Joseph H. Smith, "Justification the Great Thing," *God's Revivalist*, July 4, 1940, p. 2.
377. Joseph H. Smith, "Question Box," *Heart and Life*, March-April, 1933, p. 19.
378. Smith, "Question Box," *Heart and Life*, March-April, 1933, p. 19.
379. Joseph H. Smith, "Expository Preaching," *Heart and Life*, January, 1931, p. 21.
380. Charles R. Eberhardt, *The Bible in the Making of Ministers*, p. 99.
381. *Ibid.*, p. 103.
382. *Ibid.*, *passim*.
383. Joseph H. Smith, "Two Studies," *Heart and Life*, January, 1930, p. 6f.
384. Abdel Ross Wentz, *A New Strategy for Theological Education*, p. 11; *supra*, pp. 25, 26.
385. Eberhardt, *op. cit.*, *passim*.
386. *Ibid.*; Smith, "Study," *God's Revivalist*, January 22, 1942, p. 2.
387. Joseph H. Smith, "Pastoral Evangelism," *Heart and Life*, September, 1927, pp. 8–9.
388. *Ibid.*
389. Rom. 12:11; Tit. 2:14; II Tim. 1:6; I Pet. 1:22; 4:8.
390. Joseph H. Smith, "Consecration in the Concrete, or Holiness Applied," *Heart and Life*, April, 1921, p. 7.
392. *Ibid.*
393. *Ibid.*
394. *Ibid.*
395. Smith, "The Menace to Our Evangelism," *Heart and Life*, August, 1927, p. 12f.
396. *Ibid.*
397. *Ibid.*
398. Joseph H. Smith, "Anyone May Be Saved," *God's Revivalist*, October 25, 1934, p. 16.
399. *Ibid.*
400. II Tim. 4:5.
401. Matt. 28:18.
402. Smith, "The Menace to Our Evangelism," *Heart and Life*, August, 1927, pp. 14–15.
403. Joseph H. Smith, "Office of An Evangelist Scripturally Considered," *The Pentecostal Herald*, January 1, 1908, pp. 3ff.
404. Smith, "The Menace to Our Evangelism," *Heart and Life*, August, 1927, p. 12f.
405. Joseph H. Smith, "Holiness Evangelism to All Christendom," *Heart and Life*, November, 1940, pp. 4–6.
406. Rom. 14:17.

FOOTNOTES

407. Smith, "Holiness Evangelism For All Christendom," *Heart and Life,* November, 1940, pp. 4–6.
408. *Ibid.*
409. Smith, "The Holiness Movement and Missions," *Heart and Life,* September, 1926, pp. 31f.
410. *Ibid.*
411. Joseph H. Smith, "The Compensation of Consecration," *God's Revivalist,* December 7, 1933, p. 3.
412. John and Emily Thomas, Correspondence between Joseph H. Smith and, dated April 15, 1913.
413. *The Pentecostal Herald,* January 5, 1938, p. 13.
414. J. C. McPheeters, "Joseph H. Smith," *The Pentecostal Herald,* July 3, 1946, p. 8; J. W. Beeson, "Holiness Union Convention," *The Pentecostal Herald,* November 16, 1904, pp. 4–5.
415. Joseph H. Smith, "What I Found at Meridian," *The Pentecostal Herald,* September 30, 1908, p. 12; Joseph H. Smith, "Another Revival at the Meridian Colleges," *The Pentecostal Herald,* April 22, 1908, p. 4.
416. J. C. McPheeters, "Sent As Jesus Was Sent," *The Pentecostal Herald,* October 25, 1950, p. 8.
417. *The Pentecostal Herald,* June 23, 1909, pp. 10–11.
418. Joseph H. Smith, Correspondence between J. Hunter Smith and, dated November 21, 1942.
419. J. C. McPheeters, "Joseph H. Smith," *The Pentecostal Herald,* July 3, 1946, p. 8.
420. *Yearbook of Chicago Evangelistic Institute,* 1914, pp. 8–9; Joseph H. Smith, "Educationalism or Evangelism," *The Christian Witness,* April 22, 1937, pp. 4–5.
421. Joseph H. Smith, "Educational Limitation in the Holiness Movement," A sermon preached at Cleveland Bible Institute, Cleveland, Ohio, May 28, 1922.
422. *Ibid.*
423. *Ibid.*
424. Appendix B.
425. H. C. Morrison, *Some Chapters of My Life Story,* pp. 193–194.
426. Smith, "His Grace . . Not in Vain," *God's Revivalist,* December 3, 1925, p. 2.
427. J. Hunter Smith, Interview between author and, Balboa Island, California, June 10, 1949.
428. Joseph H. Smith, "That Good and Perfect Will of God," *God's Revivalist,* December 13, 1923, p. 3.
429. C. W. Butler, Interview between author and, Detroit, Michigan, July 11, 1950.
430. Joseph H. Smith, "Thanksgiving Always for All Things," *God's Revivalist,* November 21, 1940, p. 4.
431. Joseph H. Smith, "Contentment," *Heart and Life,* March, 1940, pp. 4–5; Joseph H. Smith, "Contentment and Conquest," *God's Revivalist,* May 6, 1937, pp. 4, 14.

432. Joseph H. Smith, "God's Call to Holiness," *God's Revivalist*, August 15, 1929, p. 2.
433. Joseph H. Smith, "The Call To God's Work," *Heart and Life*, November, 1927, p. 10f.
434. Smith, "Study," *God's Revivalist*, January 22, 1942, p. 2; Joseph H. Smith, "Learn of Me," *Heart and Life*, November, 1930, p. 7.
435. Smith, "The Things of the Spirit," *Heart and Life*, May, 1920, pp. 5–7.
436. Joseph H. Smith, "The Leading of the Spirit," *Heart and Life*, July, 1927, pp. 10–11.
437. Smith, "Pentecostal Preaching," *Heart and Life*, June, 1941, p. 14.
438. Joseph H. Smith, "D.D.," *Christian Witness*, July 23, 1914, pp. 2–3.
439. Smith, "That Good and Perfect Will of God," *God's Revivalist*, December 6, 1923, p. 3.
440. James B. Chapman, *Bud Robinson, A Brother Beloved*, p. 63.
441. W. W. Cary, unpublished record of an interview between W. W. Cary and Joseph H. Smith, Cincinnati, Ohio, April 25, 1936.
442. Joseph H. Smith, "Lights In the World," *Heart and Life*, April, 1920, p. 10.
443. Joseph H. Smith, "Concern for the Backslidden," *God's Revivalist*, July 21, 1938, pp. 3–4.

CHAPTER FOUR

444. McClintock was co-editor with Dr. James Strong of the *Cyclopedia of Biblical, Theological, and Ecclesiastical Literature*.
445. Quoted in Olin A. Curtis, *The Christian Faith*, p. 372.
446. Joseph H. Smith, "Wise," *Heart and Life*, August, 1915, p. 9.
447. Smith, *Pauline Perfection*, p. 17.
448. *Ibid.*, p. 186.
449. *Ibid.*, pp. 185–186.
450. *Ibid.*, p. 101.
451. *Ibid.*, passim.
452. Smith, *From Glory to Glory*, p. 15.
453. Rom. 1:19–20; Joseph H. Smith, "The Light of Nature and Revelation of Scripture," *God's Revivalist*, October 31, 1940, p. 3.
454. Cannon, *The Theology of John Wesley*, pp. 154–156.
455. Joseph H. Smith, "The Spirit's Light," *The Pentecostal Herald*, September 22, 1937, p. 4.
456. Joseph H. Smith, "Wise Men," *Heart and Life*, December, 1929, pp. 6–8.
457. Smith, *From Glory to Glory*, p. 102.
458. Joseph H. Smith, "God Hath Spoken," *God's Revivalist*, June 3, 1926, p. 11.
459. Smith, *From Glory to Glory*, pp. 40, 41.
460. Joseph H. Smith, unpublished article in F. S. Teed collection, Ann Arbor, Michigan.
461. Cannon, *The Theology of John Wesley*, p. 20.
462. *Ibid.*, pp. 20–21.

463. Smith, *Pauline Perfection*, p. 73.
464. Smith, *From Glory to Glory*, p. 42.
465. Smith, "Wise Men," *Heart and Life*, December, 1929, p. 6f.
466. Joseph H. Smith, "Ye Shine," *ibid.*, February, 1927, pp. 8–9.
467. Smith, "The Spirit's Light," *The Pentecostal Herald*, September 22, 1937, p. 4.
468. *Ibid.*; John 14:26; 16:13–15; II Peter 3:15, 16; Joseph H. Smith, *Things Of The Spirit*, p. 69f.
469. Smith, "God Hath Spoken," *God's Revivalist*, June 3, 1926, p. 11.
470. II Tim. 3:16, 17.
471. II Peter 1:20 21; Joseph H. Smith, "Spiritual Life Suggestions," *The Christian Witness*, September 11, 1919, p. 10.
472. Joseph H. Smith, "Light On Our Pathway," *God's Revivalist*, October 24, 1929, p. 2.
473. Smith, "God Hath Spoken," *ibid.*, June 3, 1926, p. 11.
474. Joseph H. Smith, "The Scriptures and the Word of God," *Heart and Life*, August, 1923, pp. 18–19.
475. Joseph H. Smith, "The Inspiration and Interpretation of the Scripture," *ibid.*, December, 1919, pp. 13–14, 16.
476. Smith, *Things Of The Spirit*, pp. 33–34.
477. Smith, "Spiritual Life Suggestions," *The Christian Witness*, March 18, 1937, p. 10.
478. Joseph H. Smith, "Private Interpretations"; "The Holy Scriptures"; "The Word of Christ," *Heart and Life*, February, 1924, p. 7.
479. Smith, "Spiritual Life Suggestions," *The Christian Witness*, December 17, 1936, pp. 12–13.
480. Joseph H. Smith, "Be Ye Holy," *Heart and Life*, November, 1928, pp. 6, 9.
481. Smith, "The Inspiration and Interpretation of the Scriptures," *ibid.*, December, 1919, pp. 13–14, 16.
482. Smith, "Question Box," *The Christian Witness*, January 20, 1938, p. 6.
483. Smith, "The Spirit's Light," *The Pentecostal Herald*, September 22, 1937, p. 4.
484. Joseph H. Smith, "Inspiration and Illumination," *Heart and Life*, December, 1926, p. 10.
485. Joseph H. Smith, "Education! Inspiration! Illumination!" *Heart and Life*, May, 1925, p. 9.
486. Smith, *Things Of The Spirit*, p. 27f.
487. Smith, "The Spirit's Light," *The Pentecostal Herald*, September 22, 1937, p. 4.
488. Smith, "Education! Inspiration! Illumination!" *Heart and Life*, May, 1925, p. 9.
489. Smith, "Question Box," *ibid.*, December, 1920, p. 19; Smith, "The Scriptures and the Word of God," *ibid.*, August, 1923, pp. 18–19.
490. Joseph H. Smith, "Expository Suggestion," *Heart and Life*, July, 1924, p. 8f.
491. Joseph H. Smith, unpublished articles in F. S. Teed collection, Ann Arbor, Michigan.

492. Smith, "Expository Suggestion," *ibid.*, July, 1924, pp. 8–9.
493. Joseph H. Smith, "Question Lecture Drawer," *ibid.*, March, 1918, p. 13.
494. Smith, unpublished articles in F. S. Teed collection, Ann Arbor, Michigan.
495. Smith, "Question Lecture Drawer," *Heart and Life*, March, 1918, p. 13.
496. Smith, "The Inspiration and Interpretation of the Scripture," *ibid.*, December, 1919, pp. 13–14, 16.
497. Smith, "Education! Inspiration! Illumination!" *ibid.*, May, 1925, pp. 8–9.
498. Joseph H. Smith, "Cardinal Doctrines of the Bible," *ibid.*, March, 1921, p. 6f.
499. Smith, *Pauline Perfection*, pp. 106–107; Joseph H. Smith, "What Christ Plans For His Own," *God's Revivalist*, November 2, 1933, p. 4.
500. Augustus Hopkins Strong, *One Hundred Chapel Talks to Theological Students*, p. 24.

CHAPTER FIVE

501. Smith, *From Glory to Glory*, pp. 50–53.
502. Joseph H. Smith, "He Came to Show Us God," *Heart and Life*, August, 1924, p. 10.
503. Smith, *From Glory to Glory*, pp. 50–59.
504. *Ibid.*; Smith, "He Came to Show Us God," *Heart and Life*, August, 1924, p. 10.
505. Joseph H. Smith, "Growing Godlike," *God's Revivalist*, September 26, 1929, p. 3; Joseph H. Smith, "A Quiet God," *The Free Methodist*, February 16, 1934, pp. 2–3.
506. H. Orton Wiley, *Christian Theology*, vol. I, pp. 370–371, 381–382.
507. Joseph H. Smith, "Ohio State Camp Meeting, Eighth Day," *The Christian Witness*, October 19, 1899, p. 3.
508. John 14:17; Harold William Perkins, *The Doctrine of Christian or Evangelical Perfection*, p. 213.
509. Smith, *Things of the Spirit*, pp. 16, 19.
510. Heb. 11:3; II Cor. 4:6; Joseph H. Smith, "Spiritual Life Suggestions," *The Christian Witness*, March 25, 1937, p. 10.
511. I Cor. 15:51, 52; Smith, "Spiritual Life Suggestions," *The Christian Witness*, March 25, 1937, p. 10.
512. *Ibid.*
513. Smith, "A Quiet God," *The Free Methodist*, February 16, 1934, pp. 2–3.
514. *Ibid.*
515. *Ibid.*
516. Joseph H. Smith, "God's Will and Ours," *Heart and Life*, July, 1926, p. 6.
517. Smith, "Spiritual Life Suggestions," *The Christian Witness*, March 7, 1935, p. 10; Smith, *Things of the Spirit*, p. 48; Joseph H. Smith, "Our Glorification," *The Herald of Holiness*, September 17, 1938, p. 5.
518. Joseph H. Smith, "Easter Thoughts," *God's Revivalist*, April 9, 1936, p. 14.

FOOTNOTES

519. *Ibid.*; Smith, "Spiritual Life Suggestions," *The Christian Witness*, March 7, 1935, p. 10.
520. Joseph H. Smith, "Heaven's Interest in Man's Redemption," *God's Revivalist*, March 6, 1941, p. 16; Joseph H. Smith, "Are We in Touch with the Spirit World," *Heart and Life*, May-June, 1938, pp. 4–5.
521. Smith, *From Glory to Glory*, p. 58.
522. *Ibid.*, p. 90.
523. *Ibid.*, pp. 108–109.
524. Smith, *Things of the Spirit*, p. 48; Joseph H. Smith, "This Thy Day," *The Christian Witness*, February 6, 1936, pp. 4, 5.
525. Joseph H. Smith, "The Glory Road—Ephesians 1:1–14," *The Pentecostal Herald*, March 3, 1946, p. 4.
526. Joseph H. Smith, "Opening Our Christmas Gift," *God's Revivalist*, December 20, 1934, pp. 4, 18, 19.
527. Smith, "Spiritual Life Suggestions," *The Christian Witness*, March 25, 1937, p. 10.
528. Smith, *From Glory to Glory*, p. 15.
529. *Ibid.*, p. 16.
530. Smith, "The Glory Road—Ephesians 1:1–14," *The Pentecostal Herald*, March 6, 1946; Smith, *Things of the Spirit*, pp. 23, 53.
531. Rev. 20: 2; Matt. 4:3; I John 5:18; Joseph H. Smith, "The Accuser of the Brethren," *Heart and Life*, February, 1927, pp. 10, 11.
532. Smith, "Preservation is More Than Sanctification," *The Christian Witness*, May 30, 1935, p. 2.
533. Smith, "Easter Thoughts," *God's Revivalist*, April 9, 1936, p. 3; Joseph H. Smith, "Sins and Sin," *ibid.*, July 20, 1939, p. 2; Joseph H. Smith, "Wiles of the Devil," *ibid.*, April 29, 1937, p. 9; Smith, *Things of the Spirit*, p. 82.
534. Smith, "Question Box," *The Christian Witness*, September 7, 1939, p. 6; Joseph H. Smith, "Depression," *Heart and Life*, December, 1927, pp. 10, 11.
535. Smith, "Spiritual Life Suggestions," *The Christian Witness*, December 19, 1935, p. 3; Joseph H. Smith, "Keeping Our Bodies Under," *Heart and Life*, April, 1921, p. 9; Joseph H. Smith, "Proving the Will," *The Christian Witness*, October 25, 1934, p. 2.
536. Smith, *From Glory to Glory*, p. 67; Smith, "The Cardinal Doctrines of the Bible," *Heart and Life*, March, 1921, pp. 6, 7.
537. Smith, "Spiritual Life Suggestions," *The Christian Witness*, May 21, 1936, p. 10.
538. Joseph H. Smith, "Sin," *Heart and Life*, August, 1919, pp. 11, 12, 30.
539. Smith, *From Glory to Glory*, p. 64.
540. *Ibid.*, p. 52.
541. *Ibid.*
542. Joseph H. Smith, "Impure Hearts," *God's Revivalist*, January 5, 1933, pp. 2, 12; Smith, "Question Box," *Heart and Life*, October, 1929, p. 19.
543. Smith, "Sin," *ibid.*, August, 1919, pp. 11, 12, 30; Smith, *Pauline Perfection*, p. 130; Smith, *From Glory to Glory*, pp. 64ff.; Smith, "The Ministry of Prayer," *Heart and Life*, October, 1920, p. 10.
544. *Ibid.*

545. Joseph H. Smith, "Evil Turned to Good," *God's Revivalist*, June 27, 1935, p. 3.
546. Smith, *Pauline Perfection, passim*.
547. *Ibid.*; Smith, "Sins and Sin," *God's Revivalist*, July 20, 1939, p. 2.
548. *Ibid.*; Mark 7:21-23.
549. Smith, "Impure Hearts," *God's Revivalist*, January 5, 1933, pp. 2, 12.
550. Smith, "Spiritual Life Suggestions," *The Christian Witness*, January 2, 1936, p. 10.
551. Joseph H. Smith, "Death Sin," *Heart and Life*, July, 1921, pp. 8, 9; Smith, "Question Box," *The Christian Witness*, June 6, 1935, p. 6; Joseph H. Smith, "Conviction for Holiness," *Friends' Expositor*, April, 1888, pp. 131-133.
552. *Ibid.*; Joseph H. Smith, "Death," *The Pentecostal Herald*, July 12, 1933, p. 7; Smith, "Sins and Sin," *God's Revivalist*, July 20, 1939, p. 2.
553. Smith, "Death Sin," *Heart and Life*, July, 1921, pp. 8, 9.
554. *Ibid.*
555. Smith, *From Glory to Glory*, p. 81.
556. Smith, "The Glory Road—Ephesians 1:1-14," *The Pentecostal Herald*, March 6, 1946, p. 4.
557. Smith, "Sin," *Heart and Life*, August, 1919, pp. 11, 12.
558. Smith, *Things of the Spirit*, pp. 78, 79; Smith, "Spiritual Life Suggestions," *The Christian Witness*, April 15, 1937, p. 10.
559. Joseph H. Smith, "The Seed of the Woman," *Heart and Life*, January-February, 1935, p. 4.
560. Gen. 3:13-21; Smith, "The Glory Road—Ephesians 1:1-14," *The Pentecostal Herald*, March 6, 1946, p. 4; Smith, "Death," *ibid.*, July 12, 1933, p. 7.
561. Smith, "Spiritual Life Suggestions," *The Christian Witness*, April 15, 1937, p. 10; Smith, *Things of the Spirit*, p. 82.
562. Joseph H. Smith, "The Curse of Christ," *Heart and Life*, June, 1921, pp. 6, 7.
563. Smith, "Spiritual Life Suggestions," *The Christian Witness*, March 25, 1937, p. 10.
564. *Ibid.*
565. Smith, "Cardinal Doctrines of the Bible," *Heart and Life*, March, 1921, pp. 6, 7.
566. Joseph H. Smith, "Christmas From John Three Sixteen," *God's Revivalist*, December 19, 1935, p. 3.
567. Smith, "Cardinal Doctrines of the Bible," *Heart and Life*, March, 1921, pp. 6, 7; "Sermon by Rev. Joseph H. Smith," *ibid.*, May, 1928, pp. 7, 8.
568. Smith, *From Glory to Glory*, pp. 20-22.
569. *Ibid., passim*.
570. Joseph H. Smith, "Questions," *The Christian Witness*, February 13, 1936, p. 6.
571. *Ibid.*
572. *Ibid.*
573. Smith, "Spiritual Life Suggestions," *The Christian Witness*, August 5, 1937, p. 10.

FOOTNOTES

574. *Ibid.*
575. Smith, *From Glory to Glory*, pp. 22, 23.
576. *Ibid.*, p. 73.
577. *Ibid.*, p. 69; Smith, "Spiritual Life Suggestions," *The Christian Witness*, February 20, 1936, p. 13.
578. Smith, *From Glory to Glory*, p. 71.
579. Smith, "Question Box," *The Christian Witness*, June 7, 1934, p. 6; Joseph H. Smith, "The Elect," *God's Revivalist*, February 28, 1935, p. 1; Joseph H. Smith, "Election," *The Pentecostal Herald*, October 12, 1949, p. 9.
580. Joseph H. Smith, "Every Man," *God's Revivalist*, November 2, 1939, p. 2.
581. H. Orton Wiley, *Christian Theology*, vol. 2, pp. 169ff.
582. Joseph H. Smith, "The Holy Ghost At the Birth of Christ," *God's Revivalist*, December 19, 1929, pp. 3, 14; Joseph H. Smith, "Thou Art Peter," *Heart and Life*, February, 1920, pp. 10, 11.
583. Joseph H. Smith, "No Reputation," *The Christian Witness*, May 13, 1937, p. 3.
584. Joseph H. Smith, "He Dwelt Among Us," *Heart and Life*, December, 1928, pp. 8, 9.
585. *Ibid.*, p. 3; Joseph H. Smith, "He Came to Show Us God," *Heart and Life*, August, 1924, pp. 10ff.
586. *Ibid.*
587. Smith, "The Question Box," *The Christian Witness*, November 27, 1919, p. 6; Smith, "Spiritual Life Suggestions," *ibid.*, January 9, 1936, p. 10.
588. Joseph H. Smith, "After Easter," *Heart and Life*, April, 1940, pp. 10ff.; *ibid.*, May, 1940, p. 16.
589. Joseph H. Smith, "Am I Going To Get To Heaven?" *The Christian Witness*, April 18, 1935, p. 4.
590. Joseph H. Smith, "Christ's Intercession, 'I Pray For Them,'" *God's Revivalist*, August 4, 1938, p. 2; Joseph H. Smith, "Christ's Ministry To Sinners," *ibid.*, January 30, 1930, p. 3.
591. Joseph H. Smith, "Sin and Sorrow," *Heart and Life*, December, 1922, p. 9.
592. Smith, "Spiritual Life Suggestions," *The Christian Witness*, March 28, 1935, p. 10.
593. *Ibid.*
594. *Ibid.*, March 4, 1937, p. 12.
595. Joseph H. Smith, "A Living Savior," *Heart and Life*, September, 1925, p. 9; Joseph H. Smith, "The Faith Whereby We Are Sanctified," *God's Revivalist*, October 26, 1922, pp. 2–4.
596. Smith, "Thou Art Peter," *Heart and Life*, February, 1920, p. 11f.
597. *Ibid.*
598. *Ibid.*, p. 43.
599. Smith, *Pauline Perfection*, p. 130.
600. Smith, *From Glory to Glory*, pp. 56ff.; Joseph H. Smith, "The Precious Blood—I Peter 1:19," *God's Revivalist*, April 18, 1935, p. 4f.

298   A THEOLOGY OF CHRISTIAN EXPERIENCE

601. Smith, *From Glory to Glory*, p. 56.
602. *Ibid.*; John 1:14; Mark 10:45.
603. *Ibid.*, pp. 56, 57.
604. *Ibid.*, pp. 57ff.
605. *Ibid.*
606. H. Orton Wiley, *Christian Theology*, vol. 2, pp. 232ff.
607. "Sermon by Rev. J.H.S., Delivered at the C.E.I.," *Heart and Life*, May, 1928, pp. 7-8.
608. *Ibid.*
609. *Ibid.*
610. Smith, "Question Drawer," *Heart and Life*, February, 1919, p. 13.
611. Joseph H. Smith, "The Precious Blood," *ibid.*, November, 1920, pp. 10, 11.
612. Joseph H. Smith, "The Precious Blood—I Peter 1:19," *God's Revivalist*, April 18, 1935, p. 4f.
613. *Ibid.*
614. *Ibid.*
615. *Ibid.*
616. *Ibid.*
617. *Ibid.*
618. Smith, *Pauline Perfection, passim.*
619. Smith, "Question Box," *The Christian Witness*, June 6, 1935, p. 6.
620. Smith, *Pauline Perfection*, pp. 93-94, 148-149.
621. Smith, "Christ's Intercession, 'I Pray For Them,'" *God's Revivalist*, August 4, 1938, pp. 2, 3.
622. *Ibid.*
623. *Ibid.*
624. *Ibid.*
625. Joseph H. Smith, "A Living Saviour," *Heart and Life*, September, 1925, p. 9.
626. Joseph H. Smith, "The Excellency of the Knowledge of Christ," *God's Revivalist*, June 19, 1924, p. 2.
627. Joseph H. Smith, "Not Meat and Drink," *Heart and Life*, June, 1920, p. 6.
628. Joseph H. Smith, "Christ's Kingdom Now," *ibid.*, January, 1940, pp. 11ff., 24, 25.
629. Smith, "Not Meat and Drink," *ibid.*, June, 1920, p. 7.
630. *Infra*, pp. 183-187.
631. Joseph H. Smith, "What Christ Plans for His Own," *God's Revivalist*, November 2, 1933, pp. 4, 12; Joseph H. Smith, "Judgment, Begun At The House of God," *Heart and Life*, May, 1919, pp. 10, 16.
632. Joseph H. Smith, *Things of the Spirit*, pp. 11, 16; Joseph H. Smith, "Holiness Simplified," *The Christian Witness*, July 25, 1935, p. 2.
633. Smith, *From Glory to Glory*, p. 131.
634. Heb. 10:29; I Pet. 4:14; Ps. 84:11.
635. Smith, "Spiritual Life Suggestions," *The Christian Witness*, March 19, 1936, p. 10.
636. *Ibid., June* 13, 1935, p. 10.

637. Smith, *From Glory to Glory*, pp. 131–134; Smith, *Pauline Perfection*, p. 127.
638. Smith, *Things of the Spirit*, pp. 35f.
639. *Ibid.*, pp. 12, 13.
640. Smith, "Spiritual Life Suggestions," *The Christian Witness*, January 17, 1929, p. 10; Smith, *From Glory to Glory*, p. 133.
641. *Ibid.*
642. *Ibid.*
643. *Ibid.*, p. 134.
644. Smith, *Things of the Spirit*, p. 22; Smith, *Pauline Perfection*, p. 21.
645. *Ibid.*, p. 41; Smith, *From Glory to Glory*, pp. 134, 135; II Cor. 3:6.
646. Smith, *From Glory to Glory*, p. 65.
647. *Ibid.*, pp. 69, 70; Smith, "Spiritual Life Suggestions," *The Christian Witness*, December 24, 1936, p. 10.
648. Smith, *From Glory to Glory*, pp. 66–69.
649. *Ibid.*, p. 68.
650. Smith, *Things of the Spirit*, p. 33.
651. Smith, *From Glory to Glory*, p. 66.
652. *Ibid.*, pp. 83, 84.
653. *Ibid.*, p. 137.
654. Joseph H. Smith, "Witness of the Spirit," *God's Revivalist*, August 2, 1928, pp. 4, 5.
655. Joseph H. Smith, "The Fulness of the Gospel," *The Pentecostal Herald*, June 28, 1944, p. 9.
656. Smith, *From Glory to Glory*, p. 137; Heb. 10:22; 6:11; Col. 2:2.
657. Joseph H. Smith, "The Witness of Our Own Spirit, of the Holy Spirit," *Heart and Life*, October, 1922, p. 14f.
658. Smith, "The Witness of the Spirit," *God's Revivalist*, August 2, 1928, p. 4f.
659. *Ibid.*, p. 5.
660. *Ibid.*, August 9, 1928, p. 4.
661. *Ibid.*
662. *Ibid.*
663. Smith, "Witness of the Spirit," *God's Revivalist*, August 2, 1928, p. 3f.
664. Smith, "The Witness of the Spirit," *ibid.*, pp. 3, 4.
665. *Ibid.*, August 9, 1928, p. 4; Smith, *From Glory to Glory*, p. 137.
666. *Ibid.*, p. 137f.
667. Smith, "The Witness of the Spirit," *Heart and Life*, November, 1923, p. 9.
668. Joseph H. Smith, "Insensible Guidance," *Heart and Life*, December, 1924, p. 9.
669. Smith, *From Glory to Glory*, pp. 138, 139.
670. Smith, *Pauline Perfection*, pp. 122–131.
671. *Ibid.*; Smith, *From Glory to Glory*, *passim*.
672. Smith, *Things of the Spirit*, pp. 43ff.
673. Smith, *From Glory to Glory*, p. 141.
674. Smith, *Pauline Perfection*, p. 127.
675. *Ibid.*
676. *Ibid.*, p. 129.

677. Smith, *Things of the Spirit*, p. 45.
678. *Ibid.*, p. 76f.; Smith, *Pauline Perfection*, p. 130.
679. Smith, *Things of the Spirit*, pp. 76, 77; see II Cor. 6:16.
680. Smith, *Pauline Perfection*, p. 130.
681. Smith, *Things of the Spirit*, p. 48.
682. *Ibid.*, pp. 48, 49.
683. Smith, *From Glory to Glory*, pp. 144, 145.
684. Joseph H. Smith, "The Setting of Sanctification," *Heart and Life*, February, 1930, pp. 6–8.
685. Smith, "Led of the Spirit," *Heart and Life*, October, 1927, p. 8.
686. Smith, *From Glory to Glory*, p. 155; Joseph H. Smith, "Faith in Divine Guidance," *God's Revivalist*, October 24, 1935, p. 9.
687. Joseph H. Smith, "Guidance," *Heart and Life*, November, 1921, p. 5.
688. *Ibid.*, pp. 5ff.
689. *Ibid.*, p. 6f.
690. Smith, "Faith in Divine Guidance," *God's Revivalist*, October 24, 1935, p. 9.
691. Smith, *From Glory to Glory*, p. 151.
692. Smith, "Faith in Divine Guidance," *God's Revivalist*, October 24, 1935, p. 9.
693. Smith, *From Glory to Glory*, pp. 153, 154.
694. Smith, "Faith in Divine Guidance," *God's Revivalist*, October 24, 1935, p. 9.
695. *Ibid.*
696. *Ibid.*
697. *Ibid.*
698. *Ibid.*
699. Smith, "Insensible Guidance," *Heart and Life*, December, 1924, p. 9.
700. Joseph H. Smith, "Guidance," *ibid.*, November, 1921, p. 5f.
701. Joseph H. Smith, "Trying the Spirits," *The Pentecostal Herald*, January 28, 1931, p. 4.
702. *Ibid.*
703. Joseph H. Smith, "Question Drawer Lecture," *Heart and Life*, October, 1917, p. 13.
704. *Ibid.*
705. Smith, *From Glory to Glory*, p. 152.
706. *Ibid.*, p. 152f.
707. Smith, "Question Box," *The Christian Witness*, January 2, 1936, p. 6; Smith, *From Glory to Glory*, p. 121; Smith, *Pauline Perfection*, p. 38.
708. Smith, *Things of the Spirit*, pp. 64, 65.
709. Smith, "Spiritual Life Suggestions," *The Christian Witness*, October 4, 1928, p. 10.
712. Smith, *Things of the Spirit*, p. 66.
713. Smith, *Pauline Perfection*, p. 65.
714. *Ibid.*, pp. 177, 178.
715. Smith, "A Letter About the Tongues' Movement," *Heart and Life*, April, 1927, pp. 12–14.
716. *Ibid.*, p. 14.

717. Smith, "Spiritual Life Suggestions," *The Christian Witness*, January 2, 1936, p. 10; *ibid.*, February 21, 1935, p. 10.
718. Smith, *Things of the Spirit*, p. 67.
719. *Ibid.*
720. Smith, "Spiritual Life Suggestions," *The Christian Witness*, May 2, 1935, p. 10; Joseph H. Smith, "Christian Unity Rests Upon Divine Union—John XVII:21, 23," *Heart and Life*, August, 1921, p. 10.
721. *Ibid.*
722. *Ibid.*
723. Joseph H. Smith, "Churches in Competition," *The Pentecostal Herald*, May 11, 1938, p. 5.
724. *Ibid.*
725. Smith, "Spiritual Life Suggestions," *The Christian Witness*, May 2, 1935, p. 10.
726. Joseph H. Smith, "Some Sort of Division is Inevitable," *Heart and Life*, May, 1926, p. 12.
727. "Ohio State Camp-Meeting, Eighth Day," *The Christian Witness*, October 19, 1899, p. 3.
728. Smith, "Churches in Competition," *The Pentecostal Herald*, May 11, 1938, p. 5.
729. Joseph H. Smith, "His High Priestly Prayer," *Heart and Life*, November, 1922, p. 33.
730. Smith, *Things of the Spirit*, pp. 63, 64.
731. Joseph H. Smith, "Praying in the Holy Ghost," *The Free Methodist*, December 4, 1942, p. 2.
732. Joseph H. Smith, "More About Prayer," *Heart and Life*, March, 1925, p. 8.
733. Joseph H. Smith, "Christians As Priests," *God's Revivalist*, September 26, 1935, p. 2.
734. *Ibid.*
735. Joseph H. Smith, "Praying in the Holy Ghost," *God's Revivalist*, August 17, 1933, p. 1; Joseph H. Smith, "Praying In the Holy Ghost," *Heart and Life*, January, 1927, pp. 12, 13.
736. Smith, "Praying in the Holy Ghost," *The Free Methodist*, December 4, 1942, p. 2.
737. Smith, *Things of the Spirit*, pp. 103, 104.
738. *Ibid.*
739. *Ibid.*
740. Smith, "Spiritual Life Suggestions," *The Christian Witness*, May 30, 1935, p. 10.
741. Smith, *Things of the Spirit*, pp. 85ff.
742. *Ibid.*
743. *Ibid.*, p. 87.
744. *Ibid.*, pp. 85, 86.
745. *Ibid.*, p. 87, 88.
746. Joseph H. Smith, *Holiness Text-Book*, pp. 172, 173.
747. Smith, *Things of the Spirit*, pp. 85ff.; Joseph H. Smith, "Making Little of Sin," *The Christian Witness*, May 28, 1936, p. 2.
748. Smith, *Things of the Spirit*, p. 84.

302   A THEOLOGY OF CHRISTIAN EXPERIENCE

749. Smith, "Question Box," *The Christian Witness*, February 21, 1935, p. 6.
750. Smith, *Things of the Spirit*, p. 68.
751. *Ibid.*, p. 69.
752. *Ibid.*, p. 71.
753. Smith, *Things of the Spirit*, pp. 71ff.; Smith, "Spiritual Life Suggestions," *The Christian Witness*, December 16, 1937, p. 10.
754. *Ibid.*, February 14, 1935, p. 10.
755. *Ibid.*, December 16, 1937, p. 10.
756. Smith, *Things of the Spirit*, pp. 71–73.
757. *Ibid.*, pp. 73–75.
758. *Ibid., passim.*

CHAPTER SEVEN

759. Smith, *From Glory to Glory*, p. 69.
760. *Supra*, p. 118.
761. Smith, "Cardinal Doctrines of the Bible," *Heart and Life*, March, 1921, pp. 6, 7.
762. *Ibid.*
763. *Ibid.*
764. *Ibid.*
765. *Ibid.*
766. *Ibid.*
767. *Ibid.*
768. *Ibid., passim;* Joseph H. Smith, "Holiness Progressive and Instantaneous," *Friends' Expositor*, October, 1891, pp. 575–577.
769. Smith, "Spiritual Life Suggestions," *The Christian Witness*, February 10, 1937, p. 10.
770. *Ibid.*, May 2, 1935, p. 10.
771. Joseph H. Smith, "The Calls of the Master," *Heart and Life*, January, 1928, p. 12.
772. *Ibid.*
773. Joseph H. Smith, "Saved From Wrath," *The Pentecostal Herald*, May 17, 1944, p. 4; Smith, *From Glory to Glory*, p. 82.
774. *Ibid.*
775. Smith, "Spiritual Life Suggestions," *The Christian Witness*, October 22, 1936, p. 10.
776. Smith, "Saved From Wrath," *The Pentecostal Herald*, May 17, 1944, p. 4.
777. *Ibid.*
778. *Ibid.*
779. Smith, *Pauline Perfection*, p. 52; Smith, "Spiritual Life Suggestions," *The Christian Witness*, November 12, 1936, p. 10.
780. Smith, *From Glory to Glory*, pp. 35, 36.
781. *Ibid.*, pp. 33–35.
782. *Ibid.*
783. *Ibid.*
784. Joseph H. Smith, "A Revival of Repentance," *God's Revivalist*, September 10, 1925, p. 2f.; Joseph H. Smith, "David's Repentance, Psalm Fifty-One," *Heart and Life*, October, 1939, pp. 4, 5.

785. *Ibid.*
786. Smith, *From Glory to Glory*, pp. 35, 36.
787. Smith, *Things of the Spirit*, p. 33.
788. Joseph H. Smith, "The Power of the Gospel," *Heart and Life*, September, 1921, pp. 7–9.
789. Smith, *From Glory to Glory*, p. 98.
790. Smith, *Things of the Spirit*, pp. 33, 34.
791. Joseph H. Smith, "Faith—A Factor," *God's Revivalist*, November 5, 1936, p. 3.
792. *Ibid.*
793. Smith, "Spiritual Life Suggestions," *The Christian Witness*, October 22, 1936, p. 10.
794. Smith, *From Glory to Glory*, p. 83.
795. Smith, "The Question Box," *The Christian Witness*, August 28, 1919, p. 5.
796. Smith, "Question Box," *Heart and Life*, November, 1929, p. 9.
797. Smith, *From Glory to Glory*, pp. 93, 94, 118.
798. Smith, "Spiritual Life Suggestions," *The Christian Witness*, November 29, 1934, p. 13; Joseph H. Smith, "Your Righteousness—Matthew 5:20," *The Free Methodist*, March 6, 1936, p. 3; Rom. 8:3, 4.
799. *Ibid.*; Smith, *Things of the Spirit*, p. 49.
800. Smith, *From Glory to Glory*, pp. 93, 94.
801. *Ibid.*
802. Smith, "The Glory Road—Ephesians 1:1–14," *The Pentecostal Herald*, March 6, 1946, p. 4; Smith, "Spiritual Life Suggestions," *The Christian Witness*, January 17, 1929, p. 10.
803. *Ibid.*; Smith, *Pauline Perfection*, p. 43.
804. Smith, "Question Box," *The Christian Witness*, February 21, 1935, p. 6.
805. Smith, "Spiritual Life Suggestions," *ibid.*, January 17, 1929, p. 10.
806. Smith, "Witness of the Spirit," *God's Revivalist*, August 2, 1928, pp. 3, 4.
807. *Ibid.*; Smith, *From Glory to Glory*, p. 138.
808. Joseph H. Smith, "The Witness of Our Own Spirit, of the Holy Spirit," *Heart and Life*, October, 1922, p. 14f.
810. *Ibid.*
811. *Ibid.*
812. Smith, *From Glory to Glory*, p. 138.
813. Smith, "Spiritual Beginnings," *God's Revivalist*, September 28, 1933, p. 5.
814. Joseph H. Smith, "A Revivalist of Repentance," *ibid.*, September 10, 1925, p. 2f.
815. Smith, "Spiritual Life Suggestions," *The Christian Witness*, April 15, 1937, p. 6.
816. Joseph H. Smith, "Questions and Answers," *Heart and Life*, October, 1923, p. 12.
817. Smith, "Spiritual Life Suggestions," *The Christian Witness*, April 15, 1937, p. 6.
818. *Ibid.*

819. *Ibid.*, November 1, 1934, p. 10.
820. *Ibid.*
821. *Ibid.*; Smith, "Making Little of Sin," *ibid.*, May 28, 1936, p. 2.
822. *Ibid.*
823. *Ibid.*
824. Joseph H. Smith, "The Uttermost Salvation," *The Pentecostal Herald*, April 25, 1945, p. 4.
825. Joseph H. Smith, "Judgment Begun at the House of God," *Heart and Life*, May, 1919, p. 10.
826. Joseph H. Smith, "Trials and Temptations," *God's Revivalist*, February 10, 1938, p. 3.
827. *Ibid.*
828. Smith, "Spiritual Life Suggestions," *The Christian Witness*, April 1, 1937, p. 10.
829. Smith, "Are We in Touch with the Spirit World," *Heart and Life*, May-June, 1938, pp. 4, 5.
830. Smith, *From Glory to Glory*, pp. 156–166.
831. *Ibid.*, p. 152.
832. *Ibid.*, pp. 156, 157.
833. *Ibid.*
834. *Ibid.*, pp. 158, 159.
835. Smith, *From Glory to Glory*, p. 160f.
836. *Ibid.*, p. 161.
837. *Ibid.*, pp. 161, 162.
838. Smith, "A Living Savior," *Heart and Life*, September, 1925, p. 9.
839. Joseph H. Smith, "On Sanctification," *Heart and Life*, February, 1929, pp. 18, 19.
840. *Ibid.*; Smith, "Question Box," *The Christian Witness*, June 6, 1935, p. 6.
841. Joseph H. Smith, "What is Christian Holiness and How Obtained," *The Free Methodist*, October 22, 1937, p. 2.
842. Smith, *From Glory to Glory*, p. 95.
843. Joseph H. Smith, "Peter's Four Reasons for our Sanctification," *The Free Methodist*, April 13, 1934, p. 2f.
844. Smith, *Pauline Perfection*, p. 47.
845. *Ibid.*, p. 4.
846. *Ibid.*, pp. 4, 5.
847. *Ibid.*, p. 5.
848. *Ibid.*, pp. 4, 5.
849. *Ibid.*, passim.
850. Smith, *From Glory to Glory*, p. 97.
851. *Ibid.*
852. *Ibid.*, p. 98; Smith, "Your Righteousness," *The Free Methodist*, March 6, 1936, p. 3.
853. Smith, "Peter's Four Reasons for our Sanctification," *The Free Methodist*, April 13, 1934, p. 2f.
854. Smith, *From Glory to Glory*, pp. 32, 33.
855. Smith, *Pauline Perfection*, pp. 47, 48.
856. *Ibid.*, p. 75.

FOOTNOTES

857. Joseph H. Smith, "Conviction for Holiness," *Friends' Expositor*, April, 1888, p. 131.
858. *Ibid.*, p. 132.
859. *Ibid.*, p. 133.
860. Smith, *From Glory to Glory*, p. 98; Joseph H. Smith, "Entire Sanctification," *God's Revivalist*, May 11, 1933, pp. 2, 3.
861. Smith, *Holiness Text-Book*, p. 26.
862. *Ibid.*
863. *Ibid.*; Joseph H. Smith, "Paul's Consecration," *Heart and Life*, June, 1922, p. 7.
864. Joseph H. Smith, "Their Own Selves," *God's Revivalist*, February 25, 1943, p. 5.
865. Smith, "Question Box," *Heart and Life*, April, 1916, p. 9.
866. Smith, "Faith that Sanctifies," *The Christian Witness*, August 27, 1914, pp. 3, 4.
867. Smith, *Holiness Text-Book*, p. 56.
868. *Ibid.*, p. 57.
869. Smith, "Faith That Sanctifies," *The Christian Witness*, August 27, 1914, pp. 3, 4.
870. Smith, *Pauline Perfection*, pp. 118, 119; Smith, *Holiness Text-Book*, p. 57.
871. Smith, "Question Box," *Heart and Life*, August, 1916, p. 11.
872. Smith, "Entire Sanctification," *God's Revivalist*, May 11, 1933, pp. 2, 3.
873. Smith, "The Setting of Sanctification," *Heart and Life*, February, 1930, p. 6f.
874. Joseph H. Smith, "Spiritual Purity," *The Pentecostal Herald*, February 14, 1912, p. 2.
875. *Ibid.*
876. Joseph H. Smith, "Desires," *Heart and Life*, May, 1924, p. 6.
877. Joseph H. Smith, "Pureness," *ibid.*, December, 1921, p. 6.
878. Joseph H. Smith, "Charity is Perfect Love," *The Christian Witness*, January 23, 1936, p. 2f.
879. Joseph H. Smith, "Perfect Love," *The Pentecostal Herald*, June 14, 1905, p. 2.
880. *Ibid.*
881. Smith, "Spiritual Purity," *The Pentecostal Herald*, February 14, 1912, p. 2.
882. Smith, "Perfect Love," *ibid.*, June 14, 1905, p. 2.
883. Joseph H. Smith, "Perfection and Progression," *Heart and Life*, November, 1924, pp. 9, 10; Joseph H. Smith, "A Pattern for the Perfect Mind," *ibid.*, May, 1920, pp. 10, 11; Smith, *Pauline Perfection*, p. 167.
884. Joseph H. Smith, "Perfection Perplexity," *Heart and Life*, August, 1918, pp. 14, 15.
885. Smith, "Perfection and Progression," *ibid.*, November, 1924, pp. 9f.
886. Smith, *From Glory to Glory*, p. 80.
887. *Ibid.* p. 81.
888. Smith, "Holiness Progressive and Instantaneous," *Friends' Expositor*, October, 1891, p. 575f.

889. *Ibid.*
890. Smith, *From Glory to Glory*, pp. 119, 120.
891. Smith, "Deepening of the Spiritual Life," *God's Revivalist*, July 27, 1933, p. 2.
892. *Ibid.*
893. Smith, "Charity is Perfect Love," *The Christian Witness*, January 23, 1936, p. 2f.; Joseph H. Smith, "Christian Perfection," *Heart and Life*, August, 1932, pp. 4, 5.
894. Joseph H. Smith, "More to Follow," *God's Revivalist*, September 5, 1935, pp. 4, 13.
895. Smith, *From Glory to Glory*, pp. 126–127.
896. Smith, "Holiness Progressive and Instantaneous," *Friends' Expositor*, October, 1891, p. 576f.; Joseph H. Smith, "Perfection Not the End of Progression," *The Free Methodist*, February 7, 1936, pp. 2, 3.
897. *Ibid.*
898. Joseph H. Smith, "The Wonderful Epistle of Jude," *God's Revivalist*, March 1, 1934, pp. 2–4; Smith, "Question Box," *The Christian Witness*, August 1, 1935, p. 6.
899. Joseph H. Smith, "Expository Lines on Philippians 2:12–16," *God's Revivalist*, January 18, 1945, p. 1.
900. Smith, "The Wonderful Epistle of Jude," *ibid.*, March 1, 1934, pp. 2f.
901. *Ibid.*
902. Joseph H. Smith, "The Prophecy of Jude," *ibid.*, March 17, 1938, p. 9.
903. Joseph H. Smith, "Preservation is More Than Sanctification," *The Christian Witness*, May 30, 1935, p. 2.
904. Smith, *Things of the Spirit*, pp. 93–95; Smith, *Pauline Perfection*, p. 148.
905. Smith, "Spiritual Life Suggestions," *The Christian Witness*, November 12, 1936, p. 10.
906. *Ibid.*
907. Joseph H. Smith, "The Crown of Life," *Heart and Life*, August, 1926, p. 8.
908. Joseph H. Smith, "His Will," *The Pentecostal Herald*, October 13, 1943, p. 3; Joseph H. Smith, "Creed and Character," *The Christian Witness*, January 2, 1936, p. 3.
909. Smith, "Our Glorification," *Herald of Holiness*, September 17, 1938, p. 6.
910. Smith, "The Question Box," *The Christian Witness*, July 15, 1920, p. 3.
911. I Cor. 15; Smith, *Pauline Perfection*, p. 65.
912. Joseph H. Smith, "The Body Kept Under," *God's Revivalist*, September 12, 1935, p. 4.
913. Smith, *From Glory to Glory*, p. 171.
914. *Ibid.*, p. 177; Smith, *Things of the Spirit*, pp. 76–81.
915. *Ibid.*, passim; Smith, *From Glory to Glory*, passim.
916. Smith, "Our Glorification," *Herald of Holiness*, September 17, 1938, p. 6.
917. Smith, *From Glory to Glory*, p. 88.
918. Smith, *Pauline Perfection*, p. 7; Smith, *Things of the Spirit*, p. 51.

FOOTNOTES

919. Smith, "Our Glorification," *Herald of Holiness*, September 17, 1938, p. 5.
920. Rom. 14:17.
921. Smith, "Spiritual Life Suggestions," *The Christian Witness*, August 28, 1919, p. 10; Smith, "Question Box," *ibid.*, November 8, 1934; p. 6.
922. Smith, "Spiritual Life Suggestions," *The Christian Witness*, August 15, 1935, p. 10.
923. Joseph H. Smith, "Spoiled Christianity," *Friends' Expositor*, July, 1889, p. 272f.
924. Joseph H. Smith, "A Wider View of the Church," *Heart and Life*, May-June, 1934, p. 4f.
925. Joseph H. Smith, "The Loveliness of Zion is in Her Spirituality," *Friends' Expositor*, July, 1892, p. 677f.
926. Joseph H. Smith, "The Beginning of the Christian Church," *God's Revivalist*, June 6–13, 1929, p. 2; Smith, *Pauline Perfection*, p. 92f.; Joseph H. Smith, "An Holy Nation," *The Pentecostal Herald*, April 19, 1911, p. 2; Joseph H. Smith, "Holiness and the Church," *The Pentecostal Herald*, May 13, 1908, pp. 2–9.
927. Smith, "The Beginning of the Christian Church," *God's Revivalist*, June 6–13, 1929, p. 2.
928. Smith, "A Wider View of the Church," *Heart and Life*, May-June, 1934, p. 5.
929. Smith, "Holiness and the Church," *The Pentecostal Herald*, May 13, 1908, pp. 2, 3.
930. Smith, "Spiritual Life Suggestions," *The Christian Witness*, December 2, 1937, p. 10.
931. *Ibid.*
932. *Ibid.*, November 26, 1942, p. 4.
933. *Ibid.*, December 2, 1937, p. 10.
934. Smith, "The Loveliness of Zion is in Her Spirituality," *Friends' Expositor*, July, 1892, pp. 675–677.
935. Smith, "Spiritual Life Suggestions," *The Christian Witness*, November 8, 1934, p. 10.
936. *Ibid.*, August 28, 1919, p. 10.
937. *Ibid.*, November 8, 1934, p. 10.
938. *Ibid.*
939. Smith, "A Wider View of the Church," *Heart and Life*, May-June, 1934, p. 4.
940. *Ibid.*, 5f.
941. *Ibid;* Smith, "The Loveliness of Zion is in Her Spirituality," *Friends' Expositor*, July, 1892, pp. 675–677.
942. Smith, "Wheat and Tares," *God's Revivalist*, May 28, 1936, pp. 4, 8; Joseph H. Smith, "Ending the Old and Entering the New," *ibid.*, January 17, 1935, p. 2f.
943. Smith, "Holiness Evangelism To All Christendom," *Heart and Life*, November, 1940, p. 4f.
944. Smith, "A Wider View of the Church," *Heart and Life*, May-June, 1934, p. 4f.
945. Smith, "Every Man," *God's Revivalist*, November 2, 1939, p. 2.

946. *Ibid.*
947. Joseph H. Smith, "Why Should I Remain in an Unholy Church?" *Heart and Life*, October-November, 1912, pp. 7, 8.
948. Joseph H. Smith, "Wheat and Tares," *God's Revivalist*, May 28, 1936, p. 4, 8.
949. Smith, "Why Should I Remain in an Unholy Church," *Heart and Life*, October-November, 1912, pp. 7, 8.
950. Smith, "Wheat and Tares," *God's Revivalist*, May 28, 1936, pp. 4, 8.
951. *Ibid.*
952. Smith, "Spiritual Life Suggestions," *The Christian Witness*, August 31, 1939, p. 10.
953. Joseph H. Smith, "Gifts For the Perfecting of the Saints," *God's Revivalist*, January 25, 1923, pp. 2-4; Joseph H. Smith, "The Spirit's Making of the Minister," *Heart and Life*, March, 1929, pp. 15, 16.
954. Smith, "Wise," *Heart and Life*, August, 1915, p. 10.
955. Smith, *Pauline Perfection, passim.*
956. Mrs. F. S. Teed, Interview between author and, Ann Arbor, Michigan, July 11, 1950.
957. Smith, *Pauline Perfection*, pp. 189-190.
958. Smith, "The Loveliness of Zion is in Her Spirituality," *Friends' Expositor*, July, 1892, pp. 675-677.
959. *Ibid;* Joseph H. Smith, "Spirituality, The Core of the Gospel, and Evangelism, the Work of the Ministry," *Heart and Life*, March, 1924, pp. 8, 9.
960. Smith, "The Loveliness of Zion is in Her Spirituality," *Friends' Expositor*, July, 1892, p. 677.
961. Smith, "A Wider View of the Church," *Heart and Life*, May-June, 1934, p. 4f.
962. Smith, "Spiritual Life Suggestions," *The Christian Witness*, November 26, 1942, p. 4.
963. Smith, "A Wider View of the Church," *Heart and Life*, p. 4f.
964. *Ibid.*, p. 5f.
965. Smith, "Spiritual Life Suggestions," *The Christian Witness*, May 23, 1935, p. 10.
966. *Ibid.*
967. Smith, *From Glory to Glory*, p. 160f.
968. Smith, "Spiritual Life Suggestions," *The Christian Witness*, May 23, 1935, p. 10.
969. Smith, "Spiritual Life Suggestions," *The Christian Witness*, December 6, 1934, p. 10f.
970. *Ibid.*, October 4, 1934, p. 10.
971. Joseph H. Smith, " 'The Work of An Evangelist,' " *ibid.*, October 20, 1927, p. 1.
972. Joseph H. Smith, "The Spirit's Making of the Minister," *Heart and Life*, March, 1929, pp. 15, 16.
973. Smith, *From Glory to Glory*, pp. 102, 103.
974. Joseph H. Smith, " 'Is Evangelism Dying?' " *The Christian Witness*, February 3, 1938, p. 2.
975. Smith, "Spiritual Life Suggestions," *ibid.*, August 31, 1939, p. 10.

976. Smith, "'The Work of An Evangelist,'" *ibid.*, October 20, 1927, p. 1.
977. *Ibid.*
978. Joseph H. Smith, "'A Good Minister of Jesus Christ,'" *Heart and Life*, April, 1919, pp. 9–11.
979. Joseph H. Smith, "A World-Wide Holiness Movement," *God's Revivalist*, March 31, 1932, p. 2.
980. *Ibid.*
981. Smith, "Spiritual Life Suggestions," *The Christian Witness*, January 30, 1936, p. 10.
982. *Ibid.*
983. *Ibid.*
984. *Ibid.*
985. Joseph H. Smith, "After War Winds, And Ballast Against Them," *Heart and Life*, September, 1920, p. 11.
986. Smith, *From Glory to Glory*, pp. 132ff.
987. Smith, "'A Good Minister of Jesus Christ,'" *Heart and Life*, April, 1919, pp. 9–11.
988. Joseph H. Smith, "An Evangelist's Equipment," *ibid.*, October, 1913, pp. 3, 4.
989. Quoted in *An Account of Pentecostal Services at Mountain Lake Park, Maryland*, July, 1896, pp. 63–70.
990. Joseph H. Smith, "Concerning Holiness," *Heart and Life*, June, 1928, p. 4.
991. Smith, "Holiness and the Church," *The Pentecostal Herald*, May 5, 1908, pp. 2, 3.
992. Smith, "Creed and Character," *The Christian Witness*, January 2, 1936, p. 3.
993. Smith, *Pauline Perfection*, pp. 25, 117, 199, 200.
994. *Ibid.*, pp. 92, 198.
995. Smith, "Sanctification," *Heart and Life*, February and March, 1912, pp. 10, 11.
996. Joseph H. Smith, "Consistency with Holiness," *ibid.*, May, 1927, p. 14.
997. Joseph H. Smith, "An All-World Revival Beginning at Christendom," *God's Revivalist*, August 18, 1932, p. 1.
998. Smith, "Holiness and the Church," *The Pentecostal Herald*, May 13, 1908, pp. 2–3.
999. Smith, "Spiritual Life Suggestions," *The Christian Witness*, February 4, 1937, p. 10.
1000. Smith, *Pauline Perfection*, pp. 92–93.
1001. Joseph H. Smith, "Doctrine and Duty," *ibid*, March 5, 1936, p. 4.
1002. Joseph H Smith, "The Touchstone," *The Pentecostal Herald*, February 9, 1921, pp. 3, 4.
1003. Smith, "Spiritual Life Suggestions," *The Christian Witness*, March 19, 1936, p. 10.
1004. Joseph H. Smith, "The Coming Revival," *The Free Methodist*, July 5, 1935, p. 2.
1005. Smith, "Spiritual Life Suggestions," *The Christian Witness*, September 9, 1937, p. 10.
1006. Smith, *Pauline Perfection*, p. 104.

1007. *Ibid.*, pp. 93, 104.
1008. Smith, *From Glory to Glory*, pp. 15, 16.
1009. *Ibid.*; Smith, "Glorification," *Herald of Holiness*, September 17, 1938, p. 5.
1010. Smith, *From Glory to Glory*, pp. 170, 177.
1011. Joseph H. Smith, "Hope of Heaven," *God's Revivalist*, February 8, 1934, p. 9.
1012. Smith, "Creed and Character," *The Christian Witness*, January 2, 1936, p. 4.
1013. Smith, "The Menace to Our Evangelism," *Heart and Life*, August, 1927, p. 12f.
1014. *Ibid.*; Smith, "Creed and Character," *The Christian Witness*, January 2, 1936, p. 4; Smith, *From Glory to Glory*, p. 171f.
1015. *Ibid.*, p. 174.
1016. *Ibid.*, pp. 171ff.
1017. Smith, "Our Glorification," *Herald of Holiness*, September 17, 1938, p. 5.
1018. Smith, *From Glory to Glory*, pp. 175–178.
1019. Smith, "Our Glorification," *Herald of Holiness*, September 17, 1938, p. 5.
1020. Smith, *Things of the Spirit*, p. 59.
1021. Smith, *From Glory to Glory*, p. 173.
1022. *Ibid.*
1023. Smith, "Question Box," *Heart and Life*, May, 1921, pp. 6, 7.
1024. Wilbur M. Smith, *Therefore Stand*, p. 443.
1025. Smith, "The Curse of Christ," *Heart and Life*, June, 1921, pp. 6, 7.
1026. *Ibid.*
1027. Smith, *From Glory to Glory*, pp. 170, 171.
1028. Smith, "Christ's Intercession, 'I Pray for Them,'" *God's Revivalist*, August 4, 1938, pp. 2, 3; Smith, "Our Glorification," *Herald of Holiness*, September 17, 1938, p. 5.
1029. Smith, *From Glory to Glory*, p. 113.
1030. Joseph H. Smith, "The Risen and Reigning Christ," *God's Revivalist*, April 10, 1941, p. 7; Smith, "Question Box," *Heart and Life*, May, 1921, pp. 6, 7.
1031. Smith, *Things of the Spirit*, p. 109.
1032. Smith, *From Glory to Glory*, passim.
1034. Harris, Rev. Wallace H., Correspondence between author and, dated June 9, 1948; enclosing a copy of the "Memoir" to Joseph H. Smith in 1946 Philadelphia Conference Minutes of the Methodist Church, prepared by Rev. Robert M. Anderson.

Bibliography

PRIMARY SOURCES

Books

1. A. J. E., *The Holiness Revival of the Past Century*, [n.p.], Philadelphia, [n.d.].
2. Bowman, Rev. H. J., *Voices on Holiness from the Evangelical Association*, Publishing House of the Ev. Association, Cleveland, Ohio, 1882.
3. Cary, W. W., *Story of the National Holiness Missionary Society*, National Holiness Missionary Society, Chicago, Ill., 1940.
4. Chapman, J. B., *A History of the Church of the Nazarene*, Nazarene Publishing House, Kansas City, Mo., 1926.
5. Clark, Dougan, and Joseph H. Smith, *David B. Updegraff and His Work*, Revivalist Office, Cincinnati, 1895.
6. Danford, S. A., *Spreading Scriptural Holiness, or, The North Dakota Movement*, The Christian Witness, Chicago, 1913.
7. *The Doctrines and Discipline of the Methodist Episcopal Church, 1880*, Harris, Bishop, editor, Walden & Stowe, Cincinnati, 1880.
8. *Echoes of the General Holiness Assembly*, Shaw, S. B., editor, S. B. Shaw, Publisher, Chicago, Ill., [n.d.].
9. *An Essay on Camp-Meetings*, Published by Lane & Scott, New York, 1849.
10. *Flames of Living Fire*, Smith, Bernie, compiler, Beacon Hill Press, Kansas City, Mo., 1950.
11. Godbey, W. B., *Bible Theology*, God's Revivalist Office, Cincinnati, Ohio, 1911.
12. Goreham, Rev. B. Weed, *God's Method With Man: or Sacred Scenes Along the Path to Heaven*, B. Weed Goreham, Boston, 1885.
13. Haney, M. L., *Pentecostal Possibilities, or Story of My Life*, The Christian Witness Co., Chicago, 1906.
14. Haynes, B. F., *Tempest-Tossed On Methodist Seas*, Pentecostal Publishing Company, Louisville, Ky., 1921.
15. Hughes, George, *The Beloved Physician, Walter C. Palmer*, Palmer and Hughes, New York, ca. 1884.
16. _____, *Days of Power in the Forest Temple, 1867 to 1872*, John Bent & Co., Boston, ca. 1873.
17. _____, *Fragrant Memories of the Tuesday Meeting and The Guide to Holiness and their Fifty Years' Work for Jesus*, Palmer & Hughes, New York, 1886.
18. *Hymnal of the Methodist Episcopal Church*, Phillips & Hunt, New York, 1883.
19. Inskip, J. S., *Methodism Explained and Defended*, H. S. & J. Applegate, Cincinnati, 1851.

20. Jernigan, C. B., *Pioneer Days of the Holiness Movement in the Southwest*, Pentecostal Nazarene Publishing House, Kansas City, Mo., 1919.
21. Jessop, H. E., *We the Holiness People*, Chicago Evangelistic Institute, Chicago, Illinois, 1948.
22. Keen, Rev. S. A., *Praise Papers*, Published for the Author by Cranston & Curts, 1895.
23. McDonald, William, *Scriptural Way of Holiness, or The Path Made Plain*, The Christian Witness Co., Chicago, 1904.
24. McLaughlin, George Asbury, *Autobiography of George Asbury McLaughlin*, The Christian Witness Co., Chicago, [n.d.].
25. McDonald, W., and John E. Searles, *The Life of Rev. John S. Inskip*, The Christian Witness Co., Chicago, 1885.
26. Mahan, Asa, *The Baptism of the Holy Ghost*, Pickett Publishing Co., Louisville, Ky., 1870.
27. Morrison, Henry Clay, *Life Sketches and Sermons*, Pentecostal Publishing Co., Louisville, 1903.
28. _____, *Some Chapters of My Life Story*, Pentecostal Publishing Co., Louisville, Ky., 1941.
29. *The National Association for the Promotion of Holiness: 1932–1936*, The Christian Witness Co., Chicago, Ill., [n.d.].
30. Osborn, Mrs. W. B., *Pioneer Days of Ocean Grove*, Methodist Book Concern, New York, [n.d.].
31. Palmer, Mrs., *Four Years in The Old World*, Pickett Publishing Co., Louisville, Ky., [n.d.].
32. _____, *The Way of Holiness*, Foster and Palmer, Jr., New York, 1867.
33. *Penuel; or Face to Face with God*, McLean, Rev. A. and Rev. J. W. Eaton, editors, W. C. Palmer, Jr., Publisher, New York, 1871.
34. Pickett, L. L., *Plea for the Present Holiness Movement*, Pentecostal Publishing Co., Louisville, [n.d.].
35. Robinson, Bud, *Sunshine and Smiles*, The Christian Witness Co., Chicago, 1903.
36. Roche, John A., *The Life of Mrs. Sarah A. Lankford Palmer*, George Hughes & Co., New York, N.Y., 1898.
37. Smith, Joseph H., *From Glory to Glory*, Christian Standard Co., Ltd., Philadelphia, 1898.
38. _____, *Holiness Text-Book*, God's Bible School and Revivalist, Cincinnati, O., 1922.
39. _____, *Pauline Perfection*, The Christian Witness Co., Chicago, Ill., 1913.
40. _____, *Things Behind and Things Before in the Holiness Movement*, Evangelist Institute Press, Chicago, 1916.
41. _____, *Things of the Spirit*, The Chicago Evangelistic Institute, Chicago, Illinois, 1940.
42. _____, *Training in Pentecostal Evangelism*, Christian Standard Co., Ltd., Philadelphia, 1897.
43. *True Method of Promoting Perfect Love: From Debates in the New York Preachers' Meeting of the Methodist Episcopal Church, on the*

Question, What Are the Best Methods of Promoting the Experience of Perfect Love? Foster & Palmer, Jr., New York, 1867.
44. Upham, Thomas C., *Principles of the Interior or Hidden Life*, Harper & Brothers, New York, 1873.
45. Wallace, Rev. Adam, *A Modern Pentecost: Embracing a Record of the Sixteenth National Camp-Meeting For Promotion of Holiness, held at Landisville, Pa., July 23rd to August 1st, 1873.* Methodist Home Journal Publishing House, Philadelphia, 1873.
46. Wesley, John, *Plain Account of Christian Perfection*, McDonald, Gill & Co., Boston, Mass., [n.d.].
47. Wheatley, Rev. Richard, *Life and Letters of Mrs. Phoebe Palmer*, W. C. Palmer, Jr., New York, N.Y., 1876.
48. Williams, Mrs. E. E., *Pentecostal Services...at Mountain Lake Park* (Garret Co., Maryland)...1896. Published by Rev. John Thompson, Philadelphia, [n.d.].
49. Wood, J. A., *Auto-Biography of Rev. J. A. Wood*, The Christian Witness Company, Chicago, 1904.
50. _____, *Perfect Love; or...Christian Holiness*, Revised edition, The Christian Witness Co., Chicago, 1910.
51. *Yearbook of the Holiness Union containing A Full Report of the Holiness Convention Held at Memphis, Tenn., October 11-14, 1904.* Bromley, W. W., compiler, Pentecostal Herald Print, Louisville, Ky., [n.d.].

PERIODICALS AND PAMPHLETS

52. *Advocate of Christian Holiness*, McDonald, William, editor. Vols. I-V, 1870-1874, *passim*.
53. Cary, W. W., "Sychar, An Holiness Camp Meeting." The Pentecostal Publishing Co., Louisville, Ky., [n.d.].
54. *The Christian Witness*, McDonald, William; Fowler, C. J., McLaughlin, G. A.; Butler, C. W., editors. New Series, Vol. XV-Vol. LXIV, 1897-1946.
55. *The Free Methodist*, Howland, Carl, editor. Vols. 67-75, 1934-1942.
56. *Friends' Expositor*, Updegraff, David B., editor. Vols. I-VI, 1887-1892.
57. *God's Revivalist*, Stanley, M. G., editor. Vols. 26-58, 1914-1946.
58. *Heart and Life*, Vennard, Iva Durham, and Jessop, H. E., editors. Vols. 1-33, 1911-1946.
59. *Herald of Holiness*, Corlett, D. Shelby, editor. Vol. 27, 1938.
60. *The Pentecostal Herald*, Morrison, H. C., and McPheeters, J. C., editors. Vols. 10, 16, 17, 20, 21, 23, 24, 25, 29, 33, 36, 37, 40, 42, 43, 44, 45, 49, 50, 55, 56, 58, 61. 1898-1950.
61. Smith, Joseph H., "Educational Limitation in the Holiness Movement," A sermon preached at Cleveland Bible Institute, Cleveland, Ohio, May 28, 1922, [n.p.].

MANUSCRIPTS

62. Smith, Joseph H., "Consecration More Than Consecration," unpublished article in the F. S. Tweed collection. Ann Arbor, Michigan.

63. _____, "Faith and Facts," *ibid.*
64. _____, "Paul's Definition and Explanation of Faith," *ibid.*
65. _____, "A Peculiar People," *ibid.*
66. _____, "Preservation," *ibid.*

Official Minutes

67. *Minutes of the Annual Conferences of the Methodist Episcopal Church, for the Year 1875*, Nelson and Phillips, New York, N.Y., 1875.
68. *1906 Year Book and Minutes of the Iowa Holiness Association*, published by the General Secretary, Globe Presses, Oskaloosa, Iowa, 1906.
69. *Official Minutes of the National Association for the Promotion of Holiness, for 1907*, unpublished record, Trevecca Nazarene College, Nashville, Tennessee.
70. *Ibid.*, for 1926–1928.

Letters

71. Smith, Joseph H., Correspondence between J. Hunter Smith, and, dated March 10, 1927.
72. _____, Correspondence between J. Hunter Smith, and, dated November 21, 1942.
73. Thomas, John and Emily, Correspondence between Joseph H. Smith, and, dated April 15, 1913.

Personal Interviews

74. Butler, C. W., Interview between author and, Detroit, Michigan, June 20–26, 1952.
75. _____, Interview between author and, Detroit, Michigan, July 11–12, 1950.
76. Smith, J. Hunter, Interview between author and, Balboa Island, California, June 10, 1949.

Miscellaneous

77. Cary, W. W., Unpublished record of an interview between Joseph H. Smith, and, Cincinnati, Ohio, April 25, 1936.
78. Smith, Joseph H., Phonographic recordings of chapel addresses at Chicago Evangelistic Institute, September 21, 1942, and September 11, 1944, by, Chicago Evangelistic Institute, University Park, Iowa.

SECONDARY SOURCES

Books

79. Beardsley, Frank Granville, *A History of American Revivals*, second edition, American Tract Society, New York, 1912.
80. Bowie, Mary Ella, *Alabaster and Spikenard, The Life of Iva Durham Vennard, D.D.*, Chicago Evangelistic Institute, Chicago, 1947.

81. Brown, Charles Ewing, *The Meaning of Sanctification*, The Warner Press, Anderson, Indiana, 1945.
82. Burtt, Edwin Arthur, *Types of Religious Philosophy*, Harper & Bros., New York, 1939.
83. Candler, Warren A., *Great Revivals and the Great Republic*, Publishing House of the M. E. Church, South, Lamar & Barton, Agents, Nashville, Tenn., 1924.
84. Cannon, William Ragsdale, *The Theology of John Wesley*, Abingdon-Cokesbury Press, New York, 1946.
85. Chapman, J. B., *Bud Robinson, A Brother Beloved*, Beacon Hill Press, Kansas City, Mo., 1943.
86. Clark, Elmer T., *The Small Sects in America*, Revised edition, Abingdon-Cokesbury Press, New York, 1949.
87. Coulter, E. Merton, *A Short History of Georgia*, The University of North Carolina Press, Chapel Hill, N.C., 1933.
88. Curtis, Olin Alfred, *The Christian Faith*, Eaton & Mains, New York, 1905.
89. *Cyclopedia of Methodism*, Simpson, Matthew, editor, Louis H. Everts, Philadelphia, 1880.
90. Douglass, Paul F., *The Story of German Methodism*, The Methodist Book Concern, New York, 1939.
91. Davies, Rev. E., *Bishop of Africa, or Life of William Taylor*, Holiness Book Concern, Reading, Mass., 1885.
92. Eberhardt, Charles Richard, *The Bible in the Making of Ministers*, Association Press, New York, 1949.
93. Fitzgerald, O. P., *The Class-Meeting*, Publishing House of the M. E. Church, South, Nashville, Tenn., 1911.
94. Flew, R. N., *The Idea of Perfection in Christian Theology*, Oxford University Press, London, 1934.
95. Hills, A. M., *Holiness and Power, For the Church and the Ministry*, Revivalist Office, Cincinnati, 1897.
96. Horton, Walter M., *Toward a Reborn Church*, Harper & Bros., New York, 1949.
97. Koeberle, Adolf, *The Quest for Holiness*, Translated from the 3rd German edition by J. C. Mattes, Augsburg Publishing House, Minneapolis, Minnesota, 1938.
98. Lindstrom, Harald, *Wesley and Sanctification*, Translated by H. S. Harvey, Nya Bokforlage Aktiebolaget, Stockholm, Sweden, 1946.
99. Luccock, Halford E., and Paul Hutchinson, *The Story of Methodism*, The Methodist Book Concern, New York, 1926.
100. McDonald, William, *John Wesley and His Doctrine*, The McDonald & Gill Co., Boston, 1893.
101. Mahan, Asa, *The Baptism of the Holy Ghost*, Pickett Publishing Co., Louisville, Ky., 1870.
102. Neve, J. L., *Churches and Sects of Christendom*, The Lutheran Literary Board, Burlington, Iowa, 1940.
103. Orr, J. Edwin, *The Second Evangelical Awakening in Britain*, Marshall, Morgan & Scott, Ltd., London, 1949.

104. Paul, John, *The Soul Digger, or Life and Times of William Taylor*, Taylor University Press, Upland, Indiana, 1928.
105. *Pennsylvania, A Guide to the Keystone State*, American Guide Series, Oxford University Press, New York, 1940.
106. Perkins, Harold W., *The Doctrine of Christian or Evangelical Perfection*, The Epworth Press, J. Alfred Sharp, London, 1927.
107. Redford, M. E., *The Rise of the Church of the Nazarene*, Nazarene Publishing House, Kansas City, Mo., [n.d.].
108. Rees, Paul S., *Seth Cook Rees, The Warrior-Saint*, The Pilgrim Book Room, Indianapolis, Ind., 1934.
109. Ridgaway, H. B., *The Life of the Rev. Alfred Cookman*, Harper & Bros., New York, 1873.
110. _____, *The Life of Edmund S. Janes, D.D., L.L.D.*, Phillips & Hunt, New York, 1882.
111. Sangster, W. E., *The Path to Perfection*, Abingdon Press, New York, 1938.
112. Schwab, Ralph Kendall, *The History of the Doctrine of Christian Perfection in the Evangelical Association*, George Banta Publishing Company, Menasha, Wisconsin, 1922.
113. Strong, Augustus H., *One Hundred Chapel Talks to Theological Students*, American Baptist Publication Society, Philadelphia, 1913.
114. Sweet, William W., *Methodism in American History*, The Methodist Book Concern, New York, 1933.
115. _____, *Revivalism in America*, Charles Scribner's Sons, New York, 1944.
116. _____, *The Story of Religion in America*, Harper & Brothers, New York, 1939.
117. Stevens, Abel, *History of the Methodist Episcopal Church*, 4 Vols., Published by Carlton & Porter, New York, 1867.
118. _____, *Life and Times of Nathan Bangs, D.D.*, Carlton & Porter, New York, 1863.
119. Smith, Wilbur M., *Therefore Stand*, Moody Press, Chicago, 1945.
120. Tipple, Ezra S., *Drew Theological Seminary, 1867-1917*, The Methodist Book Concern, New York, 1917.
121. Turner, George Allen, *The More Excellent Way*, Light and Life Press, Winona Lake, Indiana, 1952.
122. Tyerman, Luke, *Life and Times of the Rev. John Wesley, M.A.*, 3 Vols., Harper & Bros., New York, 1872.
123. Warfield, B. B., *Perfectionism*, 2 Vols., Oxford University Press, New York, 1931.
124. Wieman, Henry Nelson, and Bernhard Eugene Meland, *American Philosophies of Religion*, Willett, Clark & Co., 1936.
125. Wiley, H. Orton, *Christian Theology*, 3 Vols., Beacon Hill Press, Kansas City, Mo., 1940.
126. Wood J. A., *Christian Perfection as Taught by John Wesley*, McDonald & Gill, Boston, Mass., 1885.

PERIODICALS AND PAMPHLETS

127. "Asburians Assist in Philadelphia Revival," *Asbury Alumnus*, Vol. 24, No. 3, November, 1949, pp. 1, 3.
128. Butler, C. W., "Memorial Issue," *The Christian Witness*, New Series, Vol. LXIV, No. 14, June 6, 1946, pp. 1–2.
129. Haines, Paul E., "'And Their Works Do Follow Them,'" *The Missionary Standard*, 50th Anniversary of The Oriental Missionary Society, March, 1951, p. 3.
130. Johnson, Z. T., "The New Revival Movement in Methodism," *The Pentecostal Herald*, Vol. 62, No. 4, January 24, 1951, p. 4.
131. McPheeters, J. C., "Joseph H. Smith," *ibid.*, Vol. 58, Nos. 25–28, June 19–July 17, 1946, p. 8.
132. _____, "The General Conference of the Methodist Church," *The Herald*, Vol. 63, No. 22, May 28, 1952, pp. 1, 5.
133. _____, "Holiness and Social Reform," *ibid.*, Vol. 61, No. 48, December 6, 1950, pp. 1, 13.
134. Nall, T. Otto, "Evangelism in the Nation's Capitol," *The Christian Advocate*, Vol. 127, No. 14, April 3, 1953, pp. 5, 26.
135. Nixon, Lloyd H., "The American Camp Meeting," *Heart and Life*, Vol. 26, No. 9, June, 1940, pp. 10–13.
136. "Obituary," *The Christian Witness*, New Series, Vol. LXIV, No. 14, June 6, 1946, pp. 5, 9.
137. Paul, John, "Star Dust and Ashes, or Historic Sketches of 'The Movement' and of H. C. Morrison, one of its Bright 'Stars,'" *The Pentecostal Herald*, Vols. 59–60, Nos. 31–49, 1–4, August 6, 1947, to January 28, 1948, pp. 9ff.
138. "Preachers and Workers," *Program, Forty-Ninth Annual Camp Meeting for the Three Chicago Districts, Des Plaines, July 15–27, 1908*, [n.d.], p. 8.
139. "Rev. Timothy Merritt," *Advocate of Bible Holiness*, Vol. XIII, No. 7, July, 1882, pp. 193–195.
140. Sangster, W. E., "The Church's One Privation," *Religion in Life*, Vol. XVIII, No. 4, Autumn Number, 1949, pp. 493–502.
141. Thomas, Frank M., "Doctor Gross Alexander," *The Methodist Review*, Vol. 65, No. 1, January, 1916, pp. 3–19.
142. Turner, George A., "Holiness in the Calvinistic and Arminian Traditions," *Heart and Life*, Vol. 34, No. 2, November, 1947.
143. _____, *ibid.*, No. 3, December, 1947, pp. 15, 16, 30, 31.
144. *Yearbook of Chicago Evangelistic Institute*, 1914, [n.n.], Chicago, Illinois, 1914.

THESES AND DISSERTATIONS

145. Bletscher, Robert Dale, "The History of the Holiness Revival," unpublished B.D. thesis, Western Evangelical Seminary, 1950.
146. Carr, Catharine Delores, "The Early Background and a Brief History of Chicago Evangelistic Institute," unpublished M.A. thesis, Chicago Evangelistic Institute, Chicago, Illinois, now located at University Park, Iowa, 1932.

147. Dewey, Clifford Sherwood, "A History of John Fletcher College with special Reference to its Religious Traditions," unpublished M.A. thesis, State University of Iowa, 1940.
148. Gaddis, Merrill Elmer, "Christian Perfectionism in America," unpublished Ph.D. dissertation, University of Chicago, 1929.

LETTERS

149. Harris, Wallace H., Correspondence between author and, dated June 9 and 17, 1948.

PERSONAL INTERVIEWS

150. Teed, Mrs. F. S., Interview between author and, Ann Arbor, Michigan, July 11–13, 1950.
151. Turner, George A., Interview between author and, Wilmore, Kentucky, July 20, 1949.
152. Wesley, Bishop Arthur, Interview between author and, Chicago, Illinois, July 9, 1948.

MISCELLANEOUS

153. Anderson, Robert M., Memoir in 1946 Philadelphia Conference Minutes of the Methodist Church by, pp. 465–466; sent to the author by Wallace H. Harris, biographical secretary for the Philadelphia Conference.

Index

Adams, B.M.—68
Advocate of Christian Holiness—67
Albright, Jacob—60
Alexander, Gross—117
America—50-53
American Holiness Movement—15
American Methodism—18, 27
American Protestantism—26
Anglican—27
Anti-perfectionism—26
Armstrong, C. I.—77
Asbury College—71, 73, 106
Asbury Theological Seminary—116, 117
Australia—65

Babcock, Charles—270
Baker, Sheridan—68
Ballard, A. E.—68
Band Meetings—26
Bangs, Nathan—36, 37, 47
Baptism with the Holy Spirit—20, 21, 58
Baptists—36, 37, 62
Beauty of Holiness—48
Bethel Mission of Shanghai—126
Biblical Seminary in New York—118
Boardman, W. E.—37, 47, 48
Bombay—64, 65
Boole, W. H.—68
Booth, William—30, 50
Bresee, P. F.—68
Bringing in the Sheaves—48
Brodhead, George M.—270
Brooks, D. F.—68
Butler, C. W.—77, 113

Camp Meeting(s)—28, 29, 31, 32, 34, 41, 43, 47, 50, 52, 53, 55, 56, 63, 66, 68, 74, 99, 110, 121, 130.
Canada—40, 48, 63
Carradine, Beverly—68
Caughey, James—47, 48
Central Idea of Christianity—48

Central Methodist Episcopal Church, Philadelphia—80-82, 88
Chautauqua—99, 101
Chicago Evangelistic Institute—101, 128
Christian Perfection—15, 17, 25, 27, 48, 61, 115
Christian Purity—48
Christian Standard—108, 114
Christian Witness—114
Church, The
 Fact of—239f
 Foundation of—241ff
 Features of—244ff
 Function of—249ff
 Faith of—254ff
 Failure of—257
 Future of—257f
Church of England—23, 24
Clarke, Dougan—68
Clark, E. T.—109
Class Meetings—26, 28
Cleveland Bible Institute—129
Cooke, Sarah—68
Cookman, Alfred—47, 52, 68, 270
Court Street Methodist Episcopal Church, Philadelphia—49
Cullis, Charles—47
Degan, H. V.—38
Dempster, John—36
DeJernett, E. C.—72
Des Plaines Camp—98, 106
Dickinson College—54, 56
Divine Guidance—133, 190-193
Divine Union—118
Dodge, W. A.—71
Douglass, Paul H.—28
Drake, Mrs. Harriet E.—50
Drew Theological Seminary—31, 48, 105, 137
Dunham, E. S.—66
Dunn, L. R.—60, 68
Dutch Reformed Church—36

Earle, A. B.—48
Earnest Christianity—48
Eaton Rapids Camp—97, 98, 106
England—15, 23, 26, 30, 31, 40, 41, 48, 53

Entire Sanctification—20, 32, 41, 43, 49, 50, 57, 58, 69, 70, 73, 85, 110, 121, 222, 266
Evangelical Alliance—30
Evangelical Association—60
Evangelical Awakening—23
Epworth Evangelical Institute—101
Evangelistic Institute—99
Expository Principles—118ff

Finney, Charles G.—48
Finney Revivals—29, 35
Fisk, Wilbur—30
Flew, R. Newton—17
Flynn, Mrs. B. A.—269
Foster, R. S.—48
Fowler, C. J.—68, 69, 74, 75, 76, 101, 103
Fox, D. O.—64
Free Methodist—114
Friday Holiness Meeting—270
Friends Church—47
Friends Expositor—114
Full Salvation—20, 21, 39, 41, 60, 63
Fundamentalism—17

Gaddis, Merrill E.—26, 48, 69, 98, 109
Garrett Biblical Institute—98
German Methodism—37
Gill, Joshua—68
Glide, Mrs. J. H.—73
God
  His Nature—151
  His Attributes—152
  His Tri-personal Being—152f
Godbey, W. B.—68, 72, 73
God's Revivalist—114
Goreham, B. W.—49, 68
Graham, Billy—111
Great Britain—30, 50, 63
Green Street Methodist Episcopal Church, New York—50
Guide to Christian Perfection—38
Guide to Holiness—38-40, 46-48, 67

Hamline, Bishop—47, 48
Haney, M. L.—68
Harlow, Wm. T.—68
Healing—132

Heart and Life—114, 115
Heart Purity—57, 189
Herald of Holiness—58, 114
Higher Life—48
Highway and Banner—74
Hill, William—49
Hills, A. M.—68
Holiness—20, 21, 23, 24, 31
Holiness of Heart—85
Holiness Union of the South—71, 75
Holy Club—23, 27
Holy Spirit
  Strivings of—180f
  Illumination of—181f
  Birth of—182ff
  Witness of—184ff
  Sanctification of—187ff
  Guidance of—190ff
  Gifts of—193ff
  Unity of—195ff
  Intercession of—198ff
  Grieving of—200f
  Supply of—201f
Horton, Walter M.—18
Huffman, J. A.—117
Hughes, George—46, 53
Hughes, J. W.—68

Ireland—26, 30, 36, 43
India—63, 64
Indian Springs Camp, Georgia—71, 106
Inskip, John S.—47, 50, 53, 54, 56-58, 60-63, 65-68, 73, 76, 92, 109, 112, 113, 126
Iowa Holiness Association—74, 75
Itinerant Institute—101, 103, 104, 127

Janes, E. S.—30, 31, 41, 47
Jarrell, A. J.—71
Jones, E. Stanley—72
Joyce, I. W.—68, 108

Keen, S. A.—39, 68, 97, 107, 109
Kittleville Camp—49
Kincaid (Smith), Jean—269
Knapp, M. W.—68

Ladies' Repository—36, 40

Lake Junaluska—110
Lankford, Thomas A.—32
Lankford, Sarah Worrall—32, 34, 37, 38, 41
Lawhead, Millie—68
Layman's Revival—34, 42
Levy, E. M.—37
Lowrey, Asbury—47, 68

McCabe, Bishop—108
McClintock, John—137
MacDonald, William—63-65, 67, 68, 97, 109, 114, 126
McLaughlin, G. A.—68
McLean, A. M.—68
McPheeters, J. C.—117, 128
Mahan, Asa—47, 48, 68
Mallalieu, W. F.—68, 108, 109
Malone, J. Walter—68
Man, Ruin of
  Origin of Evil—158f
  Original Sin—159ff
  Twofold Nature of Sin—161f
  Penalty and Effects of Sin—163
  Extended Probation—164
  Cursed Earth—164f
Man, Redemption of
  Law of God—167f
  Gospel of Grace—169
  Gracious Redeemer—169ff
Manheim, Pennsylvania—60, 61
Markle, Miss Sallie A.—91, 269
Meridian Male College—127, 128
Meridian Women's College—128
Merritt, Timothy—30, 32, 38
Methodism—15, 22, 23, 26, 27, 30-32, 37, 39, 46, 47, 48, 109, 110, 137
Methodism Explained and Defended—57
Methodist Church—29, 32, 39, 40, 45, 47-49
Methodist Review—117
Methodists—17, 26, 27, 36, 41
Methodist Societies—26, 28, 31
Morrison, H. C.—68, 106-108, 117, 130
Morse, Deacon George—68
Mt. Lake Park Camp—94-98, 100, 101, 105, 106, 108
Nast, William—68

National Association for the Promotion of Holiness—69, 70
National Association of Evangelicals—21
National Camp Meetings—63, 65, 106
National Camp Meeting Association for the Promotion of Holiness—15, 45, 46, 52, 53, 60-64, 66-69, 71, 74, 92, 99, 112, 265
National Holiness Association—19-22, 25, 47, 101, 109, 114, 265
National Holiness Camp Meetings—60, 74
National Holiness Movement—16, 19, 106, 109
National Publishing Association—66, 67
Non-Wesleyan denominations—48

Ocean Grove Camp, New Jersey—46, 71, 97, 111, 133
Oldham, Bishop—68
Olin, Stephen—30, 36, 41, 47
Oriental Missionary Society—126
Orr, J. Edwin—42, 45
Osborn, William B.—50, 64, 65
Oxford University—23, 26

Pacific Bible College—128
Palmer, Mrs. Phoebe Worrall—32-37, 39-46
Palmer, Dr. Walter—47, 48, 57, 109
Paul, John—128
Peck, J. T.—47, 48, 67
Pentecostal—21, 102, 105, 107f
Pentecostal Herald—106, 114, 117
Pentecostal Movement—17, 20
Pepper, E. I. D.—66, 68, 81, 97, 101, 112, 114, 270
Perfection—24-26, 28, 29, 48
Perfectionistic Revivals—27
Perfect Love—20, 29, 32, 33, 40, 41, 48, 57, 82, 149, 233
Philadelphia—50
Philadelphia Conference—92
Pickett, L. L.—68
Plain Account of Christian Perfection—85
Pitman Grove, New Jersey—97, 98

Presbyterian Church—47, 49, 62

Quakers—26

Red Bank, New Jersey—50
Rees, Seth C.—101
Reid, Isaiah—68, 70
Revelation
  Scholarship and the Scriptures—142f
  Scriptural Doctrine of the Scriptures—143f
  Revelation and Inspiration—144ff
  Inspiration and Illumination—147f
  Illumination and Interpretation—148ff
  Central Figure in Scripture—150
Ridout, George—68
Roche, John A.—36
Ross, Fred H.—270
Round Lake Camp, New York—63
Ruth, C. W.—68
Roberts, Evans—45
Sanctification—24, 40, 56, 135, 187f
School of Prophets—105, 106, 113, 270
Scotland—26, 36
Scott, Levi—54
Scriptural Holiness—16, 20, 24, 34, 41, 46, 59, 107
Sebring Camp, Ohio—106
Second Crisis—20
Second Work of Grace—29
Shaw, S. B.—68
Simpson, Bishop Matthew—53, 63
Sing Sing Camp, New York—56, 57
Smith, Amanda—60
Smith, Joseph H.—15-22, 79-81, etc.
Smith, J. Hunter—269
Smith, John J.—269
Smith, Grace—269
Small Sects in America—109
Steele, Daniel—68
Sweet, W. W.—69
Sychar Camp, Ohio—98, 106, 133

Talmadge, T. Dewitt—45
Taylor, Bishop William—37, 39, 47, 48, 68, 91, 126, 269
Texas Holiness Meeting—72, 74
Thoburn, Bishop—68
Thompson, John—68, 270
Tongues Movement—20, 195
Torrey, R. A.—45
Troy Conference, New York—30
Tuesday Meeting—32-37, 39, 40, 46, 47-49, 54, 57, 59
Tyerman, Luke—19

United States—30, 36, 40, 42, 44, 48
Urbana Camp, Ohio—98
University Park, Iowa—98
Updegraff, David—37, 47, 68, 97, 114
Upham, Thomas—34, 35, 37, 39, 47, 48

Vineland, New Jersey—52, 53
Vineland Camp, New Jersey—59, 60
Vennard, Iva Durham—101, 128

Wales—26, 44
Walker, E. F.—68
Watson, George D.—68, 97
Way of Holiness—40
Wesleyan Perfection—18, 31, 38
Wesleyan Methodist—114
Whitecomb, A. L.—68
Winona Lake, Indiana—117
Witness of the Spirit—33, 184f
Wesley, Charles—23
Wesley, John—15, 18, 19, 23-28, 31, 35, 38, 39, 102, 133, 265
Wesley, Samuel and Susannah—23, 31
White, Wilbert W.—118, 120
Worall, Henry—31
World Gospel Mission—126
Wood, J. A.—82, 97, 126